THE
ROTATION
DIET
COOKBOOK

MARTIN KATAHN, PH.D.

Director, Vanderbilt Weight Management Program

and TERRI KATAHN

Illustrations by Heather L. Warren

W · W · Norton & Company · New York · London

The text of this book is composed in Caledonia, with
display type set in Perpetor.
Composition and manufacturing by The Haddon Craftsmen, Inc.
Book design by B. Klein
First Edition

ISBN 0-393-02457-1

W. W. Norton & Company, Inc., 500 Fifth Avenue, New York, N. Y. 10110
W. W. Norton & Company Ltd., 37 Great Russell Street, London WC1B 3NU

1 2 3 4 5 6 7 8 9 0

To Enid Katahn,
wife and mother to this team,
with much love.

Contents

Preface: Why Write a Cookbook?

Wherever I go to give a talk about the problem of obesity, the most frequently asked personal question is, "Have you been following the Rotation Diet ever since you lost your own weight?" And, of course, the answer is no. I haven't dieted in twenty-four years, except for research purposes in the Vanderbilt Weight Management Program.

I think the question reflects the dieting mentality of the American public. Evidently, most people believe that if you are overweight and go on a weight-loss diet, whether it's the Rotation Diet or any other diet, and if you are successful in losing weight, you must resign yourself to "dieting" for the rest of your life.

Nothing is farther from the truth, and that is why I'm writing a cookbook.

I would like to show you how I, as a former fat man, have learned to prepare just about anything my heart desires, from soup to nuts, without "dieting." This is how I keep the 75 pounds that I lost twenty-four years ago from creeping back around my hips, which, by the way, used to be 55 inches around.

I would also like to show you how my daughter, Terri, and a small army of friends learned to cook and plan menus in accordance with my low-fat, low-salt principles, as they jumped in to help me create recipes of all kinds that would also be in accordance with *their own* tastes. The results, as you will discover as you experiment with the recipes in this book, are proof positive: all low-calorie cooking does not have to be bland and taste the same! You can adapt your favorite recipes, using the same principles, to suit *your* tastes.

You will find as you examine the book that there is not one dietetic food, artificial sweetener, or any other artificial ingredient used in any of the recipes. I have always felt that such concoctions do no good when it comes to weight management. And now there is research to support my claims that, if anything, people who use artificial sweeteners tend to gain more weight in a given time period than those who don't.* I want to show you how to use the "good stuff"—the genuine, tasty foods—in a way that will help you control your weight.

The approach to food preparation and menu planning that you will find in *The Rotation Diet Cookbook* is designed to have other health benefits. By being low in overall fat and salt content, and high in vitamins, minerals, and dietary fiber, the approach I take follows the most up-to-date guidelines for preventing heart disease and cancer.

There is, however, one important, indisputable fact that you must accept if you are going to lose weight and keep it off forever. If you are an overweight person and want to weigh even five pounds less for the rest of your life, you must DO SOMETHING DIFFERENT from what you have been doing, for the rest of your life. You cannot return to your present life-style after losing even five pounds, without going right back to square one.

If you are a sedentary person, an increase in physical activity can give you a reasonable margin in your calorie intake. It's a margin of several hundred calories that's lacking in your present life-style. That's why this may be one of the only cookbooks in history that has a chapter devoted to physical activity! Just taking a brisk walk for 45 minutes each day will permit you to enjoy one of our dessert recipes every day, or a couple of glasses of wine with dinner, with no fear of gaining weight.

*For instance, check the summary of the research findings of the American Cancer Society in the September 1986 edition of *Wellness Letter* (volume 2, no. 12), a health newsletter published by the University of California at Berkeley.

But my goal in writing this cookbook goes beyond simple weight management. The increase in physical activity that I recommend, as important as it is in helping to control your weight, does not ensure the health benefits of reducing fat (and possibly sodium) in your diet. When it comes to reducing the risk of heart disease and cancer, the meal plans and style of food preparation that I suggest are *at least as important,* and possibly even more important, than an increase in physical activity. Fortunately, when you learn to reduce the fat content of your diet, you accomplish both objectives: you reduce the risk of disease and at the same time make it much easier to control your weight.

The basic principles that Terri and I have used in developing our recipes are:

1. Keep fat at a minimum but still come up with tasty dishes. Our goal here is to show you how to design a meal plan and then prepare the foods so that you end up with around 25 to 30 percent of your daily calories, on the average, coming from fat. If we were to go further than that in reducing fat calories, we don't think it would be possible to develop tasty recipes and to design a comprehensive dietary plan that a majority of persons (including ourselves) could live with for the rest of our lives.

2. Reduce the amount of sugar. Rather than use any artificial sweetener, we prefer to use moderate amounts of sugar as a sweetener (or honey or molasses, when appropriate). It tastes better and it is more satisfying.

3. Demonstrate how the wise use of herbs and spices can add to the attractiveness of your dishes, while avoiding such an exotic or complicated approach to cooking that no one but a full-time cook would have the time to pursue it. So, we focus on the use of spices and herbs, the latter used in their most easily found form, which is often dried rather than fresh. Of course, if fresh is available, all the better.

As for salt, we include minimal amounts because salt helps bring out the flavor of other ingredients. You can prove this to yourself by mixing up a blend of herbs, tasting the mixture, then adding just a pinch of salt. Suddenly, there is an explosion of flavor.

In general, our recipes include about half the salt that a salt-adapted taste might expect, so you may find yourself taking a little time getting used to the new blend of flavors. Do take the time, because, as you reduce salt in your diet, your sensitivity to its flavor will probably increase. You'll want less as you get used to using less!

In our opinion, the weight of scientific evidence suggests that healthy persons who do not have a familial tendency to hypertension can use salt in moderation, without danger to their health. However, if you are on a salt-restricted diet, be sure to check with your physician about the use of salt in our recipes before including the recommended amount.

4. Finally, we wanted dishes that are, for the most part, relatively simple and quick to prepare. Although we were fortunate to obtain the enthusiastic cooperation of several professional chefs and bakers in the development of our recipes, we ourselves are not professionals. Both Terri and I work full-time and we rarely wish to put a great deal of time into preparing meals at the end of a long working day. (We do, of course, enjoy spending several hours creating special meals for festive occasions.) If you learn to organize your approach to cooking as we suggest, you will find that most dishes that we have included in this book take less than 20 or 25 minutes to prepare (not including final cooking time). A few of the more elaborate may take an hour, although some of the preparation can be done in advance so that the time required for the final steps just before meal time is reduced.

Think of this book as a course in healthy food preparation as well as a cookbook. We show you a number of daily meal plans with different calorie totals. Try our way of low-fat cooking, then adapt any of your own favorite recipes and design your own healthy meal plans.

Martin Katahn, Ph.D.
Nashville, Tennessee
January 1987

Acknowledgments

Just as the Rotation Diet itself became a community-wide weight-loss program, first in our hometown of Nashville, and then in hundreds of other cities all over the country, so this cookbook has become, in some ways, a community-wide effort. So many devoted people helped to make this book possible that it is difficult for us to know where to begin to express our appreciation. Perhaps we should start with the three people who, in addition to ourselves, created, cooked, and tested most of the recipes.

Joyce Weingartner, friend, master baker, and enthusiastic teacher of the art of baking fine breads, has contributed her bread recipes in the past (to *The Rotation Diet*), and really entered into the present project by testing, and in part creating, over one hundred of the recipes. Joyce and her family were some of our best taste-testers, as were several of her friends who were on the Rotation Diet, and who would stop off at her house each week for the plunder, armed with paper bags full of plastic containers.

Donna Kamler and Patty Smith, chefs at Robert Orr/Sysco, cooked, tested, sampled, and retested over two-hundred recipes in the Robert Orr/Sysco Kitchen. We deeply appreciate both the friendship and cooperation of Burt Hummell, president of Robert Orr/Sysco, for making the company kitchen and his staff available to us, and for seeing to it that we had the very finest quality meats and produce at our fingertips for all of our recipes.

Many others responded to our calls for help in illustrating specific approaches to food preparation. Margaret Nofziger Dotzler prepared most of our tofu recipes and several meatless dishes. Jewel Coburn brought us a number of exciting recipes from around the world, including her native Australia. Patti Bereyso, Kim Harrison, Trey Kuhn, Patricia Lipman, Denni Llovet, Patricia Sommers, George and Betty Schnitzer, and June Stevenson also contributed their favorite low-calorie, low-fat recipes.

We also want to thank the Kellogg Company for providing some of the recipes for breakfast foods, muffins, and breads, several of which were created especially for this book. In particular, we'd like to thank Dr. Shirley Chen, research nutritionist at the Kellogg Company, for providing important information on recent research in nutrition.

Several Nashville restaurants answered our requests for illustrations of how they prepare low-calorie, low-fat dishes for their customers who wish to order such foods when eating out. The recipes that they provided for this cookbook are unique and instructive, and appear in print for the first time. In some cases we had to adjust the recipes for home preparation (not many of us will prepare Court Bouillon by the gallon!). But we can testify that, with a little practice, we can all become adept at recreating what the finest chefs have originated. So thanks to Mr. Jaime Camara and Chef Tom Allen at Arthur's; Mr. John Haggard, Head Chef Sylvain le Coguic, and Maître d' Hoyt Hill at Julian's; Ms. Bonnie Chen and Chef Wang Chia Hsin at Peking Gardens; Chef Kem Ramovich at Villa Romano; and Manager Casey Ishida at Kobe Steak House.

Jamie Pope, M.S., R.D., now the nutritionist at the Vanderbilt Weight Management Program, gave willingly of her time and energy in compiling the substitution and fiber lists that appear at the end of this book. She also got into the spirit of things and helped create some great recipes.

Mary Bomar performed indispensible work, especially in analyzing all of our recipes at least once on one of our Tandy 1200HD computers, using *The Food Processor* Computerized Nutrition System from ESHA Research. Marilyn Blair was our all-around "do-anything-and-everything" production assistant, who helped us keep our overflowing files in order, and kept mountains of food and paperwork moving between our offices, the post office (and hence, the publisher), Robert Orr/Sysco, Vanderbilt, and so on, throughout Nashville.

Enid Katahn, wife and mother, and David Katahn, son and brother, also helped either by cooking in every spare moment, or by tasting (and tasting twelve to fifteen dishes at a time requires quite a taste tolerance!). David also pitched in with analyzing recipes when we needed extra help at the last minute. Enid has our special thanks, along with master carpenter and designer Mitch MacKay, for remodeling the kitchen at the "Katahn Homestead" into what has to be the most beautiful and efficient kitchen anyone could wish for.

Once again, it's a pleasure to thank our literary agents, Arthur and Richard Pine, for all they have done for us during the writing of this book, and for their help with our health-promotion activities in general. What began as a professional relationship between literary agents and author six years ago has developed into a valued friendship.

And thanks once again to our editor at W. W. Norton, Starling Lawrence. This is his fourth book with one or more of the Katahn family, and he provided, as usual, invaluable advice on format, style, and content. Star loves to cook as much as we do, and we share an interest in improving the quality of our diets, without sacrificing the enjoyment found in good food, tastefully prepared. As with our literary agents, our relationship with Star has gone far beyond the usual business and professional relationship between publishing company, author, and editor. It is wonderful to work with all of the friendly and helpful people at W. W. Norton, and we want to express our appreciation to Fran Rosencrantz, publicity director, Eddie Gunn, publicity associate, Anthony Levintow, Debra Makay, Nancy Palmquist, and Patty Peltekos of the editorial department, art director Hugh O'Neill, and production manager Andy Marasia for the special roles they have played in making this book a reality.

Finally, an undertaking such as this would have taken at least four times longer and caused fifty times the headaches without the help of our friendly Tandy computers. From a single Model II in 1981, we have grown to a "fleet" of twelve various models (in our home offices and the Weight Management Office at Vanderbilt University). We want to thank Doug Stallings in particular for his personal attention to our needs during the past six years, and our thanks to Ralph Kirkland, Rita Baughman, and Andrew McCluskey of the Tandy Area Training and Support Group, who answer the "crisis" telephone number when any of us call for advice in an emergency.

THE
ROTATION
DIET
COOKBOOK

What Is the Rotation Diet?

Although *The Rotation Diet Cookbook* is designed to show you how to maintain desirable weight for the rest of your life without depriving yourself of the enjoyment of good food, we're sure that at least some of our readers may want to lose a few pounds at the outset. And what better way than with the Rotation Diet!

So, let's start with an explanation of that diet.

The Rotation Diet has certain unique features and several advantages over other approaches to losing weight. It's a quick-weight-loss plan that:

1. does not lower the metabolic rate;
2. is time limited and highly motivating;
3. includes a wide variety of healthy foods from all four food groups;
4. and is safe for overweight adults who are otherwise in good health.

When you make up your mind to lose weight using the Rotation Diet, you set a target of time—three weeks—in which you rotate caloric intake. In addition, if you are a sedentary person, you GET ACTIVE. This is what protects you from the "starvation response," that is, a lowering of your metabolic rate. When you use other low-calorie diets and neglect to increase physical activity, your need for food can drop 35 or even 40 percent in the space of three weeks. You can't eat like a normal human being after those diets without gaining weight even faster than you lost it!

During the Rotation Diet, women follow a core diet of approximately 600 calories for three days, 900 for four, and 1200 for a week. Then, in the third week, you return to the calorie levels of the first week. The version for men contains 600 calories more at each level. You eat a wide variety of healthful foods: fruits, vegetables, whole grains, low-fat milk products, lean meat, fish, and poultry. Although there are recommended menus, you can substitute freely, as long as you stay within the same food group. Using the substitution rules and the guidelines for food preparation, you design the diet to suit your personal tastes and food preferences.

In addition to the core diet, there is an "insurance policy" that greatly increases the nutritional value of the diet. The insurance policy (explained on pages 394–95) enables most people to follow the diet for the full three weeks and obtain an average weight loss of two-thirds of a pound a day. At any meal (or for snacks, if you choose) you can eat all you want of just about any vegetable. I call these *free vegetables* because your consumption can be virtually unlimited. In addition, you choose a *safe fruit,* one that you really like so that you don't feel deprived because you're dieting. Any time you need a lift or are in need of a snack for any reason, have a *safe fruit.*

In the original version of the Rotation Diet, I suggested that you choose only one fruit (apples, for example) as your *safe fruit* so as not to be tempted to overeat. I suggested that you set an upper limit on the fruit at three servings per day. The reason for these suggestions about *free vegetables* and the *safe fruit* is that the vegetables listed in the original version contain 10 calories or less per half cup, while the fruit might average 60 calories for a medium-size piece. I have, however, relaxed the rule on the *safe fruit* as a result of the experience people have had on the diet. As long as you stick with three fruit snacks a day, in addition to the meals on the core menu, it is perfectly all right to vary the fruit and enjoy yourself.

I also relaxed the restrictions on the *free vegetables.* Experience showed that just about any vegetable could be used as a *free vegetable,* including all those that contain fewer than 25 calories per half cup. Perhaps the most important thing that people who use the Rotation Diet learn is that they—and you —can't get fat on fruits and vegetables! These foods, together with whole grains, should comprise 55 to 60 percent of your total daily calorie intake. The complete *free vegetable* and *safe fruit* lists are given on pages 394 and 395.

On pages 403–9 are some suggestions for 600-, 900-, 1200-, 1500-, and 1800-calorie menus, as well as directions for men, and for couples who want to diet together. When friends and families that need to lose some weight do it together, they have more fun, and are generally more successful because of the support they can give one another.

The menus refer to specific recipes, but all of our recipes list the caloric values as well as other important nutrient information, so that you can easily choose the recipes that are especially good for low-calorie days in case you want to make substitutions and design your own weight-loss plan.

I want to repeat, however, that this is a cookbook designed to illustrate a way of "cooking for life"—not "dieting for life." The 1800-calorie menus on pages 406–9 illustrate basic maintenance menus, and instructions are given for increasing portion sizes for men, who will end up needing an average of between 2100 and 2400 calories per day.

Our recipes show you how to eat just about everything, maximizing flavor and sound nutrition, while cutting back on fat, sugar, and salt, so that you have a nutrition plan you can live with. Just take a look at some of the recipe headings: there are recipes for everything from appetizers to desserts. We really concentrated on developing desserts, because that is what most people expect to give up the moment anyone says "weight management."

We recognize that many others have created healthful dietary plans for weight reduction and the permanent control of obesity, as well as for the prevention of those diseases that are related to an overconsumption of fat. The problem with these plans (and we are sure you know what we mean when we say this) is that the "cure" is often worse than the disease! They require sacrifices that are just too hard to live with. If the recommendations don't "feel good"—and in the case of a cookbook, if the recipes don't taste good—and if the payoff is not worth whatever sacrifices are involved, there is no way you will stick with the program.

The Rotation Diet has a BIG payoff. And the recipes taste so good we think you will be able to stick with our suggestions for a lifetime of good cooking whether you use them for weight reduction or not.

So, enjoy!

NUTRITION NOTE

With each recipe we include information on calorie content, cholesterol, dietary fiber, total fat, and sodium. Thus if you use our recipes for your daily menus you will find it easy to calculate totals and design a special diet should you wish to limit calories for weight reduction, or determine whether your diet falls within the guidelines for cholesterol, fat, sodium, and dietary fiber recommended by the major health organizations. Our sample menus, (pp. 403–9) are designed with these guidelines in mind although on a given day they can be a little above or below the exact recommendations for any given nutrient (as would be typical of a normal approach to eating in which no one can be expected to tie a calculator to one's fork!).

We feel that, on the average, no more than 30 percent of calories should come from fat; about 55 to 60 percent should come from carbohydrate, and about 15 percent from protein.

An average of 300 milligrams of cholesterol per day is a goal to aim for, with the American Heart Association now suggesting that it is even better to regulate cholesterol in relation to your total daily caloric intake, with no more than 100 milligrams cholesterol per 1000 calories.

We think the latest American Heart Association recommendation will be difficult, and certainly tedious, to implement. Barring existing heart disease or a familial history, the general goal of 300 milligrams per day seems reasonable.

According to the National Cancer Institute, dietary fiber should fall between 20 and 35 grams per day, with many health authorities suggesting that you gradually increase to the upper level of this range provided that amount of fiber does not make you uncomfortable. We, too, think this is a good idea since consumption of foods relatively high in dietary fiber has extra value for weight control, because of their bulk and the tendency of fiber to bind with and prevent the absorption of a small amount of the fat in your diet.

A healthy range for sodium lies between 1100 and 3300 milligrams per day, although the American Heart Association now ties sodium intake to total daily calories, suggesting 1000 milligrams per 1000 calories. In the past, most medical authorities considered moderate sodium intake to mean 2000 milligrams per day. One teaspoon of salt contains about 2200 milligrams of sodium, so we tend to use very little in our recipes, and add a bit to taste at the table.

A "no" in our nutrient analyses indicates less than 0.5 gram fat or fiber, and less than 0.5 milligrams cholesterol or sodium. We round up in other cases (0.5 to 1.49 will be listed as 1, 1.5 to 2.49 will be listed as 2, etc.). Recipes that contain tiny bits of fiber (for example, from small amounts of vegetables or nuts) will thus say "no" fiber even though up to 0.49 gram is present, and the same will be true of fat up to 0.49 gram. The decision to round was arbitrary and was made to avoid confusing decimal values that would contain a small amount of error anyway due to the way nutritional analyses are performed in the laboratory.

We used standard varieties of soy sauce and bouillon in

our analyses, since these are the most easily available in all supermarkets. However, compared with commercial bouillons (powders and cubes) which contain from 900 to 1500 milligrams of sodium in the quantities used per cup of water, plus sweeteners, homemade stock will tend to be much lower in sodium, sugars, and other additives. You may always substitute a commercial low-sodium soy sauce or bouillon, if you wish, and you will reduce the sodium content of the relevant recipes by a significant amount. Read the labels of the substitute products, since these products usually contain more sweetener than the meat or soy product named on the label. They may also use potassium chloride in place of sodium chloride (table salt) and some people find this flavor objectionable. Please check our Basic Soup Stocks (pages 64 to 67) for several simple recipes that can be used whenever bouillon or stock is called for. Once you discover how good your homemade stock can be, we think you will rarely fall back on the commercial product.

Many of our recipes call for skim or low-fat milk. Our analyses are based on 2% milk, when the choice is given, since that is what we find most palatable. Per cup of milk, each percent butterfat adds roughly 20 calories to the recipe, or slightly over 2 grams of fat. When you divide this by 4 to 8 servings, we think this is an insignificant amount of fat for a significant increase in flavor and texture.

All preparation times listed are rough estimates, since everyone cooks at a different pace. The second or third time you prepare a recipe will not take as long as the first. Cooking times also vary slightly, since some ovens run hotter than others. We hope our advice on how to organize your kitchen, and to assemble all ingredients prior to starting meal preparation, will help move things along more quickly if you tend to be somewhat inefficient.

The Efficient Kitchen

The joy of cooking begins in an efficient kitchen that makes the preparation of food as pleasurable in the doing as in the eating. It's so much easier to prepare healthful meals for yourself and for your family when you work in an environment that's equipped to facilitate your efforts and that gives you the rewards that creative cooking so richly deserves.

Ask yourself this question:

How many times have you started to prepare a meal, whether it's after a long, late day at work when you're tired and hungry, or whether it's a joyously anticipated holiday celebration when you have the whole day to cook, and found yourself getting tense and irritable?

Your change in mood may have occurred for several reasons, all of which are easily corrected if you take a little time to examine what happened.

Did you run out of counter space? Couldn't find the oregano? The knife was so dull you couldn't trim the meat without trimming your fingers? You twisted your back when you bent over and tried to crawl into the corner of a bottom cabinet to reach the roasting pan? You cut into a lemon and it squirted all over the toaster, which, for some reason, has for twenty years managed to stay smack at the rear of your work space and is still splattered with a sprinkle from yesterday's grapefruit?

Annoyances like these can quickly destroy the joy of cooking. We know it as well as anyone. *Every single one of these aggravations has happened to us!*

Finally, since we really love to cook, we learned to pay a little attention to the organization of our kitchens and the preparation process itself. There's no question about it: inferior utensils, a poorly laid-out kitchen, inefficient storage, lack of essential ingredients, and poor cooking strategies can all make meal preparation an aggravating chore.

Here are some suggestions that have helped make meal preparation easier and a source of pleasure for us.

EQUIPMENT

Knives and Related Utensils

When it comes to knives, buy the very best you can afford! For years I was as susceptible to cheap promotions as anyone. For example, I only recently disposed of a set of impossible kitchen carving knives and steak knives that I received at our neighborhood service station for a dollar and ten gallons of gasoline during a promotion when our family first came to Nashville twenty-five years ago! We tried them once. They didn't have

enough body to cut a hamburger, and for ugliness they couldn't be beat, so they were stuck in the back of a drawer, taking up space needed for more important household goods.

There is a tremendous difference between fine knives and inferior knives. Haven't you always marveled at the ease with which your butcher trims a steak or roast, or skins a chicken? You can do the same if you treat yourself to Henckels or Wusthof knives, which I use, or something of similar quality. Keep them sharp with a good steel, or with a ceramic sharpening stick, which we think is superior to either steel or stone. I like the Crock Stick, manufactured by Chicago Cutlery, although there are larger, more expensive ones available.

Our most used knives are:

10-inch chef's knife (for the heavy duty jobs such as splitting a winter squash or carving a big roast);

10-inch slicing knife (thinner blade more convenient for slicing turkey, for example);

6½-inch utility knife (better on carrots, potatoes, and larger vegetables than a paring knife); and

4-inch paring knives (I like to have two since they are in constant use).

It pays to keep your knives right next to the point of use in a wooden knife block. With this set up, you won't have to leave your work area or reach across sink or stove whenever you need one.

Never put your knives in the dishwasher. This will ruin the handles and dull the blades as well, since they knock up against the other cutlery while washing.

I keep a large assortment of serving spoons, spatulas (mostly wooden, a few plastic, all of which will not scratch our pots and pans), and other implements stored upright in a canister, as a "bouquet," on a counter near the stove. Terri keeps hers in a large drawer right next to the stove. So small utensils such as the can opener and corkscrew don't jam and jumble, they fit in a deep drawer near the stove.

Pots and Pans

We have had a set of copper-bottom cookware in the family for thirty-five years, and while I may still occasionally use a saucepan, or the 6-quart covered stockpot when I cook spaghetti, I feel that lightweight copper- or aluminum-clad stainless cookware is just not suitable for either simple or serious cooking.

I prefer pots and pans made of an extra-thick, heavy-duty aluminum alloy, such as the Leyse or Mirro brands, while Terri has a set of pots and pans made of heavy-duty porcelain enamel over steel. A heavy-cast aluminum with a Silverstone, nonstick interior also works well. My 10-inch and 12-inch Leyse skillets have received lots of use, and I keep a complete set of nonstick Silverstone in my motor home, since it is so much easier to clean when I am traveling.

Recently we were introduced to 7-ply stainless steel, which is excellent for waterless cooking; a 2-quart saucepan and 10-inch skillet are now the mainstays for food preparation in my household. A 5- or 7-ply stainless-steel bottom spreads the heat evenly, and, once the pan is hot, you can continue cooking on very low heat. I use these two pots for covered dishes, as the "whistle" vent on the cover, which lets steam escape, tells me when the interior is maintaining the right temperature. Even when panbroiling, food does not stick in the 7-ply skillet, as it will in a thinner stainless skillet. Let the pan get hot before you add any oil, and then add the meat, poultry, or other ingredients.

Most people will find that 2- and 4-quart covered saucepans and a 10-inch and 12-inch skillet are indispensable. We have never needed a stockpot larger than 6 quarts. As with your knives, buy the best you can afford, but keep function in mind, and your own preference for equipment. Don't buy things you won't use and don't keep things that you aren't using. Look in your cupboard right now—you may find pots you haven't used in years! I just got rid of two very heavy cast-iron skillets that many chefs swear by, but they didn't "feel right" or suit my style.

We use a variety of deep, porcelain-on-steel, covered roasting pans, ranging in interior size from $9\frac{1}{2} \times 14$ inches to $11\frac{1}{2} \times 17$ inches. Those extra inches really make a difference, since the smallest is right for roasting a chicken, while the largest takes care of a 22-pound turkey. A heavy-weight, porcelain-on-steel roasting pan can be used on top of the stove, since it will spread the heat quite evenly. My smallest roaster has a rack, which makes it excellent for steaming everything from fish to vegetables. And the largest one comes in handy for mixing great batches of stuffing when I prepare that 22-pound turkey for Thanksgiving. I also use a covered roasting pan to make stews (as well as roasts) in the oven, with a low heat setting.

Terri uses a plain carbon-steel wok for stir-frying, while I prefer a skillet, mainly because my electric-stove instructions warn against burning out the elements when using a stove-top wok. The skillet works fine, but the texture and flavor always seem to be better in the wok, as it heats faster and the "hot spot" makes for crisper vegetables in the stir-fry.

Casseroles and Other Pots

Our favorite earthenware casseroles and baking dishes, as well as soup bowls and coffee mugs, are made by two of Nashville's fine potters, Burneta Clayton and Lenore Vanderkooi. Their work is available in many shops around the country, so if you're fortunate enough to see one of their pots, treat yourself!* I also find a 3½-quart glass casserole, recently introduced by Corning Glass, to be very useful, and for the biggies, I use a 5-quart stoneware casserole, one of those brown monstrosities that have been around for generations. Earthenware, glassware, and stoneware are also excellent for microwave cooking. We also have quite a large assortment of other baking dishes and, of course, muffin tins. (We are very fond of muffins, as you will note when you examine our recipes.)

Miscellaneous

We have a few other items in both our kitchens that do special jobs particularly well.

A **microwave oven** is particularly useful for cooking vegetables. Microwave cooking requires little water, while more nutrients are retained through microwave cooking than through any other cooking method. The microwave is also useful for reheating foods, making cheese toast, baking a potato or two, and making scrambled eggs and omelettes. We do not rely on

*You can also order cookware by mail from Burneta Clayton by writing to her at Clay Works, 4515 Harpeth Hills Drive, Nashville, Tennessee, 37215. Write to Lenore Vanderkooi at 1412 Graybar Lane, Nashville, Tennessee, 37215. Also look for handmade cookware from potters in your area.

it for most of our food preparation, however. Most of our main courses, roasts, stews, casseroles, and poached and steamed foods, are best prepared on the stove top or in the convection oven.

We have both a **blender** and **food processor.** The food processor does everything from grating Parmesan to slicing vegetables when we have great quantities to slice (we still prefer our fine knives and a manual approach for a few stalks of celery or an onion or two). It also works well for chopping something like a large quantity of Brazil nuts, or for making crumbs out of zwieback or graham crackers. But when it comes to *blending* or *pulverizing,* the blender does a better job than the food processor.

Big wooden salad bowls are essential. Salads don't look right and don't seem to taste as well in glass or metal. A modest-size walnut bowl, about 4 inches deep and 14 inches across the top, is fine for a family and for small dinner parties, but for a buffet, a festive way to serve a gigantic salad is in a truly generous bowl, 8 inches deep and 18 inches across at the summit!

Serving platters have been passed along in our family since our ancestors immigrated from Russia and Lithuania at the turn of this century. Among them is an English porcelain platter (the imprint of origin is now illegible) and another is a gold-leafed Standard whose finish is beautifully cracked. What a joy it is to display a 22-pound glistening red turkey made tandoori style on the outdoor grill, or a beef bourguignon, surrounded by an arrangement of colorful vegetables, new potatoes, and mushrooms, on one of these platters before serving dinner to family and friends! The platters have held such a wealth of goodness over the years that, each time we use them, we experience again the feelings of thanksgiving we have at being together as a family and living in the United States of America.

For many years I always minced, and never pressed, fresh garlic. Of course, in many recipes, minced garlic is just fine. Finally, however, my wife Enid got tired of a surprise piece of garlic in her food and purchased an Ahner garlic press. It is now a mainstay in Terri's kitchen as well as ours. It handles cloves of all sizes, presses easily and completely, and, thank goodness, is easy to clean. You should have a fine garlic press since fresh garlic is a completely different experience from garlic powder. The powder will do in a pinch, as we demonstrate in some of our recipes, but fresh is best!

A piece of two-by-four is quite serviceable for pounding meat (I've done it) but it's not quite as good as an honest-to-goodness **meat pounder** when it comes to our wonderful veal recipes. It's worth the investment of four or five dollars, and you can use it for poultry and beef as well. A large **wooden cutting board,** well seasoned, and used for all pounding and cutting, is a must. I have a built-in oak board, 24 inches × 27 inches, next to the sink, and its convenience makes these jobs a joy. Some bakers prefer a marble slab for pastry-making, but we have never used one.

Other utensils that we find useful include a **pepper mill** (fresh-ground is far more flavorful than the canned ground pepper, which we never use); a **coffee grinder,** since fresh-ground coffee is also a completely different experience from pre-ground; and a **mortar and pestle,** which we use for grinding herbs, spices, and seeds when we mix recipes such as Herb Salt (pp. 334–35). I have a mortar and pestle of attractive black marble, and Terri has a small lightweight wooden one that cost a dollar in a health-food store about ten years ago. If you don't wish to buy a mortar and pestle, you can use a bowl and a heavy spoon.

GENERAL INSTRUCTIONS FOR BAKING AND ROASTING

We specifically indicate the instances in which baking or roasting requires a preheated oven. Although the probability is very low, earthenware or heat-resistant glass can crack when exposed to an extreme change in temperature. Therefore, we do not preheat our oven when we plan to use such cookware.

HERBS AND SPICES

Here is a guide to the use of herbs and spices that can add to your cooking and eating pleasure. I keep my herbs and spices handy in a wine-rack-style holder on the counter top at the rear of my work area, together with garlic and onion powder, and a few homemade blends that I use frequently. I keep others on three revolving shelves in the cupboard over the work area: one shelf for seeds of various kinds, another for liquid seasonings, and the third for infrequently used items. We have not tried all of the various foods with all of the suggested herbs and spices in the following list. But we think you will find one or two uses for all of them, as we do. You will find what we think are some particularly good suggestions in our recipes.

Allspice—Meats, fish, gravies, relishes, tomato sauce
Anise—Fruit
Basil—Green beans, onions, peas, potatoes, summer squash, tomatoes, lamb, beef, shell fish, eggs, sauces
Bay Leaves—Artichokes, beets, carrots, onions, white potatoes, tomatoes, meats, fish, soups and stews, sauces, and gravies
Caraway Seed—Asparagus, beets, cabbage, carrots, cauliflower, cole slaw, onions, potatoes, sauerkraut, turnips, beef, pork, noodles, cheese dishes
Cardamom—Melon, sweet potatoes
Cayenne Pepper—Sauces, curries
Celery Seed—Cabbage, carrots, cauliflower, corn, lima beans, potatoes, tomatoes, turnips, salad dressings, beef, fish dishes, sauces, soups, stews, cheese
Chervil—Carrots, peas, salads, summer squash, tomatoes, salad dressings, poultry, fish, eggs
Chili Powder—Corn, eggplant, onions, beef, pork, chili con carne, stews, shell fish, sauces, egg dishes

Chives—Carrots, corn, sauces, salads, soups

Cinnamon—Stewed fruits, apple or pineapple dishes, sweet potatoes, winter squash, toast

Cloves—Baked beans, sweet potatoes, winter squash, pork and ham roasts

Cumin—Cabbage, rice, sauerkraut, chili con carne, ground beef dishes, cottage or cheddar cheese

Curry Powder—Carrots, cauliflower, green beans, onions, tomatoes, pork and lamb, shell fish, fish, poultry, sauces for eggs and meats

Dill Seed—Cabbage, carrots, cauliflower, peas, potatoes, spinach, tomato dishes, turnips, salads, lamb, cheese

Dillweed—Vegetables, salads, poultry, soups

Ginger—Applesauce, melon, baked beans, carrots, onions, sweet potatoes, poultry, summer and winter squash, beef, veal, ham, lamb, teriyaki sauce

Mace—Carrots, potatoes, spinach, summer squash, beef, veal, fruits, sauces

Marjoram—Asparagus, carrots, eggplant, greens, green beans, lima beans, peas, spinach, summer squash, lamb, pork, poultry, fish, stews, sauces

Mustard—Asparagus, broccoli, Brussels sprouts, cabbage, cauliflower, green beans, onions, peas, potatoes, summer squash, meats, poultry

Mustard Seed—Salads, curries, pickles, ham, corned beef, relishes

Nutmeg—Beets, Brussels sprouts, carrots, cabbage, cauliflower, greens, green beans, onions, spinach, sweet potatoes, winter squash, sauces

Oregano—Baked beans, broccoli, cabbage, cauliflower, green beans, lima beans, onions, peas, potatoes, spinach, tomatoes, turnips, beef, pork, veal, poultry, fish, pizza, chili con carne, Italian sauces, stews

Paprika—Salad dressings, shell fish, fish, gravies, eggs

Parsley Flakes—All vegetables, soups, sauces, salads, stews, potatoes, eggs

Pepper—Most vegetables, meats, salads

Poppy Seeds—Salads, noodles

Rosemary—Mushrooms, peas, potatoes, spinach, tomatoes, vegetable salads, beef, lamb, pork, veal, poultry, stews, cheese, eggs

Saffron—Rice

Sage—Eggplant, onions, peas, tomato dishes, salads, pork, veal, poultry, ham, cheese

Savory—Baked beans, beets, cabbage, carrots, cauliflower, lima beans, potatoes, rice, squash, egg dishes, roasts, ground meat dishes

Sesame Seed—Asparagus, green beans, potatoes, tomatoes, spinach

Tarragon—Asparagus, beets, cabbage, carrots, cauliflower, mushrooms, tomatoes, salads, macaroni and vegetable combinations, beef, poultry, pork

Thyme—Artichokes, beets, carrots, eggplant, green beans, mushrooms, peas, tomatoes, pork, veal, poultry, cheese and fish dishes, stuffings

Turmeric—Mustards and curries, chicken

ORGANIZING THE KITCHEN

We know a number of people who unpacked their dinnerware and kitchen utensils when they moved into their homes and put things away "temporarily," until they could find the time "to get organized." Twenty years later they are still scrambling all over the kitchen for things they use every day and reaching over things they haven't used in a year.

Here are some hints that can increase your efficiency and decrease some of the frustrations that can arise during food preparation.

1. Keep frequently used items as close as possible to their point of use (pots and pans by the stove, glasses near the sink, and so on).

2. Rearrange your kitchen so that cooking utensils, dishes, and other paraphernalia you use every day, or almost every day, are up front, at eye level in their storage areas and so you don't have to move anything else to reach them. Then, take the items you use perhaps once or twice a year, and put them in the farthest, least convenient reaches of your storage areas. Everything left over, those items you might use once or twice a month, should be put in intermediate areas. (While reorganizing your kitchen, you might consider throwing out anything you haven't used for a year or more. Or, if you have an attic or basement that you don't mind cluttering, stick these little-used items there and throw them out next year if you haven't used them by then!)

3. Don't clutter work space on your counter tops with kitchen equipment. Pick a space at least two feet wide and keep it completely clear for working. This spot is usually best placed either to the right or left of the sink. If at all possible, this should be a hardwood cutting-board surface of oak or maple. Then, clear another counter space to be used as a holding area for the cooking ingredients you assemble prior to cooking, and clear a third spot to be used, if necessary, as a holding area for partly finished dishes that are not yet ready to pop on or into the stove or microwave. If your counter tops are deep enough, you can store canisters and frequently

used small appliances in less used areas, but don't let them cramp your preparation space.

4. If your stove top is not large enough for hot pots when you take them off burners or out of the oven, prepare another area right next to the stove with a fully heat-resistant surface, such as a portable slab of stainless steel. If you are lucky enough to be able to design your own kitchen, build it in (along with that cutting board next to your sink).

5. Efficient kitchen work-centers have sink, refrigerator, and stove all within a step or two of each other but on different walls, forming a triangle of space for you to work in.

6. Set up a logical system for storing canned goods and boxes of foods. Arrange spices in alphabetical order (some people find an alphabetical order good for canned goods, too). The best storage systems for spices have the jars laid on their sides, wine-storage style, with removable, replaceable labels on the tops so that you can add and delete spices when necessary. You can save a great deal of money buying spices in reasonable amounts from a store that sells spices in bulk. Keep the spices in your own jars.

7. Always assemble the ingredients you will need for cooking and lay them out, in order of use, in your holding area before starting to prepare your meal.

8. I have already mentioned that a convenient way to store serving spoons, spatulas, and other large items in constant use is as a "bouquet" in an open canister, vase, or jug near the stove. Silverware needs a drawer only about 2½ inches deep, while small utensils, such as can openers, cork screws, jar openers, etc., can be kept in one deep drawer, about 4" deep, set aside for this purpose, using drawer organizers or cigar box bottoms to group them so they won't jumble and jam as you open the drawer.

9. Open wall space can be used to hang utensils or hang them from the ceiling.

10. Label and date foods that you put in the freezer, and organize the freezer so that you know where things are. Some foods are best used within a few months, while others may last up to a year. For comprehensive advice on how long frozen foods last, check the classic cookbook, *Joy of Cooking*, by Irma S. Rombauer and Marion R. Becker, published by Bobbs-Merrill.

11. A butcher-block-topped table on lockable casters, at counter height, can do double- or even triple-duty and is one of the most useful things you can have in your kitchen: the table is extra work space, it can be used to cart things from kitchen to eating area(s), and it can serve as a kitchen table for light meals. Attaching a 2-inch thick maple top, 24 inches × 36 inches or 48 inches, to a trestle base will allow room for your knees and thighs underneath. Lightweight, easily movable stools can serve as seating for meals, food preparation, or dishwashing.

If you have the opportunity to redo your kitchen or your entire home, or if you have been telling yourself that it's time to "get organized" in just about any aspect of your life, we recommend looking into a book that we found helpful and entertaining: *Getting Organized: The Easy Way to Put Your Life in Order*, by Stephanie Winston, published by W.W. Norton. Some of our ideas are based on her suggestions.

Breakfast Foods

Many nutritionists consider breakfast the most important meal of the day. I think eating in the morning is important in a very special way for persons who are trying to manage their weight: When you skip breakfast, you tend to build up a "hidden hunger" that shows itself in overeating at night.

There is some research evidence that people who eat breakfast are more alert and better problem-solvers in the morning, and that eating a nutritious breakfast helps to avoid the afternoon blahs.

Although some people who wake early really don't feel comfortable if they eat before ten or eleven, or even noon, we think you should give breakfast a try. Experiment for two weeks with a breakfast such as you will find on one of our menus (pp. 403–9) and see if you feel and work better. If you tend to eat from the moment you get home from work until you hit the sack, that tendency to nibble all night might decrease once you start eating breakfast. You must, however, give the experiment a full two weeks to take effect, since it can take your system that long to readjust if you have been skipping breakfast for a long time. There are many hormones and enzymes that mobilize our bodies for the day and that aid in digesting food. They may be slightly out of rhythm, and it can take a while to retrain them. If you find yourself uncomfortable at the end of two weeks, well, go back to what you were doing! It must be right for you.

I like cereal with fruit and milk, or bread and cheese along with a piece of fruit, as my two "standard" breakfasts. Terri prefers yogurt and fresh fruit. Both of us like a good cup of fresh-ground coffee, followed by a second cup! In order to keep our caffeine intake at reasonable levels, we often mix decaffeinated with regular coffee; I usually drink only a half cup at a time. We rarely have eggs, and I cannot remember the last time I had bacon or sausage, although it might have been about a year and a half ago on a camping trip. (Yes, I must admit it: there is something wonderful about the smell and the taste of bacon or sausage and pancakes on the grill out there in the woods, and I don't intend to forego that pleasure permanently!) But these foods are too high in fat and cholesterol to be part of my daily diet.

We include here some "special" breakfast foods for special occasions: pancake recipes with interesting blends of different flours and cereals; French toast; yogurt and fruit; and unusual ways to make eggs.

If you like plain fried or scrambled eggs for breakfast, you can prepare them with very little added fat by using a nonstick vegetable cooking spray or a nonstick-surface pan. Then, too, a plain boiled egg can be delectable if you know how to boil it properly. As you will see below, there really is a trick to it!

Boiled Egg

PREPARATION TIME: 5 MINUTES.   COOKING TIME: 15 MINUTES

Place the egg in a saucepan with enough water to cover. Bring to a boil. Then cover immediately, *remove from the heat,* and let stand 15 minutes for a hard-boiled egg with a light, almost fluffy texture, and no sulfurous green ring. (The green ring results from the interaction of continuous high heat with the sulfur in the egg.) Soft-boiled eggs should stand about 4 to 5 minutes when prepared this way.

Per Egg: 79 calories, 274 mg. cholesterol, no dietary fiber, 6 g. fat, 69 mg. sodium.

Basic Pancake Mix

PREPARATION TIME: 15 MINUTES.   COOKING TIME: 20 TO 30 MINUTES.

For your own, homemade, nutritious pancake mix, you can mix together the dry ingredients listed below, and store the mix in an airtight container. Add the wet ingredients when you're ready to cook.

The mix:

4 cups whole-wheat flour
3 cups all-purpose flour
1½ cups soy flour
2 cups wheat germ

1 teaspoon salt
1 cup instant low-fat dry milk
⅓ cup baking powder

The pancakes:

1½ cups mix
2 eggs, beaten well
1 cup skim milk or water

1 tablespoon oil
Nonstick vegetable cooking
 spray (optional)

1. Combine the mix with the eggs, milk or water, and oil. The batter will be slightly lumpy.
2. Heat a Teflon pan, or other pan sprayed with cooking spray, over medium heat. Pour about ¼ cup of batter per pancake into the pan. When the cakes are bubbly on top and brown on the bottom, flip them and brown the other side.

Makes 12 pancakes. 6 servings.

Per Serving, 2 pancakes: 146 calories, 92 mg. cholesterol, 2 g. dietary fiber, 4 g. fat, 44 mg. sodium.

Mexican Eggs

PREPARATION TIME: 5 TO 10 MINUTES.   COOKING TIME: 5 MINUTES.

Try serving this with warm Whole-Wheat Tortillas (pp. 316–17), and/or Spanish Rice (p. 287). A tablespoon of Avocado Dip (p. 53) goes well with it, too.

Nonstick vegetable cooking
  spray
1 small onion, chopped
1 large tomato, chopped
1 or 2 mild green chilis
  (canned, drained), chopped
  fine

4 eggs, beaten
Dash of salt

1. Spray the skillet with vegetable spray. Add the chopped vegetables, cover, and cook over low heat until tender, stirring occasionally.
2. Push the vegetables to one side of the pan. Add the eggs, and scramble them. When the eggs are almost cooked, mix the vegetables in with them. Add a dash of salt, if desired.

4 servings.

Per Serving: 98 calories, 274 mg. cholesterol, 2 g. dietary fiber, 6 g. fat, 141 mg. sodium.

Bran and Raisin Pancakes

PREPARATION TIME: 10 MINUTES.   COOKING TIME: 25 TO 30 MINUTES.

¾ cup all-purpose flour
2 tablespoons sugar
1 tablespoon baking powder
½ teaspoon salt
1 egg, slightly beaten

1¼ cups skim milk
1 cup All-Bran or Bran Buds
  cereal
3 tablespoons margarine
½ cup raisins

1. In a bowl, mix together the flour, sugar, baking powder, and salt. Set aside.
2. In a large bowl, mix together the egg, milk, cereal, and 2 tablespoons of melted margarine. Let stand 1 to 2 minutes, or until the liquid is absorbed. Stir in the raisins.
3. Add the flour mixture all at once to the cereal mixture, and stir until moistened. The batter will be lumpy.
4. Heat the remaining tablespoon of margarine in a large frying pan over medium heat. Drop the batter in, using 2 tablespoons of batter per pancake. Cook until golden brown, turning once, about 3 minutes on each side.

Makes 18 pancakes. 9 servings.

Per Serving, 2 pancakes: 160 calories, 30 mg. cholesterol, 4 g. dietary fiber, 5 g. fat, 430 mg. sodium.

Bran Scones

PREPARATION TIME: 20 MINUTES.   COOKING TIME: 20 MINUTES.

2 cups whole-wheat flour
1 cup All-Bran or Bran Buds
  cereal
1 tablespoon baking powder
1 tablespoon sugar

½ teaspoon salt
¼ cup margarine
1 egg
½ cup skim milk

1. In a large bowl, mix together the whole-wheat flour,

cereal, baking powder, sugar, and salt. Cut in the margarine until the mixture resembles coarse meal.

2. Beat together the egg and milk. Add to the flour mixture, and stir until well combined.

3. Knead on a lightly floured surface for 2 to 3 minutes, or until smooth. Roll out the dough ½-inch thick, and cut with a 2-inch biscuit or cookie cutter.

4. Place the scones in a heated, lightly greased or Teflon frying pan. Cook over low heat for 10 minutes, turn, and cook 10 minutes more.

Makes 14 scones. 14 servings.

Per Serving: 115 calories, 20 mg. cholesterol, 3 g. dietary fiber, 4 g. fat, 500 mg. sodium.

Breakfast Rice

PREPARATION TIME: 1 TO 2 MINUTES.   COOKING TIME: 10 MINUTES.

1 cup cooked brown rice or other whole grain
½ cup skim or low-fat milk

1 tablespoon raisins
Dash cinnamon or nutmeg

1. Heat the rice in the milk in a saucepan over medium-low heat until warmed. Do not boil.

2. Add the raisins, and heat another minute or two. Pour into a bowl, and top with a dash of cinnamon or nutmeg.

1 serving.

Per Serving: 274 calories, 2 mg. cholesterol, 5 g. dietary fiber, 1 g. fat, 64 mg. sodium.

Brancakes

PREPARATION TIME: 15 MINUTES.   COOKING TIME: 20 TO 25 MINUTES.

1 egg
2 cups skim milk
¾ cup All-Bran or Bran Buds
  cereal

1½ cups all-purpose flour
1 tablespoon baking powder
¼ teaspoon salt
2 tablespoons sugar

1. Beat the egg until foamy. Stir in the milk and the cereal. Let stand 5 minutes.
2. Stir together the flour, baking powder, salt, and sugar in a medium mixing bowl. Add the cereal mixture, stirring to combine, and let stand 5 minutes.
3. Drop the batter, using ¼ cup for each pancake, onto a lightly greased, preheated griddle. Cook, turning once, until golden brown on both sides.

Makes 12 pancakes. 12 servings.

Per Serving: 95 calories, 24 mg. cholesterol, 2 g. dietary fiber, 1 g. fat, 220 mg. sodium.

French Toast

PREPARATION TIME: 5 MINUTES.   COOKING TIME: 7 TO 10 MINUTES.

This is good served with fresh fruit, applesauce, or of course, a tablespoon or two of real maple syrup.

1 egg
1 tablespoon skim milk
¼ teaspoon cinnamon

2 slices whole-grain bread
Nonstick vegetable cooking
  spray

1. Beat the egg and the milk with the cinnamon. Dip the bread in the egg mixture, coating both sides.
2. Spray a skillet with nonstick cooking spray, and heat over medium heat. Fry the bread in the pan, turning once, until golden brown on both sides.

VARIATIONS: Omit the cinnamon, and substitute ¼ teaspoon of grated lemon or orange peel.

1 serving.

Per Serving (without syrup): 247 calories, 279 mg. cholesterol, 3 g. dietary fiber, 10 g. fat, 399 mg. sodium.

Yogurt and Fresh Fruit

PREPARATION TIME: 2 TO 3 MINUTES.

Plain low-fat yogurt mixed with fresh fruit is one of Terri's standard foods for breakfast or for lunch. You can take it with you to work in a plastic container, if there is a refrigerator available for storing it until lunchtime.

Store-bought varieties of yogurt containing fruit also contain large amounts of sugar. Mixing your own means your fruit is fresh, and you can control the amount of sugar. Terri never uses any sweetener besides dried fruit or an occasional bit of sweetened coconut—which actually tastes too sweet to her now.

Her favorite combinations include raisin-apple-almond, raisin- or date-orange-pecan, and raisin-orange-banana with a dash of coconut.

You can use canned fruit, as long as it is unsweetened and canned in its own juices. Canned pineapple with coconut is very good.

You may like to experiment with spices. A dash of cinnamon,

nutmeg, allspice, cardamom, clove, or mace, or a combination of a couple of these, will heighten the sweetness without adding calories.

Some fruits, however, such as apples or bananas, do turn brown when exposed to air, so they are best eaten right away.

Here's the basic recipe:

1 cup plain low-fat yogurt
1 medium-sized piece of fruit, chopped OR ½ cup sliced mixed fruit

1 tablespoon raisins, or other chopped dried fruit
1 tablespoon chopped nuts of choice

1. Combine all the ingredients in a serving bowl, and it's ready to eat.

1 serving.

Per Serving: 296 calories, 14 mg. cholesterol, 4 g. dietary fiber, 8 g. fat, 161 mg. sodium.

Scrambled Eggs and Cheese

PREPARATION TIME: 3 TO 5 MINUTES.   COOKING TIME: 5 MINUTES.

By using an extra egg white you can extend the amount of egg, without using another whole egg. By using very little fat and a low-fat cheese, you also save calories. The difference? 140 calories versus 300!

1 egg
1 egg white
1 ounce low-fat cheese (part-skim mozzarella, Swiss, etc.), grated

Nonstick vegetable cooking spray (optional)

1. Beat together the egg and the egg white. Pour into a nonstick pan, or a pan sprayed with nonstick vegetable cooking spray, and cook over medium-low heat, stirring occasionally.

2. After a minute, add the cheese. Keep cooking and stirring occasionally until done.

1 serving.

Per Serving: 175 calories, 289 mg. cholesterol, no dietary fiber, 10 g. fat, 269 mg. sodium.

Wednesday's "Sunday Breakfast"

PREPARATION TIME: 3 TO 5 MINUTES.   COOKING TIME: 2 MINUTES.

This recipe is named for the fact that it's a quick, easy way to throw together something special in the middle of the week. The original Rotation Diet menus frequently list cottage cheese and a slice or two of bread as part of the breakfast meal. Below is one of the many ways you can dress up cottage cheese without adding many calories or fat. Spread it on a slice of Italian Whole-Wheat Bread (pp. 308–9), or any other whole-grain bread.

¼ cup low-fat cottage cheese
1 small clove garlic, crushed
1 scallion, bulb only, minced

¼ teaspoon Traditional Italian
   Herb Blend (p. 335)
1 slice whole-grain bread

1. Combine the cottage cheese, garlic, scallion, and Herb Blend, and spread on the bread.
2. Broil for a couple of minutes until hot, and serve.

1 serving.

Per Serving: 148 calories, 5 mg. cholesterol, 4 g. dietary fiber, 3 g. fat, 453 mg. sodium.

Whole-Wheat Corn Cakes

PREPARATION TIME: 5 TO 6 MINUTES. COOKING TIME: 20 TO 25 MINUTES.

⅓ cup yellow cornmeal
⅓ cup whole-wheat flour
⅓ cup all-purpose flour
2 teaspoons sugar
2 teaspoons baking powder
Dash of salt

1 egg
1 cup skim or low-fat milk
2 tablespoons vegetable oil
1 teaspoon honey
Nonstick vegetable cooking
  spray

1. Combine the dry ingredients in a medium-sized bowl.
2. In another bowl, beat the egg, then beat in the milk, oil, and honey.
3. Spray a griddle or skillet with cooking spray, and heat over medium heat. When hot, spoon batter into pan to make pancakes about 4 inches in diameter. Cook until they begin to bubble and are golden brown on the bottom. Turn them over and cook until done.

Makes 8 large pancakes. 4 servings.

Per Serving, 2 pancakes: 231 calories, 70 mg. cholesterol, 2 g. dietary fiber, 9 g. fat, 297 mg. sodium.

Appetizers

I have a confession to make: it's been ages since my wife and I have served anything except fruit as an appetizer at our dinner parties. So, Terri and I had to start from scratch to create appetizers that we would be comfortable serving to our friends at our own dinner and cocktail parties.

For casual dinner parties, I enjoy serving a large bowl of fruit on the coffee table, with individual plates and knives for our guests to use for carving up their own apples, pears, or peaches as we talk in the den before dinner.

For large parties and other occasions when you need many different appetizers, consider using a monster-size Creative Fruit Salad (see page 88) as your centerpiece. Hollow out half a watermelon, if available, or use a large punch bowl filled with various fruits, such as melon balls, sliced apples, chunks of fresh pineapple or pears or both, strawberries or blueberries, grapes, and sections of a citrus fruit. Mix in a few ounces of lemon juice to preserve the color, and then add a bottle of white wine or champagne. If you don't care to use an alcoholic beverage as a mixer, use ginger ale. The beverage serves as a marinade for the fruit. Guests can use toothpicks to spear the fruit. If watermelon is not available, we use a 6-quart clear glass brandy snifter to hold our assortment.

You can feature your fruit bowl along with some of the other hors d'oeuvres from this chapter at cocktail parties, but we assure you, a creation of this kind will easily compete for attention with any appetizers that might surround it!

Some of the appetizers in this section are lowered-fat modifications of standard recipes (the Stuffed Mushrooms), while others are quite unusual. The Clam Dip illustrates how to use lower-fat dairy products in place of cream and cream cheese, and create perfectly acceptable dips with 40 percent fewer calories. The Incredibly Edible Artichoke Dip is our version of an even more incredibly edible, incredibly fattening dip. The original uses only cheese and mayonnaise and contains more than double the fat calories of our formula.

There are recipes in other sections of this book that can easily be adapted for use as appetizers. Two that seem particularly appropriate are Spinach Pizza (see pp. 250–51) and Summer Squash Pizza (see pp. 252–53). If you try these pizzas as appetizers, serving size can be determined by cutting the pie into quarters, and then cutting each quarter into eighths; the caloric and nutritional values here would be about one-eighth of those listed under the main-course recipes.

One final word of caution. Many dips and appetizers are unavoidably high in fat, and we all know how hard it is to resist a bowl or plate of those goodies, *especially* when we are hungry! A sure way to ruin a good dinner is to encourage your guests to satisfy their appetite before they even get to the table. So try making individual servings of your appetizers, or perhaps pass them a couple of times and leave the plate in the kitchen. Remember that you can do yourself and your friends a favor by at least providing the alternative of fresh fruits.

We also cut calories when serving dips by using fresh, sliced vegetables or whole-grain crackers for dipping, instead of potato chips and other high-fat snacks.

"Where in hell is today's Melon Fruit Jubilee?" DRAWING BY BOOTH; © 1985 THE NEW YORKER MAGAZINE, INC.

Avocado Dip

PREPARATION TIME: 5 MINUTES.

Though avocados are high in fat, they are nutritious, and can be eaten sparingly. Mixed with yogurt, the protein level is boosted. Go easy on the salt if you are watching your sodium intake.

Often the avocados in the supermarkets are not yet ripe. Simply leave them on the kitchen counter or a windowsill for a day or two until they feel slightly soft. You can speed the process by putting them in a brown paper bag.

Although it doesn't matter a great deal which avocado you use for this dip, the larger Florida (or West Indian) avocados are somewhat lower in fat than the California (or Mexican) avocados. Because of the difference in the size of the seed, the total usable flesh (and thus the total calories) is pretty much the same.

2 medium avocados	Garlic, cumin, salt, and
1 cup plain low-fat yogurt	fresh-ground black pepper to taste

1. Peel and mash the avocados in a medium-sized bowl. Add the remaining ingredients and mix well with a fork, or, for a very smooth consistency, use a wire whisk or blend in a blender. Serve with cut up fresh vegetables, whole-grain crackers, or Quick Tortilla Chips (p. 62).

Makes about 1½ cups. Serving size is 1 tablespoon.

Per Serving: 33 calories, no cholesterol, 1 g. dietary fiber, 3 g. fat, 31 mg. sodium (with ¼ teaspoon salt used in the complete recipe).

Cheese and Olive Party Toast

PREPARATION TIME: 8 TO 10 MINUTES.   COOKING TIME: 2 MINUTES.

¼ cup black olives, chopped
¼ cup scallion, chopped
¼ cup shredded Swiss cheese
1 tablespoon mayonnaise
¼ teaspoon Indian Spice Blend
   (p. 334) or other curry
   powder

¼ teaspoon salt
¼ teaspoon black pepper
1 tablespoon grated Parmesan
   cheese
14 slices rye party-round bread

1. Combine all ingredients except bread, and mix well.
2. Spread a scant teaspoon of the mixture on each slice of
   bread. Broil for 2 minutes, until the cheese melts.

Makes 14 rounds. 14 servings.

Per Serving: 38 calories, 3 mg. cholesterol, 1 g. dietary fiber, 2 g.
fat, 120 mg. sodium.

Eggplant Caviar

PREPARATION TIME: 1 HOUR AND 15 MINUTES.   COOKING TIME: 35
                                                   TO 40 MINUTES.

Eggplant is thought to have been cultivated first in India over
four thousand years ago. Though popular in Middle Eastern
countries, it made its way westward slowly, being regarded
with some suspicion by Europeans, who thought it might be
dangerous. John Gerard of England wrote in his *Herball* in
1597 that eggplant had "a mischievous quality." We are not

sure precisely what he meant by that, but he admonished his readers to "forsake" the eggplant.

For those who don't mind making a little mischief, serve this tasty spread chilled, with whole-grain, low-salt crackers, wedges of pita bread, or Quick Tortilla Chips (p. 62).

1 large eggplant
½ cup scallions, chopped fine
1 small bell pepper (red, green, or yellow), minced
2 cloves garlic, minced or crushed
1 tablespoon olive oil
2 medium tomatoes, chopped

½ teaspoon fresh-ground black pepper
⅛ teaspoon cayenne pepper
½ teaspoon cumin
½ teaspoon salt
Dash of Tabasco (optional)
2 tablespoons lemon juice

1. Preheat oven to 400 degrees. Pierce the eggplant several times with a fork, and place on a foil-covered baking sheet. Bake for about 1 hour, turning the eggplant occasionally.
2. When the eggplant is done, the skin will be wrinkled and soft. Take it out of the oven and let it cool. Cut it in half, scoop out the pulp, and chop it finely. Place it in a colander in the sink to drain while you prepare the other ingredients.
3. Sauté the onion, pepper, and garlic in the oil over medium heat until the onion is translucent. Add all the other ingredients except the lemon juice, stirring the eggplant in last.
4. Cover and let simmer on low heat for about 30 minutes, stirring occasionally. Then remove the cover, and let simmer until liquid is reduced.
5. Let cool, then stir in the lemon juice, and refrigerate.

Makes about 2½ cups. Serving size is 1 tablespoon.

Per Serving: 10 calories, no cholesterol, 1 g. dietary fiber, no fat, 287 mg. sodium.

Clam Dip

PREPARATION TIME: 6 TO 7 MINUTES.

We are pretty generous with the garlic when we prepare this recipe, and suggest you serve it with a large variety of fresh vegetables. Compared with recipes that use cream cheese or other dairy products with higher fat contents, this recipe has as much as 40 percent fewer calories.

4 ounces Neufchatel cheese
¼ cup plain low-fat yogurt
1½ teaspoons white
  OR red Worcestershire sauce

1 can (7 ounces) minced clams
Garlic powder, salt, and
  fresh-ground black pepper to
  taste

1. Let the Neufchatel cheese soften to room temperature, then blend it in a bowl with the yogurt and Worcestershire sauce.
2. Open the can of clams, drain and reserve the liquid, and add the clams to the dairy mixture. Add a small amount of the reserved clam liquid to make a light (but not soupy) dip.
3. Add the seasonings to taste, and chill until serving time. Serve with whole-grain crackers, celery sticks, or other fresh vegetables.

Makes about 1½ cups. Serving size is 1 tablespoon.

Per Serving: 18 calories, 9 mg. cholesterol, no dietary fiber, 2 g. fat, 46 mg sodium.

Stuffed Mushrooms

PREPARATION TIME: 20 MINUTES.   COOKING TIME: 15 MINUTES.

Here is an example of how to combine a small amount of butter, for flavoring, with other fats (in this case, olive oil) and herbs. The combination of parsley, garlic, and onions is basic to many recipes and here provides for a mild, noticeably buttery stuffing. If you prefer a spicier appetizer, add to the stuffing recipe below freshly ground black pepper or your favorite herb blend to taste, or just ONE splash of Tabasco.

24 large mushrooms (about 8 to 10 ounces)
1 small clove garlic, crushed
¼ cup onions, finely minced
¼ teaspoon dried parsley
2 teaspoons olive oil
3 heaping tablespoons

Whole-Wheat Bread Crumbs (pp. 307–8)
1 tablespoon egg white (save the rest of the egg for another recipe)
1 teaspoon melted butter

1. Rinse the mushrooms and remove the stems. Dice six of the stems and reserve.
2. Sauté the garlic, onions, and parsley in the oil, stirring constantly until onions are translucent. Carefully drain any liquid from the pan.
3. Stir in the bread crumbs, egg white, and butter, and mix thoroughly.
4. Fill the mushrooms with this mixture. Place on a foil-covered baking pan, and bake at 350 degrees for 15 minutes.

6 servings. Serving size is 4 mushrooms.

Per Serving: 48 calories, 2 mg. cholesterol, 1 g. dietary fiber, 3 g. fat, 36 mg. sodium.

Mexican-Style Hot Sauce

PREPARATION TIME: 10 MINUTES.

This is a good salsa-type dip for fresh vegetables, Quick Tortilla Chips (p. 62), or for use in any Mexican recipe. It requires no cooking, and contains no oil. We like it spicy hot, but if you prefer a milder sauce, cut back on the Tabasco . . . or the crushed red pepper . . . or the jalapeños!

1 can (28 ounces) whole tomatoes
1 can (6 ounces) tomato paste
3 to 4 scallions, finely chopped
½ medium bell pepper, diced
4 jalapeño peppers, finely chopped, plus 3 tablespoons juice

½ ounce (¼ bottle) Tabasco sauce
1 tablespoon crushed red pepper
¾ cup water

1. Pour the can of whole tomatoes into a large bowl, along with their juice. Chop the tomatoes into small pieces.
2. Add all the other ingredients, blending well. Store in a glass container in the refrigerator.

Makes about 6 cups. Serving size is 1 tablespoon.

Per Serving: 4 calories, no cholesterol, no dietary fiber, no fat, 2 mg. sodium

Roast Beef Roll-Ups

PREPARATION TIME: 15 MINUTES.

The original recipe for this cold appetizer calls for corned beef. Lean roast beef works just as well, however, and is lower in salt and fat. You can even use lean, thin-sliced turkey.

2½ ounces lean, thin-sliced roast beef or other lean meat
3 ounces Neufchatel cheese, softened to room temperature

2 teaspoons skim milk
¾ teaspoon tamari sauce OR soy sauce
1 small clove garlic, crushed
1 small scallion, minced

1. Slice the roast beef into 26 pieces about 4 inches long and 2 inches wide.
2. In a small bowl, combine the remaining ingredients. Spread a teaspoon of the mixture across each piece of beef, roll up the beef, and secure it with a toothpick. Place on a serving platter, and serve.

26 servings.

Per Serving: 13 calories, 4 mg. cholesterol, no dietary fiber, 1 g. fat, 68 mg. sodium.

Garbanzo Dip

PREPARATION TIME: 10 MINUTES.

A low-fat alternative to traditional hummous. And, by the way, if you can find the unhulled sesame seeds, they are an excellent source of calcium. They are usually available in specialty food shops. See pages 237–38 for instructions on how to toast seeds without added fat.

1 can (15 ounces) garbanzo
  beans
1 teaspoon onion powder
2 to 3 cloves garlic, crushed
¼ teaspoon salt

½ cup plain low-fat yogurt
2 tablespoons toasted sesame
  seeds, ground with mortar
  and pestle

1. Drain the garbanzos, and pour the beans into a blender or food processor.
2. Add the onion powder, garlic, salt, and yogurt, and blend until smooth.
3. Pour the mixture into a serving bowl, and top with the sesame seeds. Chill until serving time.

Makes about 2 cups. Serving size is 1 tablespoon.

Per Serving: 28 calories, no cholesterol, 1 g. dietary fiber, 1 g. fat, 20 mg. sodium.

Incredibly Edible Artichoke Dip

PREPARATION TIME: 7 TO 8 MINUTES.

For variety, this dip is also good with about ½ teaspoon of Traditional Italian Herb Blend (p. 335) in addition to the spices listed. Serve it with whole-grain crackers (Ak-Mak, a sesame cracker available in the imported foods section of supermarkets, is particularly good).

1 can (14 ounces) artichokes
¾ cup plain low-fat yogurt
1½ tablespoons mayonnaise
½ cup grated Swiss cheese
½ teaspoon garlic powder
1 tablespoon dried parsley
OR 3 tablespoons fresh
parsley, minced
2 tablespoons Parmesan cheese
Fresh-ground black pepper to
taste
Paprika (optional)

1. Drain the artichokes in a colander and rinse to remove some of the salt. Whir them in a blender or food processor for a few seconds until coarsely chopped.
2. In a medium bowl, combine the chopped artichokes with all the other ingredients except the paprika. Pour into a serving bowl, and sprinkle with paprika. Chill until serving time.

Makes about 3¼ cups. Serving size is 1 tablespoon.

Per Serving: 17 calories, 2 mg. cholesterol, no dietary fiber, 1 g. fat, 51 mg. sodium.

Salmon Mousse

PREPARATION TIME: 10 MINUTES.

Serve this as an appetizer on whole-grain crackers, or use it as a sandwich spread. It is also good on whole-grain English muffins and broiled for a couple of minutes. This is one of our new appetizers that are slightly higher in fat, but it is so delicious that it's worth showing off on occasion. The use of Neufchatel cheese in place of cream cheese helps lower the saturated fat content, and salmon is a good source of the "good" Omega III fatty acids that we discuss on page 193.

1 can (16 ounces) salmon,
   drained and flaked
8 ounces Neufchatel cheese
3 tablespoons lemon juice
2 tablespoons diced red onion
1 tablespoon fresh parsley,
   minced

2 teaspoons pure horseradish
¼ cup chopped nuts (walnuts
   or pecans are good)
Black olive or teaspoon of nuts
   for garnish (optional)

1. In a blender or food processor, combine all ingredients except the nuts, and blend until smooth.
2. Stir in the ¼ cup of nuts, then pour the mousse into a serving bowl. Chill until serving time. Garnish with a black olive in the center, or decorate with the teaspoon of nuts, if desired, and serve.

Makes about 2 cups. Serving size is 1 tablespoon.

Per Serving: 45 calories, 11 mg. cholesterol, no dietary fiber, 3 g. fat, 102 mg. sodium.

Quick Tortilla Chips

PREPARATION TIME: 5 MINUTES.   COOKING TIME: 10 MINUTES.

Keep your eye on these while they are baking, as they brown quickly.

1 or 2 tablespoons vegetable oil   1 package corn tortillas (10
   OR nonstick vegetable   6-inch rounds)
   cooking spray

1. Either spread the oil lightly on a foil-covered baking sheet with a pastry brush, or spray the sheet with nonstick cooking spray.
2. Stack the tortillas on top of each other and cut into eighths. Spread the tortilla pieces on the baking sheet, and brush or spray lightly with oil.
3. Bake at 350 degrees for about 10 minutes, or until just beginning to turn crispy and brown.

VARIATIONS: Sprinkle the chips with garlic powder, Parmesan cheese, paprika, or other seasonings before baking.

Makes 80 chips.

Per Chip: 10 calories, no cholesterol, no dietary fiber, 1 g. fat, 2 mg. sodium.

Soups

As a main meal or a first course, soups are always in season: refreshing cold soups for the summer, invigorating hot soups for the winter.

We like to start most of our soups with our own homemade chicken or vegetable stock, and we have included some basic stock recipes (see Basic Soup Stocks, pp. 64 to 67).

Another trick we like to use is to save the liquid from steaming or simmering vegetables for use in soups. Pour the liquid into a plastic freezer container, seal it, and freeze. Whenever you cook vegetables, simply add the leftover juices to the container. Then, when you want to use the stock for soups or for cooking grains or any other dish, run the container under warm water to loosen the sides, and pop the whole cube into a saucepan. Heat until you melt as much as you need for your recipe; if you don't need it all, put the rest of the cube back in the freezer for another time. We use most vegetable juices for this purpose, but we avoid stronger ones, such as asparagus, which tend to overpower the flavor of milder ingredients.

We realize that many people don't want to take the time to make their own stock and, in a pinch, we, too, will use instant bouillon granules or bouillon cubes. If you use instant, you should be aware that *the* primary ingredient in commercial preparations is *salt*. A single cube or teaspoon of granules, the measure ordinarily used to create one cup of bouillon, can contain 900 to 1500 milligrams of sodium. When we do use a commercial instant bouillon, we use Wyler's at half strength or less, or a no-salt-added bouillon by Featherweight, which relies on potassium chloride as the primary source of its salty flavor. However, Featherweight is rather sweet; it contains more sugar and corn syrup than chicken flavor in the Chicken-Flavor Instant Bouillon.

Clear soups are generally lower in calories than cream soups, but we have found that substituting skim or low-fat milk in place of cream works very well.

Cornstarch, flour, and arrowroot are good thickeners. A roux is another thickener, made with flour and butter or margarine. It should be cooked over low heat long enough to turn golden brown, or you will have a floury flavor in your food. Arrowroot is good, but I have never used it and Terri rarely uses it because it doesn't reheat well, and she likes to make enough of a recipe for leftovers. You can also mix flour or cornstarch with a small amount of water or stock to make a thin paste and add this to soups or sauces. Soups with vegetables can be thickened by whirring a few of the vegetables in a blender or food processor until puréed and stirring the mixture back into the soup.

Making a meal out of a hearty soup is one of our standard winter dinners, along with a bountiful salad and a slice of whole-grain bread. Thus, we've included a couple of chili recipes, and other warm, filling soups in this section. Also check the Beef, Lamb, Poultry, Fish, and Veal sections for some wonderful stews.

Finally, soup appears to be an excellent aid in preventing overeating. Persons who frequently include soup with their meals find it easier to lose weight and maintain their losses.

BASIC SOUP STOCKS

Soup Base

PREPARATION TIME: 15 TO 20 MINUTES.   COOKING TIME: 2 HOURS.

This is the basic stock that we use for making soups of various kinds, rice, and boiled potatoes. It is excellent for soaking and cooking beans.

Save all chicken and turkey giblets (necks, hearts, gizzards, but *not* livers). Freeze these parts immediately, first trimming skin and any fat from the necks, and hold in your freezer until you have accumulated the parts of 4 to 6 birds.

You may substitute a beef soup bone or two for the giblets, but we prefer the lighter flavor and lower cholesterol of chicken stock.

You can also freeze the soup stock in plastic containers for later use as needed.

Giblets of 4 to 6 birds
1 large bay leaf
Salt and pepper to taste
1 teaspoon each: rosemary, sage, thyme, tarragon

1 large onion, coarsely chopped
2 large stalks celery, cut into 2-inch pieces (include leaves)
2 large carrots, cut into 2-inch pieces

1. Place the giblets in a deep soup kettle, with enough water to cover (about 8 to 10 cups). Bring to a boil and skim as necessary. When finally clear of fat scum, add the remaining ingredients. You may also throw in any other greens or wilted vegetables you have on hand in your refrigerator (except for asparagus, cabbage, broccoli, and cauliflower, which taste too strong).
2. Bring to a boil once again, then reduce heat and simmer for at least 2 hours.
3. Separate the giblets and vegetables from the water. Blend the vegetables in a blender or food processor until smooth, and return to the stock. Save the cooked giblets for low-calorie snacks.

Makes about 10 to 12 cups, depending on how many giblets and how many vegetables you add.

Per Cup (10 cups): 31 calories, 20 mg. cholesterol, 1 g. dietary fiber, 1 g. fat, 82 mg. sodium.

Basic Vegetable Stock

PREPARATION TIME: 10 MINUTES.   COOKING TIME: 1 HOUR.

Here's a basic recipe for a stock made from water and a variety of fresh vegetables. You can add other vegetables, such as parsnips, turnips, leeks, etc., if desired.

3 medium carrots, cut in
  chunks
2 stalks celery, cut in chunks
3 medium onions, cut in
  chunks
3 cloves garlic, minced

⅓ cup fresh parsley, minced
1 bay leaf
6 whole peppercorns
½ teaspoon tarragon and/or
  other dried herbs
6 cups water

1. Combine all ingredients in a large soup pot, and bring to a boil. Reduce heat to simmer, cover, and let cook for about 1 hour.
2. You may strain the vegetables out and use the clear broth, or put the stock in a blender and purée for a thicker stock, adding more water if necessary.

Makes about 8 cups.

Per Cup: 24 calories, no cholesterol, 2 g. dietary fiber, no fat, 23 mg. sodium.

Onion Stock

PREPARATION TIME: 15 MINUTES.   COOKING TIME: 5 MINUTES.

If you are out of vegetable or other stock, try making a quick onion broth for soups, as follows:

1 large onion, sliced
1 tablespoon vegetable oil

5 cups water

1. Sauté the sliced onions in the oil over medium heat until golden brown, stirring often.
2. Add the water, bring to a boil, then reduce heat and let simmer for about 5 minutes. You may strain the onions

out, depending on the type of dish you are planning to combine with the stock. We usually prefer to leave the onions in, as they provide added fiber, vitamins, and minerals.

Makes about 5½ cups of stock.

Per ½ Cup: 15 calories, no cholesterol, no dietary fiber, 1 g. fat, 1 mg. sodium.

SOUPS

Asparagus Soup

PREPARATION TIME: 25 MINUTES.   COOKING TIME: 10 TO 15 MINUTES.

You may substitute canned asparagus if necessary, but, as usual, fresh is best.

1 pound fresh asparagus	½ to 1 teaspoon dry mustard
2½ cups skim milk	Fresh-ground black pepper to
1½ teaspoons onion powder	taste
½ teaspoon salt	Fresh parsley sprigs or chives

1. Wash and trim asparagus spears, and steam until just tender.
2. Chop the asparagus into 1-inch pieces, and place in a blender or food processor. Add the milk, onion powder, salt, and mustard, and blend at high speed until smooth.
3. Pour the soup into a pot, and heat over medium heat. Do not boil.
4. Pour into 4 serving bowls, grind some black pepper on top, and garnish with a couple of parsley sprigs.

4 servings. Serving size is about 1½ cups.

Per Serving: 85 calories, 2 mg. cholesterol, 2 g. dietary fiber, 1 g. fat, 351 mg. sodium.

"Before you go accepting a dinner invitation, remember their dollar stretcher gumbo with potato balls." DRAWING BY GEO. PRICE; © 1979 THE NEW YORKER MAGAZINE, INC.

Chunky Tomato Soup

PREPARATION TIME: 10 TO 15 MINUTES.   COOKING TIME: 45 MINUTES.

This is a spicy soup if you use the cumin. You may also prefer to reduce the amount of scallion, if you find it too strong.

1 tablespoon olive oil
1 cup scallion, minced
2 cloves garlic, crushed
¼ teaspoon cumin (optional)
Black pepper to taste

3 cans (28 ounces each) tomatoes, plus their juice
2 medium tomatoes, diced
2 tablespoons fresh parsley, minced

1. Heat the olive oil in a large saucepan over medium heat.

Add the onion and garlic, cover, and sauté, stirring occasionally. Add a little water if necessary to keep the ingredients from sticking.
2. Add the cumin and pepper, turn heat to low, and cover.
3. Drain the canned tomatoes and reserve the juice. In a blender or food processor, whir the canned tomatoes until smooth. Add tomatoes to the onion mixture, along with the reserved juice and the fresh tomatoes. Cover and let simmer over low heat for about 45 minutes.
4. Sprinkle with parsley and serve.

6 servings. Serving size is 2 cups.

Per Serving: 123 calories, no cholesterol, 5 g. dietary fiber, 3 g. fat, 646 mg. sodium.

Quick Clam Soup

PREPARATION TIME: 4 MINUTES.   COOKING TIME: 10 MINUTES.

2 cans (6½ ounces each) clams, with juice
2 cups vegetable or chicken stock
1 bay leaf
½ teaspoon dried thyme
Salt and fresh-ground black pepper to taste
4 teaspoons chopped chives

1. Combine the clams with their juice, the stock, bay leaf, thyme, salt, and pepper in a saucepan, and heat through.
2. Pour into 4 serving bowls and top each with a teaspoon of chives.

4 servings. Serving size is 1 cup.

Per Serving: 96 calories, 46 mg. cholesterol, no dietary fiber, 3 g. fat, 607 mg. sodium.

David's Chili

PREPARATION TIME: 35 MINUTES TOTAL.   COOKING TIME: 4½ HOURS.

This is my son David's multi-bean chili. The beans and rice combination provides protein, boosted by the judicious use of a small amount of beef.

1 cup white beans
½ cup black beans
1½ quarts water
4 to 5 cloves garlic, minced or crushed
2 teaspoons salt
2 tablespoons olive oil
¼ cup uncooked brown rice

¼ cup lentils
1 cup water
2 medium onions, quartered
2 tablespoons chili powder
1 teaspoon crushed red pepper (optional)
½ pound lean ground beef
1 can (10 ounces) tomato purée

1. Rinse the white and black beans. Place them in a 2½-quart saucepan with the 1½ quarts of water. Bring to a boil, then reduce heat to simmer.
2. Add the garlic, salt, and oil. Cover and simmer for about 2½ hours, stirring occasionally.
3. Add the rice and the lentils, along with the 1 cup of water. Bring to a boil again, then reduce the heat to simmer.
4. Add the onions, chili powder, and the red pepper if desired.
5. Cover and simmer for about 2 more hours, stirring occasionally, and adding extra water if necessary to keep the beans covered.
6. Meanwhile, brown the ground beef in a skillet. Drain off any excess fat, and stir in the tomato purée. Simmer for about 15 minutes.
7. When most of the water has cooked away from the beans, add the meat sauce, and mix well.

8 servings. Serving size is 1 cup.

Per Serving: 266 calories, 25 mg. cholesterol, 8 g. dietary fiber, 10 g. fat, 590 mg. sodium.

French Onion Soup

PREPARATION TIME: 15 TO 20 MINUTES.   COOKING TIME: 30 MINUTES.

One bowl of onion soup for dinner in a restaurant can tip the scales a couple of pounds higher in the morning. This is due to the large amount of salt usually found in these soups; the salt makes you retain water. Here's a recipe using no- or low-salt bouillon or homemade stock that eliminates some of the sodium without eliminating the soup. (The cognac helps make up for some of that lost salt flavor.)

2 medium onions, sliced in rounds
1 tablespoon butter or margarine
4 cups beef stock
1 bay leaf
1 teaspoon dried basil
½ teaspoon dried thyme
½ teaspoon salt

½ teaspoon fresh-ground black pepper
Dash of cognac or dry sherry (optional)
4 slices Whole-Wheat French Bread (pp. 310–11)
4 slices Swiss cheese, ½ ounce each
2 tablespoons grated Parmesan or Romano cheese

1. Sauté the onions in the butter or margarine until they are translucent, stirring occasionally. Add a little water if necessary to keep the onions from sticking.
2. Add the bouillon, seasonings, and the cognac if desired, and bring to a low boil. Reduce heat, and let simmer for 30 minutes.
3. Meanwhile, toast the bread on a foil-covered baking sheet under the broiler until crisp. Top each slice of bread with a slice of Swiss cheese, and broil for several minutes more, until cheese is melted. (Keep your eye on it!)
4. Place ½ tablespoon of grated Parmesan or Romano cheese in each of four soup bowls. Pour 1 cup of onion soup in each bowl, and float the bread slices on top.

4 servings. Serving size is 1½ cups.

Per Serving: 232 calories, 24 mg. cholesterol, 5 g. dietary fiber, 11 g. fat, 1382 mg. sodium.

Potato and Cheese Soup

PREPARATION TIME: 10 MINUTES.   COOKING TIME: 45 MINUTES.

Use Swiss, Jarlsberg, or Emmenthaler cheese for this one.

2 cups stock—vegetable,
  chicken, or beef
1½ cups water
1 bay leaf
½ teaspoon salt
Fresh-ground black pepper to
  taste
1 medium onion, diced
2 large potatoes, diced
2 stalks celery, diced

4 ounces fresh mushrooms,
  sliced
2 tablespoons butter or
  margarine
2 tablespoons whole-wheat
  flour
3 tablespoons fresh parsley,
  minced
4 ounces shredded cheese

1. Combine stock, water, bay leaf, salt, pepper, onions, potatoes, celery, and mushrooms in a large pot, and bring to a boil. Reduce heat, and let simmer covered for 30 minutes, or until potatoes are tender.
2. In a small saucepan, melt the butter or margarine over medium heat, and stir in the flour. Stir constantly until golden brown, then add the mixture to the soup.
3. Raise the heat to medium high, and stir the soup until it bubbles and thickens. Sprinkle with parsley and cheese, and serve.

8 servings. Serving size is 1¼ cups.

Per Serving: 164 calories, 21 mg. cholesterol, 3 g. dietary fiber, 7 g. fat, 405 mg. sodium.

Patti's Vegetable Soup

PREPARATION TIME: 30 MINUTES.   COOKING TIME: 1 HOUR.

2 tablespoons vegetable oil
4 medium white onions,
  peeled, halved, and sliced
3 leeks, trimmed, halved
  lengthwise, and sliced
4 medium carrots, sliced
2 small turnips, peeled,
  quartered, and sliced
4 stalks celery, sliced
5 large cloves garlic, minced
½ teaspoon dried thyme

¼ teaspoon dried tarragon
5 large potatoes, skins on,
  sliced
8 cups chicken stock
1½ cups skim milk
¼ teaspoon nutmeg
Fresh-ground black pepper to
  taste
1 medium bunch endive
  lettuce, well rinsed, shredded
½ cup grated Parmesan cheese

1. Heat the oil in a large kettle over medium-high heat. Add the onions, leeks, carrots, turnips, celery, garlic, thyme, and tarragon, tossing to coat. Cover and cook vegetables, stirring occasionally, until they begin to soften, about 10 minutes.
2. Stir in the potatoes and the stock. Cover and bring to a boil, then simmer, partially covered, for 45 minutes, stirring occasionally.
3. With a slotted spoon, transfer half the vegetables to a food processor or blender, and purée until smooth. Return the purée to the kettle. If the soup seems thin, purée a few more vegetables.
4. Add the milk, the nutmeg, and a generous grinding of black pepper. Return the soup to a low boil. If soup seems too thick, add a little more stock.
5. Scatter the endive on the surface of the soup, cover, and simmer about 5 more minutes. Stir, and serve, with 2 teaspoons of grated Parmesan sprinkled on top of each serving.

12 servings. Serving size is 1½ cups.

Per Serving: 146 calories, 4 mg. cholesterol, 3 g. dietary fiber, 4 g. fat, 621 mg. sodium.

Barley Chicken Soup

PREPARATION TIME: 10 TO 15 MINUTES.   COOKING TIME: 2½ HOURS.

A complete meal in one pot. Omit the cayenne pepper and crushed red pepper if you don't like spicy food. You can also decrease or omit the salt if you are trying to cut down on your sodium intake.

4 chicken breasts (or 8 thighs or drumsticks), skinned
½ cup barley
2 quarts water
3 large carrots, cut in ¼-inch slices
1 large stalk celery, sliced

1 medium onion, diced
1 teaspoon salt
½ teaspoon thyme
¼ teaspoon cayenne pepper (optional)
⅛ teaspoon crushed red pepper (optional)

1. Combine all ingredients in a large soup kettle. Bring to a boil, then reduce heat and simmer for 2½ hours.

4 servings. Serving size is 2 cups.

Per Serving: 205 calories, 73 mg. cholesterol, 4 g. dietary fiber, 4 g. fat, 656 mg. sodium.

Cold Tomato Soup (Julian's)

PREPARATION TIME: 10 MINUTES.   COOKING TIME: 45 MINUTES.

This delicious soup is the first course of a full meal prepared by the chef at Julian's, in Nashville, that contains fewer than 600 calories for the whole meal. The main course is the Grilled Duck Breast (p. 183), followed by the Crêpe with Fresh Strawberries (pp. 364–65) for dessert.

1 teaspoon unsalted butter
½ cup diced carrots
½ cup diced onions
1 clove garlic, minced

3 pounds fresh tomatoes
1 quart chicken stock
1 tablespoon chopped fresh basil

1 tablespoon chopped fresh
  parsley

½ teaspoon black peppercorns
Pinch of thyme

1. Melt the butter in a large pot, add the carrots, onions, and garlic, and cook over low heat for 2 minutes. Add all the remaining ingredients, and bring to a boil. Simmer for 45 minutes.
2. Put the soup in a blender and purée. Cool, then chill in the refrigerator. Garnish with a leaf of fresh basil, if available, before serving.

8 servings. Serving size is 1 cup.

Per Serving: 91 calories, 2 mg. cholesterol, 6 g. dietary fiber, 2 g. fat, 60 mg. sodium.

English Cucumber Soup

PREPARATION TIME: 10 TO 15 MINUTES.   REFRIGERATION TIME: 4 HOURS.

You may garnish this soup with a tablespoon per serving of either chopped hard-cooked egg, finely chopped scallions, chives, croutons (preferably whole grain), or avocado.

2 pounds cucumbers
3 cups chicken stock
3 cups plain low-fat yogurt
3 tablespoons white wine
  vinegar

1 garlic clove
2 teaspoons salt
½ teaspoon white pepper (or
  black)

1. Wash but do not peel the cucumbers. Cut them into 1-inch chunks, and purée along with the remaining ingredients in a blender or food processor.
2. Refrigerate at least 4 hours.

8 servings. Serving size is 1 cup.

Per Serving: 86 calories, 6 mg. cholesterol, 2 g. dietary fiber, 2 g. fat, 888 mg. sodium.

Gazpacho

PREPARATION TIME: 10 MINUTES.   REFRIGERATION TIME: 24 HOURS.

Serve this chilled soup in bowls with one of the following garnishes: chopped hard-boiled egg, finely chopped scallions, chives, croutons, or avocado (1 tablespoon per serving; the avocado will add more fat and calories than the other choices).

1 large tomato	2 cups tomato juice
½ small onion	3 tablespoons red wine vinegar
½ medium cucumber	½ cup white wine
½ medium green pepper	2 tablespoons basil
1 celery stalk	1 tablespoon lemon juice
2 teaspoons fresh parsley, finely chopped	1 teaspoon salt
	½ teaspoon white pepper
2 cloves garlic, minced or crushed	1 teaspoon Worcestershire sauce
	Dash of Tabasco sauce

1. Finely chop all vegetables. (A food processor is ideal for this.) Combine all remaining ingredients and refrigerate for 24 hours.

6 servings. Serving size is ¾ cup.

Per Serving (without garnishes): 42 calories, no cholesterol, 2 g. dietary fiber, no fat, 658 mg. sodium.

Minestrone Soup

PREPARATION TIME: 25 MINUTES.   COOKING TIME: 2 HOURS.

You may use 2 teaspoons or more of Traditional Italian Herb Blend (p. 335) in place of the garlic, basil, salt, and pepper in this recipe. Another handy feature is that you don't have to soak the beans overnight before cooking, as there is plenty of cooking time in the recipe itself. Try it with our Italian Whole-Wheat Bread (pp. 308–9).

3 cups chicken stock	½ cup uncooked navy beans
3 cups water	1 bay leaf

2 medium carrots, sliced
1 medium potato, diced
½ small head of cabbage, shredded
1 can (16 ounces) unsalted tomatoes
1 medium onion, diced
1 stalk celery, sliced
1 tablespoon olive oil
1 medium zucchini, cut into chunks

2 cloves garlic, minced or crushed
¾ teaspoon dried basil leaves
¼ teaspoon salt
¼ teaspoon fresh-ground black pepper
2 tablespoons fresh parsley, minced
½ cup whole-wheat macaroni, uncooked

1. In a 6-quart soup pot, combine the stock, water, navy beans, and bay leaf. Bring to a boil, then reduce heat and let simmer for 1 hour.
2. Add the carrots, potato, cabbage, and tomatoes, and let cook another 30 minutes.
3. Meanwhile, sauté the onions and celery in the oil over medium heat, until onions are translucent. Stir in the zucchini, garlic, and the other seasonings, including the parsley. Cover, and let sauté/steam until tender. Add this mixture to the beans, and let simmer together for about 15 to 20 minutes.
4. Add the macaroni, and cook until tender, about 10 minutes, adding more water if necessary.

8 servings. Serving size is 1½ cups.

Per Serving: 107 calories, no cholesterol, 5 g. dietary fiber, 3 g. fat, 464 mg. sodium.

Split-Pea Soup with Vegetables

PREPARATION TIME: 15 MINUTES.   COOKING TIME: 2 TO 2½ HOURS.

Here is a basic recipe for meatless split-pea soup. Instead of the usual ham hock or other pork meat (and fat) that is customarily added to split-pea soup, we recommend adding to this recipe a couple of whole cloves, and/or about ¼ teaspoon of sage, and/or ¼ teaspoon of rosemary. We think these additional seasonings complement the taste of the peas best, though of course you can use any other herbs that you like.

This is delicious served with Breadsticks (p. 319).

1 pound dried split peas
Water or vegetable stock
1½ cups celery, sliced into
  ½-inch pieces
1 cup carrots, sliced into
  ¼-inch pieces

3 medium red potatoes, cut
  into eighths
2 teaspoons salt
⅛ teaspoon black pepper

1. Rinse the peas and combine with 2½ quarts of water or stock. Bring to a boil, then reduce the heat and let simmer for 1 hour, stirring every 15 minutes.
2. Add 2 more cups of water, the celery, carrots, potatoes, salt, pepper, and other seasonings if desired. Return to a boil, then reduce heat again, and simmer another hour, stirring every 15 minutes. The soup is done when the peas are creamy, the vegetables are soft but hold their shape, and the soup is thick but not stiff. If necessary, add more water and simmer an additional 20 minutes.

6 servings as a main course. Serving size is 2 cups.

Per Serving: 322 calories, no cholesterol, 13 g. dietary fiber, 1 g. fat, 779 mg. sodium.

Vichyssoise

PREPARATION TIME: 30 MINUTES.   COOKING TIME: 30 MINUTES.

Again, yogurt and low-fat milk come to the rescue. Vichyssoise is a traditional French delicacy, heavy on the heavy cream. Here's our low-fat version to be served hot or cold.

2 medium potatoes
1 pound leeks
2 tablespoons butter or margarine
2 ½ cups chicken or vegetable stock

3 cups low-fat milk
1 cup plain low-fat yogurt
Fresh-ground black pepper to taste
2 tablespoons chives

1. Scrub the potatoes and dice them finely. Wash and trim the leeks, and dice them finely.
2. Melt the butter in a large saucepan or pot over medium heat. Add the potatoes and leeks, and turn the heat to low. Cover and let sauté/steam for about 10 minutes, stirring often. You may wish to add a little bit of the stock to keep the vegetables from sticking.
3. Pour in the stock, and bring to a boil. Add the milk, and reduce the heat to medium low. When milk is heated through, cover and reduce the heat to low. Let simmer for about 30 minutes, then set aside to cool for another 30 minutes.
4. Pour the soup in a blender or food processor, and add the yogurt and pepper. Blend until smooth. Chill for several hours in the refrigerator, or serve hot, sprinkled with a teaspoon of chopped chives per serving.

6 servings. Serving size is 1¾ cups.

Per Serving: 213 calories, 24 mg. cholesterol, 3 g. dietary fiber, 8 g. fat, 457 mg. sodium.

Winter Bean Soup

PREPARATION TIME: 15 MINUTES.   COOKING TIME: 2 HOURS.

Another hearty soup to warm you up in chilly weather.

2 cups navy beans
6 cups water
2 lean soup bones
½ cup chopped leeks
  OR scallions
1 large clove garlic, crushed
¼ cup green pepper, diced
2 stalks celery, diced

1½ cups carrots, sliced
4 ounces mushrooms, sliced
1 teaspoon chili powder
1 teaspoon salt
½ teaspoon black pepper
¼ teaspoon cumin
1 bay leaf

1. Soak the beans overnight in the water.
2. The next day, add all the other ingredients, and bring to a boil. Reduce heat to simmer, cover, and let cook for 2 hours, or until the beans are tender.

6 servings. Serving size is 1⅓ cups.

Per Serving: 182 calories, no cholesterol, 14 g. dietary fiber, 1 g. fat, 412 mg. sodium.

Spinach Egg-Drop Soup

PREPARATION TIME: 10 MINUTES.   COOKING TIME: 10 MINUTES.

6 cups chicken stock
1 package (10 ounces) frozen
  spinach
1 tablespoon sesame seeds,
  ground with mortar and
  pestle
1 tablespoon chives

2 eggs, lightly beaten
1 teaspoon Traditional Italian
  Herb Blend (p. 335)
Dash ginger
¼ teaspoon salt
¼ teaspoon fresh-ground black
  pepper

1. Bring the stock to a boil in a large kettle. Add the spinach and bring back to a boil.
2. Reduce heat, and let simmer until spinach is cooked.

3. Stir in the sesame seeds and chives, and bring to a boil again. Remove the pot from the heat, and slowly pour the beaten eggs in, stirring slightly. Add the seasonings, and serve.

8 servings. Serving size is 1 cup.

Per Serving: 66 calories, 69 mg. cholesterol, 1 g. dietary fiber, 3 g. fat, 697 mg. sodium.

Meatless Chili

PREPARATION TIME: 10 MINUTES.   COOKING TIME: 2½ HOURS.

You can boost the protein in this chili by topping each serving with an ounce of cheese. If desired, substitute prepared chili powder for the ground chili and cumin.

2 cups dried pinto beans	1 can (6 ounces) tomato sauce
Water	2 tablespoons ground chili
2 medium onions, quartered	1 tablespoon ground cumin
2 large cloves garlic, minced	2 teaspoons salt
1 can (15 ounces) kidney beans, drained	

1. Wash and sort the pinto beans. Cover them with water, and soak overnight.
2. The next day, pour off the water from the beans. Pour in fresh water, covering the beans with 2 inches of water. Bring to a boil. Add the onions and garlic. Reduce the heat, and simmer for 1 hour.
3. Add the drained kidney beans, tomato sauce, and seasonings. Simmer for another 1½ hours. Stir occasionally, adding a little more water as necessary to keep the beans covered. Let cook until the beans start to break down and form a gravy with the water. Adjust seasonings to taste.

6 servings as a main course. Serving size is 1½ cups.

Per Serving: 270 calories, no cholesterol, 19 g. dietary fiber, 1 g. fat, 1179 mg. sodium.

New England Clam Chowder

PREPARATION TIME: 15 MINUTES.   COOKING TIME: 20 TO 25 MINUTES.

This is a traditional favorite that substitutes skim milk for dairy products that contain more calories and have a higher fat content. The wine adds a flavorful flair and helps reduce the need for salt. For a thicker chowder, use the cornstarch.

2 cans (6 ounces each) minced clams, with liquid
1 tablespoon cornstarch (optional)
1½ cups skim milk
½ cup white wine
1 small potato, diced

4 ounces fresh mushrooms, sliced
1 medium onion, diced
1 teaspoon oregano
½ teaspoon salt
¼ teaspoon pepper

1. Pour the clams and their liquid into a large saucepan or kettle. If using the cornstarch, mix it with 1 cup of the milk in a small bowl or measuring cup. Reserve.
2. Add the other ½ cup of the milk to the clams, and begin heating over medium heat. Do not boil.
3. When the clam mixture is hot, stir in the cornstarch mixture, or the plain milk if you're not using cornstarch.
4. Add the remaining ingredients, stirring well. Cover and cook, stirring occasionally, over medium to medium-low heat until the potatoes are tender and the soup is hot, but never boiling.

4 servings. Serving size is 1¼ cups.

Per Serving: 122 calories, 55 mg. cholesterol, 2 g. dietary fiber, 6 g. fat, 354 mg. sodium.

Manhattan Clam Chowder

PREPARATION TIME: 20 MINUTES.   COOKING TIME: 20 MINUTES.

1 tablespoon vegetable oil
1 medium onion, diced
½ medium bell pepper, diced
1 stalk celery, diced
1 large clove garlic, minced or crushed
2 cans (16 ounces each) tomatoes, undrained
2 cans (6½ ounces each) minced clams, undrained

1 bay leaf
3 medium potatoes, diced, skins on
4 cups water
½ teaspoon salt
½ teaspoon black pepper
¼ teaspoon thyme

1. Heat the oil in a large soup pot over medium heat. Add the onion, bell pepper, celery, and garlic, and stir well. Cover and reduce the heat to medium low. Sauté until onions are translucent, stirring occasionally. Add a little water if necessary to prevent sticking.
2. Meanwhile, whir the tomatoes in a blender or food processor. When onions are ready, add to the onion mixture the tomatoes, the clams plus their liquid, and the remaining ingredients.
3. Bring to a boil. Reduce heat, cover, and simmer for about 20 minutes, or until potatoes are tender.

12 servings. Serving size is 1¼ cups.

Per Serving: 90 calories, 20 mg. cholesterol, 2 g. dietary fiber, 2 g. fat, 134 mg. sodium.

Salads

In America, salads are traditionally eaten before the meal, while in Europe they are served after the main courses and before the dessert to clear the palate and aid the digestion.

Salads as full meals, or on the side as appetizers, can be among the most attractive dishes on your table. We enjoy seeing the contrasting colors of the various vegetables, grains, legumes, cheeses, or meats we toss into a salad, sprinkled with an array of herbs, and glistening with our favorite dressing.

Our recipes vary from the everyday dinner salad to the more exotic Middle Eastern tabbouli, which uses bulgur wheat as its base. We include a couple of Greek-style salads, one using lettuce and one with black-eyed peas. There are more; some originate from other countries, and some from our imaginations.

Nutritionists recommend that approximately half the vegetables you eat each day should be raw. Eating vegetables uncooked preserves both bulk and nutrient content. For persons using the Rotation Diet to lose weight, we do, of course, recommend unlimited *free vegetables* with every meal and as snacks. We hope the suggestions we give you will prompt you to increase your consumption of vegetables, both cooked and raw, and to create some of your own salads to make it interesting.

Artichoke-Spinach Salad

PREPARATION TIME: 12 TO 15 MINUTES.

Jícama is a Mexican vegetable, similar to a turnip, which can be served raw or cooked. You can usually find it in the produce section of better-stocked supermarkets.

¾ pound fresh spinach
4 ounces jícama or radishes
1 can (14 ounces) artichokes,
  drained

½ medium red onion,
  sliced

1. Wash carefully and trim the spinach, and tear the leaves into bite-sized pieces. Wash, trim, and slice the jícama.
2. Toss all ingredients in a salad bowl, and serve with your favorite dressing.

4 servings. Serving size is about 2 cups.

Per Serving: 124 calories, no cholesterol, 7 g. dietary fiber, 8 g. fat, 599 mg. sodium.

"You know? . . . I think I'd like a salad." *BEYOND THE FAR SIDE.*
© 1986 UNIVERSAL PRESS SYNDICATE. REPRINTED WITH
PERMISSION. ALL RIGHTS RESERVED.

Apple-Carrot Salad

PREPARATION TIME: 10 MINUTES.

A delicious variation on the usual carrot-raisin salad.

2 medium apples, diced
1½ cups carrots, grated
⅓ cup raisins

¼ cup chopped walnuts
½ cup plain low-fat yogurt
1 tablespoon honey

1. Combine apples, carrots, raisins, and walnuts.
2. Blend the yogurt with the honey and pour over the other ingredients, mixing thoroughly.

8 servings. Serving size is about ½ cup.

Per Serving: 87 calories, 1 mg. cholesterol, 2 g. dietary fiber, 3 g. fat, 18 mg. sodium.

Garbanzo Salad

PREPARATION TIME: 10 MINUTES.   REFRIGERATION TIME: 3 TO 4 HOURS.

2 cups garbanzo beans
 (chickpeas), cooked
1 medium onion, diced
½ medium red bell pepper,
 diced
2 medium tomatoes, diced

1½ tablespoons olive oil
½ teaspoon fresh-ground black
 pepper
¼ teaspoon salt
Herb and Onion Dressing
 (p. 103)

1. Combine all ingredients in a large bowl, and refrigerate for several hours before serving.

8 servings. Serving size is about ¾ cup.

Per Serving: 96 calories, no cholesterol, 4 g. dietary fiber, 4 g. fat, 77 mg. sodium.

Chef's Salad

PREPARATION TIME: 8 TO 10 MINUTES.

The calorie content of this salad will range between 300 and 400, depending on whether you include the egg, and how much dressing you use.

¼ head of your favorite lettuce, shredded
1 medium tomato, quartered
1 slice (ring) of green pepper
¼ cup red cabbage, shredded
¼ cup shaved carrots
1 ounce Swiss cheese, cut in narrow strips
1 ounce white meat of turkey OR chicken, cut in strips

1 egg, quartered (optional)
Choice of *free vegetables* (see pp. 394–95)
Herb Salt (pp. 334–35)
Fresh-ground black pepper
Several large leaves of romaine lettuce
Your favorite no- or low-cal dressing

1. Arrange your vegetables attractively on the romaine, and sprinkle with seasonings to taste. Use 1 to 2 tablespoons of dressing.

1 serving. Serving size is about 2 cups.

Per Serving (with egg): 338 calories, 324 mg. cholesterol, 10 g. dietary fiber, 16 g. fat, 748 mg. sodium.

Creative Fruit Salad

PREPARATION TIME: 5 MINUTES.

This is called *Creative Fruit Salad* because you can create a different salad every time you make it, using whatever fruits, spices, or nuts you have on hand. Cut the fruit into chunks, and sprinkle with lemon juice to keep the fruit looking fresh and to add a bit of tang. Then, for every 2 cups of fresh fruit, add 1 tablespoon of any one of the following:

Grated coconut
Chopped unsalted nuts
  of any kind

Raisins
  OR chopped dates

Then add a sprinkle of any of the following spices:

Cinnamon
Nutmeg
Allspice

Ginger
Anise
Cardamom

A main-course serving is 2 cups of any combination of fresh fruit, plus the tablespoon of nuts or raisins. The spices, of course, add few or no calories.

Average Serving: 205 calories, no cholesterol, 7 g. dietary fiber, 3 g. fat, 8 mg. sodium.

Cucumber-Radish Salad

PREPARATION TIME: 12 MINUTES.

½ large cucumber
12 radishes
¼ large red onion, thinly sliced
4 ounces provolone
  OR Swiss cheese, grated
¼ cup fresh parsley, minced
1 tablespoon red wine vinegar

1 tablespoon Dijon
  OR spicy brown mustard
⅓ cup plain low-fat yogurt
1 tablespoon mayonnaise
2 teaspoons dried basil
⅛ teaspoon celery seed

1. Scrub cucumber clean, removing waxy substance if neces-

sary; it is preferable not to peel it. Slice the cucumber as thinly as possible. Clean, trim, and slice the radishes as thinly as possible.

2. Combine the cucumbers, radishes, and onions in a bowl, along with the cheese.
3. Add the remaining ingredients, tossing lightly. Serve chilled.

4 servings. Serving size is about 1 cup.

Per Serving: 157 calories, 31 mg. cholesterol, 1 g. dietary fiber, 11 g. fat, 339 mg. sodium.

Dinner Salad

PREPARATION TIME: 10 MINUTES.

Since salads are usually a mainstay for most dieters, and are certainly used frequently in the Rotation Diet, people often ask what constitutes a "dinner salad." Actually, you can eat unlimited quantities of almost any vegetable, so you can feel free to create your own dinner salad, but generally we tell people a dinner salad is what you would normally get along with a meal in a typical restaurant—asking for your dressing on the side, of course.

The basic dinner salad is as follows.

½ carrot, thinly sliced
1 stalk celery, thinly sliced,
    OR ¼ green pepper, diced
¼ cup shredded red cabbage
    OR 4 sliced mushrooms

2 thin slices sweet red onion
Lettuce or greens (*free
    vegetables,* see pp. 394–95)

1. Arrange all ingredients in a bowl or on a plate. Add your favorite no- or low-cal dressing (see pp. 102, 108) and flavor with Herb Salt (pp. 334–35) or other seasonings if you like.

1 serving. Serving size is about 1½ cup.

Per Serving (without dressing): 44 calories, no cholesterol, 4 g. dietary fiber, no fat, 46 mg. sodium.

Greek Black-Eyed Pea Salad

PREPARATION TIME: 6 MINUTES.   REFRIGERATION TIME: 6 TO 8 HOURS.

3 cups black-eyed peas, cooked
½ cup bell pepper, diced (red
  or yellow is attractive)
½ cup scallions, diced
1 small clove garlic, crushed
½ teaspoon dried oregano

3 tablespoons olive oil
4 tablespoons red wine vinegar
1 teaspoon lemon juice
2 tablespoons fresh parsley,
  minced
¼ teaspoon salt

1. Combine all ingredients in a large bowl. Marinate 6 to 8 hours in the refrigerator, stirring occasionally.

8 servings. Serving size is about ½ cup.

Per Serving: 123 calories, no cholesterol, 4 g. dietary fiber, 5 g. fat, 75 mg. sodium.

Peas, Beets, and Water Chestnuts

PREPARATION TIME: 5 MINUTES.   REFRIGERATION TIME: 1 HOUR.

1 can (8 ounces) baby peas,
  drained
1 can (8 ounces) beets, drained
  and diced
1 can (2½ ounces) water
  chestnuts, drained
2 tablespoons plain low-fat
  yogurt

2 tablespoons mayonnaise
¼ tablespoon tarragon
⅛ teaspoon dillweed
¼ teaspoon OR less salt
Fresh-ground black pepper to
  taste
Dash garlic powder

1. Combine all ingredients in a large bowl. Chill for 1 hour, and serve on lettuce leaves.

6 servings. Serving size is about ½ cup.

Per Serving: 81 calories, 3 mg. cholesterol, 3 g. dietary fiber, 4 g. fat, 306 mg. sodium.

Fennel Salad with Pecans

PREPARATION TIME: 10 MINUTES.

If you like licorice, you will love fennel. Raw fennel smells and tastes strongly of licorice when served alone. However, diced and added to a salad, it blends delectably, adding a touch of sweetness to a vinaigrette dressing (along with a healthy dose of potassium and vitamin A).

Look for firm fennel bulbs in the produce section of your supermarket. Test the bulbs with your thumb for firmness.

½ head Boston OR Bibb
  lettuce
½ head radicchio, escarole,
  OR other lettuce
½ medium fennel bulb
2 tablespoons pecan pieces
3 tablespoons red wine vinegar
2 tablespoons vegetable oil

1 tablespoon water
1 teaspoon mustard seed,
  ground with mortar and
  pestle
¼ teaspoon dried tarragon
¼ teaspoon salt
¼ teaspoon fresh-ground black
  pepper

1. Wash and dry the lettuce. Tear the leaves into bite-size pieces, and place in a large salad bowl.
2. Trim the tough outer leaves of the fennel. Wash and core the bulb. Dice, and add to the bowl. Add the pecans.
3. Combine the remaining ingredients in a jar. Cover and shake, then pour into the salad. Toss and serve.

4 servings. Serving size is about 1½ cups.

Per Serving: 95 calories, no cholesterol, 1 g. dietary fiber, 9 g. fat, 141 mg. sodium.

Oriental Spinach-Sesame Salad

PREPARATION TIME: 12 MINUTES.

This salad is good served chilled or at room temperature. It is at its best served the same day it is made. See pages 237–38 for instructions on how to toast seeds.

Water (about ¼ cup)
1½ pounds fresh spinach, washed thoroughly and trimmed

3 tablespoons toasted sesame seeds, ground with mortar and pestle
1 tablespoon honey
2 tablespoons tamari sauce OR soy sauce

1. Bring the water to a boil in a saucepan, toss in the spinach, cover, and cook about 30 *seconds,* until wilted.
2. Drain the spinach (reserve the liquid for other recipes, such as a soup, if you like) and rinse it in a colander in cold water. Drain well, and transfer to a serving bowl.
3. In a small bowl, combine the honey, tamari sauce, and sesame seeds. Pour this dressing over the spinach, toss, and serve.

4 servings. Serving size is about 1 cup.

Per Serving: 97 calories, no cholesterol, 7 g. dietary fiber, 4 g. fat, 649 mg. sodium.

Elegant Asparagus

PREPARATION TIME: 5 MINUTES.

This recipe is delicious with fresh, very lightly steamed asparagus. However, the canned variety works well too. You can substitute green asparagus, of course, but the white is more elegant—and more expensive.

1 can (15 ounces) white (or green) asparagus
2 tablespoons vegetable oil

1 tablespoon red wine vinegar
¼ teaspoon salt
⅛ teaspoon black pepper

½ teaspoon Dijon mustard
¼ teaspoon thyme
¼ teaspoon dried parsley

1 large clove garlic, minced or
crushed

1. Chill the asparagus.
2. Combine the remaining ingredients, cover, and chill.
3. To serve, place the asparagus on 4 salad plates. Spoon some dressing over each serving, dividing it up equally.

VARIATIONS: Try this with any of your favorite no- or low-cal dressings. Terri especially likes the Fennel Dressing (p. 103). You might also try sprinkling one-quarter of a diced, hard-boiled egg across each serving, and/or add a teaspoon of chopped nuts, such as walnuts, pecans, or almonds, or sunflower or sesame seeds.

4 servings. Serving size is about 1 cup.

Per Serving: 83 calories, no cholesterol, 2 g. dietary fiber, 8 g. fat, 511 mg. sodium.

Vegetable Slaw

PREPARATION TIME: 10 MINUTES.   REFRIGERATION TIME: ½ HOUR.

The onion and garlic can be pulverized in a food processor with the lemon juice, mayonnaise, yogurt, and salt, if desired. A food processor is wonderful for grating vegetables!

½ small onion, grated
1 clove garlic, grated
Juice of 1 lemon (about 2 tablespoons)
4 tablespoons mayonnaise
½ cup plain low-fat yogurt

½ to ¾ teaspoon salt
Black pepper to taste
1 small head cabbage, grated
1 large carrot, grated
1 medium bell pepper, grated

1. Combine all ingredients and mix well. Refrigerate for at least ½ hour. Mix well before serving.

6 servings. Serving size is about 1½ cups.

Per Serving: 119 calories, 7 mg. cholesterol, 3 g. dietary fiber, 8 g. fat, 270 mg. sodium.

Potato-Vegetable Salad

PREPARATION TIME: 20 TO 25 MINUTES.   REFRIGERATION TIME: 1 HOUR.

Simply the best potato salad we have ever tasted! Thanks to my wife Enid for coming up with this low-calorie version of an all-time American favorite.

6 medium potatoes, boiled and
  cubed
3 hard-boiled eggs, diced
½ small onion, grated
2 medium carrots, diced
1 medium bell pepper, diced
2 stalks celery, sliced thin
1 cup plain low-fat yogurt

¼ cup mayonnaise
¼ teaspoon garlic powder
Fresh-ground black pepper to
  taste
1 teaspoon tarragon
1 tablespoon Dijon mustard
1 teaspoon salt

1. Combine all ingredients, chill for at least an hour, and
   serve.

12 servings. Serving size is about ¾ cup.

Per Serving: 124 calories, 35 mg. cholesterol, 2 g. dietary fiber,
5 g. fat, 258 mg. sodium.

Greek Salad

PREPARATION TIME: 8 MINUTES.

4 ounces feta cheese
20 cherry tomatoes or 2
  medium tomatoes, sliced
1 large bell pepper, thinly
  sliced
1 medium onion, thinly sliced
1 clove garlic, minced or
  crushed

1 teaspoon dried oregano
Lettuce
Fennel Dressing (p. 103)
16 Greek olives (or use regular
  black olives)

1. One hour before preparation time, cut the feta cheese
   into chunks and soak in cold water for 1 hour to reduce salt
   content.

2. Cut the cherry tomatoes in half, or slice the regular tomatoes into wedges. Combine the tomato, pepper, onion, garlic, and oregano. Drain the feta cheese, pat dry with paper towels, and toss with the vegetables.
3. Divide into 8 servings, place on lettuce leaves, and garnish with 2 olives and 1 tablespoon of Fennel Dressing (p. 103) per serving.

8 servings. Serving size is about ¾ cup on two large lettuce leaves.

Per Serving: 64 calories, 12 mg. cholesterol, 1 g. dietary fiber, 5 g. fat, 231 mg. sodium.

Marinated Broccoli and Cauliflower

PREPARATION TIME: 15 TO 20 MINUTES.   REFRIGERATION TIME: 2 HOURS.

2 tablespoons olive oil
2 tablespoons red wine vinegar
1 cup water
2 cloves garlic, crushed
½ teaspoon fresh-ground black
  pepper
1 bay leaf
1 teaspoon dried basil
¼ teaspoon salt

½ medium cauliflower, cut
  into flowerettes
3 medium stalks broccoli, cut
  into flowerettes
1 medium red onion, chopped
½ teaspoon oregano
Fresh parsley
8 cherry tomatoes

1. Combine all the ingredients except the oregano, parsley, and tomatoes in a large saucepan. Bring to a slight boil, reduce heat, and simmer, covered, until broccoli and cauliflower are cooked *al dente*—just barely tender; about 5 to 7 minutes.
2. Chill 2 hours, then garnish each serving with a sprinkle of oregano, parsley sprigs, and 2 tomatoes.

4 servings. Serving size is about 1½ cups.

Per Serving: 98 calories, no cholesterol, 3 g. dietary fiber, 7 g. fat, 146 mg. sodium.

Japanese-Style Crab Salad

PREPARATION TIME: 12 MINUTES.

Slicing cucumbers *very* thin is easy with a special low-cost gadget made only for that purpose. Inquire at your local cookware shop for such a slicer. As for the "light soy sauce" and the rice-wine vinegar, they can be found in Oriental markets. They have a unique, delicate flavor, but if you wish to substitute, you may: use tamari sauce or regular or low-sodium soy sauce for the soy sauce, and white vinegar for the rice-wine vinegar.

2 medium cucumbers, unpeeled, sliced thin
1 package (6 ounces) frozen crab, thawed, OR 1 can (6½ ounces) crab
1 teaspoon peanut oil

3 tablespoons light soy sauce or tamari sauce
2 tablespoons rice-wine vinegar
1 tablespoon toasted sesame seeds, ground with mortar and pestle

1. Drain the sliced cucumbers well; also drain the crab.
2. Heat a small skillet over medium-low heat, and brush with the oil. Add the sesame seeds and toast, stirring constantly, until lightly browned.
3. Lightly toss all ingredients together in a bowl and serve.

6 servings. Serving size is about ½ cup.

Per Serving: 58 calories, 28 mg. cholesterol, 1 g. dietary fiber, 3 g. fat, 800 mg. sodium.

Red Bean and Pasta Salad

PREPARATION TIME: 10 MINUTES.   COOKING TIME: 1 HOUR.

All you have to do is look at the restaurant salad bars to know that pasta salads are "in." The problem with most pasta salads, when it comes to weight control, is not the pasta, but the dressings that are used. If you use our Italian Dressing or the oil and vinegar dressing, in the amount we suggest, you will be adding very few fat calories to this salad. If you find that the flavor is too mild, use additional seasoning (such as Herb Salt, or a commercial no- or low-salt seasoning) at the table, or add another splash of vinegar.

½ pound dried red beans
½ pound pasta
1 package (10½ ounces) frozen
  peas, defrosted in time for
  mixing
6 tablespoons Italian Dressing
  (p. 108)
  OR Basic Lo-Cal Salad
  Dressing (p. 102)

1 tablespoon lemon juice
1 teaspoon Traditional Italian
  Herb Blend (p. 335)
Dash of salt
Fresh-ground black pepper to
  taste
Fresh parsley for garnish

1. Soak beans overnight, cook for about 1 hour or until just tender, and drain.
2. Cook pasta, drain, and cool in cold water.
3. Mix beans, pasta, and peas with dressing in large bowl, and add lemon juice, Herb Blend, salt, and pepper.
4. Serve garnished with parsley.

12 servings. Serving size is about ½ cup.

Per Serving: 153 calories, no cholesterol, 7 g. dietary fiber, 1 g. fat, 103 mg. sodium.

Tabbouli

PREPARATION TIME: 10 MINUTES.

There are almost as many versions of this traditional Middle Eastern recipe as there are cooks. Some people like to add tomato, fresh mint leaves, or other ingredients. This is how Terri usually makes it.

The salad:
2 cups bulgur wheat
Water
¾ cup shredded
   OR finely chopped carrots
¾ cup shredded
   OR finely chopped cucumber
½ cup minced fresh parsley

The dressing:
¼ cup safflower oil
¼ cup red wine vinegar
¼ cup tamari sauce
   OR soy sauce
2 tablespoons lemon juice
3 to 4 garlic cloves, crushed

1. Soak the bulgur wheat in a bowl in enough water to cover for 3 to 4 hours. The wheat will soak up the water and become puffy and chewable.
2. In the meantime, combine all dressing ingredients and set aside. Chop the vegetables as directed.
3. When the bulgur is ready, add the vegetables, mixing well, then add the dressing. Toss and serve.

6 servings as a main course. Serving size is about 1¼ cup.

Per Serving: 301 calories, no cholesterol, 6 g. dietary fiber, 10 g. fat, 696 mg. sodium.

Vegetable-Cheese Salad with Herb Dressing

PREPARATION TIME: 15 TO 20 MINUTES. REFRIGERATION TIME: ½ HOUR.

Combine two or more of your favorite cheeses: cheddar, Swiss, mozzarella, muenster, monterey jack, gouda—whatever you prefer. Swiss and part-skim mozzarella, and other mild white cheeses, are lowest in fat. Try this with Patti's Vegetable Soup (p. 73). She did!

3 cups cheese, cut in julienne
  strips
1 medium cucumber, diced
1 medium tomato, diced
1 medium bell pepper, diced
1 scallion, minced
⅓ cup fresh parsley, chopped
Juice of one medium lime
Juice of one medium lemon

2 tablespoons mayonnaise
½ cup plain low-fat yogurt
1 teaspoon Dijon mustard
½ teaspoon horseradish
½ teaspoon dillweed
½ teaspoon tarragon
½ teaspoon marjoram
½ teaspoon basil
1 teaspoon paprika

1. Combine cheese, vegetables, and parsley in a large bowl.
2. In another bowl, blend together the remaining ingredients to make the dressing.
3. Pour the dressing over the cheese and vegetables, chill for about ½ hour, and serve.

8 servings as a main course. Serving size is about 1 cup.

Per Serving: 213 calories, 43 mg. cholesterol, 1 g. dietary fiber, 16 g. fat, 246 mg. sodium.

Dressings

A good dressing is a blessing. Here's why.

As we said in our introduction to salads, most nutritionists agree that a good percentage of our vegetables, **perhaps even 50** percent, should be eaten raw. Although many vegetables taste very good raw and without adornment, most of us prefer salad vegetables with some kind of dressing. Plain lemon juice or plain vinegar can take you only so far!

So, we place a major emphasis in this cookbook on salad dressings. Ours are generally relatively low in fat, but not all. Being fans of bleu cheese dressing, we struck a compromise in order to include one here. We have experimented with the use of yogurt, together with higher calorie ingredients, such as mayonnaise, looking for blends that considerably reduce the fat calories below those contained in mayonnaise alone.

We feel that olive oil is the best oil for salads. Fortunately, olive oil may be pretty good for you in reasonable amounts. Olive oil, as well as peanut oil, is primarily monounsaturated, and oils of this kind may have a cholesterol-reducing effect. We blend olive oil with vinegars of various kinds and water, and add herbs and spices, of course. For the most part, we aim for a low-calorie dressing, which averages around 35 calories or so per tablespoon.

Every so often we are able to obtain extra-virgin olive oil, which is quite green in color, and more than delicious in salads. But normally our brand of oil is either Bertolli or Berio; both are usually available in supermarkets.

We use wine vinegar most often in our salads, but if you can find some of the fruit vinegars, especially the strawberry and raspberry flavors, give them a try. They are not as popular as they were a few years ago, but some salads, such as a spinach salad, are especially good with fruit vinegars, as are the more delicate varieties of lettuce, such as Bibb and Boston.

You can make your own herb vinegars at home by heating vinegar and bottling it with a wide assortment of herbs. However, our No-Cal Salad Dressing (p. 108) illustrates an easy herb vinegar that requires no heating, bottling, or straining.

Mustard-Seed Dressing

PREPARATION TIME: 5 MINUTES.

In ancient times, people apparently ate mustard seeds whole, especially as a condiment to meats, without any grinding, combining, cooking, or diluting whatsoever. We sometimes add whole mustard seeds to this dressing; they provide a pleasant burst of flavor that is not as strong as you might think. However, for the less adventurous, we suggest grinding them first, which distributes the flavor throughout the dressing.

¼ cup olive oil
¼ cup red wine vinegar
¼ cup water
2 large cloves garlic, crushed
1 teaspoon whole mustard seeds
1 teaspoon thyme
½ teaspoon oregano

½ teaspoon basil
¼ teaspoon dillweed
Salt and fresh-ground black
  pepper to taste
Dash tamari sauce
  OR soy sauce

1. Grind the mustard seeds with mortar and pestle if you desire, and then blend all ingredients together. Store in the refrigerator.

Makes about ¾ cup. Serving size is 1 tablespoon.

Per Serving: 42 calories, no cholesterol, no dietary fiber, 5 g. fat, 48 mg. sodium.

Basic Lo-Cal Salad Dressing

PREPARATION TIME: 5 MINUTES.

To create a basic low-calorie dressing, one with about 35 calories per tablespoon, mix equal parts olive oil, vinegar, and water. Then, you can begin to get creative! You can make an Italian-style dressing by crushing a small amount of garlic and onion and adding the juice—or by using onion and garlic powder—plus Italian herbs (see our Traditional Italian Herb Blend, p. 335).

If you want to get a feel for the individuality of your herbs, you might try using only one at a time, such as tarragon (as we do here) or basil or oregano. We add a modest amount of salt, as in the recipe below, to help bring out the flavors of the other ingredients, as well as freshly ground black pepper. A tangier dressing is obtained by adding a teaspoon of Dijon mustard, and it gets tangier still with a teaspoon of dry mustard! A dash of cayenne pepper also seems to have a stimulating effect on the other flavorings in the dressing, and we almost always finish our blend with a dash of cayenne or Tabasco.

¼ cup fine olive oil
¼ cup water
¼ cup wine vinegar or fruit vinegar

1 clove garlic, crushed
½ teaspoon salt
1 teaspoon dried tarragon

1. Blend by shaking in a jar and let stand for several hours before using. Shake before using. This will keep for several weeks in the refrigerator, but it won't last nearly that long, because you'll want to eat it! If the oil solidifies in the refrigerator, let the jar sit on the counter to warm before serving or briefly run the jar under lukewarm water.

Makes about ¾ cup. Serving size is 1 tablespoon.

Per Serving: 41 calories, no cholesterol, no dietary fiber, 5 g. fat, 89 mg. sodium.

Fennel Dressing

PREPARATION TIME: 5 MINUTES.

½ cup water
½ cup olive oil
½ cup red wine vinegar
2 tablespoons lemon juice
2 teaspoons fennel seed,
  ground with mortar and
  pestle

1 teaspoon mustard seed,
  ground with mortar and
  pestle
¼ cup fresh parsley, minced
¼ teaspoon salt
½ teaspoon fresh-ground black
  pepper

1. Combine all ingredients in a medium-size bowl and store
   in a jar in the refrigerator.

Makes about 2 cups. Serving size is 1 tablespoon.

Per Serving: 31 calories, no cholesterol, no dietary fiber, 3 g. fat,
17 mg. sodium.

Herb and Onion Dressing

PREPARATION TIME: 5 MINUTES.

This makes a light, tart dressing that goes equally well with a
salad of your favorite greens and vegetables or over a fruit dish.

2 scallions, diced (bulbs and
  green stems)
¼ cup fresh parsley
½ cup plain low-fat yogurt

1 tablespoon mayonnaise
1 clove garlic, crushed
3 tablespoons red wine vinegar
¼ teaspoon salt

1. Blend all ingredients in blender or food processor. Store
   in the refrigerator in an airtight container.

Makes about ¾ cup. Serving size is 2 tablespoons.

Per Serving: 33 calories, 3 mg. cholesterol, no dietary fiber, 2 g.
fat, 120 mg. sodium.

Red Wine–Bleu Cheese Dressing

PREPARATION TIME: 7 MINUTES.   REFRIGERATION TIME: 12 HOURS.

It is not possible to make a truly low-fat, low-sodium bleu cheese dressing since bleu cheese is a high-fat, high-sodium cheese. This is our compromise, achieved by using yogurt rather than sour cream or greater amounts of mayonnaise. Bleu cheese dressing, however, cannot be recommended for everyday use except in very small quantities.

¼ cup crumbled bleu cheese
1 clove garlic, crushed
¼ teaspoon salt
¼ teaspoon fresh-ground
   pepper
1 scallion, minced

3 tablespoons plain low-fat
   yogurt
1 teaspoon mayonnaise
1 teaspoon red wine
1 teaspoon fresh parsley,
   minced

1. Combine all ingredients in a small bowl. Chill overnight and serve cold.

Makes about ½ cup. Serving size is 2 tablespoons.

Per Serving: 44 calories, 7 mg. cholesterol, no dietary fiber, 3 g. fat, 247 mg. sodium.

THE FAR SIDE. COURTESY CHRONICLE FEATURES, SAN FRANCISCO.

Cottage-Cheese Dressing

PREPARATION TIME: 5 MINUTES.

Another popular dressing from *The Rotation Diet,* this one is excellent with salads or on baked potatoes. For variety, add onions or ½ cup bleu cheese.

½ cup low-fat cottage cheese
½ cup plain low-fat yogurt
½ medium green pepper,
    chopped

4 radishes, sliced
2 tablespoon chives
1 tablespoon poppy seeds
Herb Salt (pp. 334–35) to taste

1. Mix all ingredients in a blender or food processor.

Makes about 1½ cups. Serving size is 1 tablespoon.

Per Serving: 10 calories, 1 mg. cholesterol, no dietary fiber, no fat, 33 mg. sodium.

Honey-Mustard Dressing

PREPARATION TIME: 5 MINUTES.

Good with a spinach salad or other green salads.

¼ cup olive oil
¼ cup white or fruit vinegar
1 teaspoon honey
1 teaspoon dry mustard
¼ teaspoon ground fennel seed
    (optional)

1 teaspoon lemon juice
Dash of salt and freshly ground
    black pepper to taste
1 tablespoon of chopped fresh
    parsley or watercress

1. Blend the dry mustard with a small amount of vinegar, and then combine all ingredients, shake, and serve. Store in the refrigerator.

Makes a little over ½ cup. Serving size is 1 tablespoon.

Per Serving: 63 calories, no cholesterol, no dietary fiber, 7 g. fat, 27 mg. sodium

Dill-Seed and Walnut Dressing

PREPARATION TIME: 3 TO 4 MINUTES.   REFRIGERATION TIME: 12 HOURS.

This tart-sweet dressing is delicious on a salad of thinly sliced cucumber, or try it with any combination of your favorite greens or raw vegetables.

1 cup plain low-fat yogurt
¼ cup raisins (golden raisins
   are nice)
1½ teaspoons dill seed
¼ cup chopped walnuts

1 clove garlic, minced
¼ teaspoon salt
⅛ teaspoon fresh-ground black
   pepper

1. Combine all ingredients in a small bowl. Chill 12 hours, and serve cold.

Makes about 1½ cups. Serving size is 2 tablespoons.

Per Serving: 39 calories, 1 mg. cholesterol, no dietary fiber, 2 g. fat, 58 mg. sodium.

Paprika Dressing

PREPARATION TIME: 5 MINUTES.

This dressing serves double-duty as a salad dressing or as a sauce for meats. You can also try using it as a moistener for sandwiches in place of mayonnaise. It's best to use a brand of horseradish with little or no added sugars, dextrose, oils, or mayonnaise.

1 cup plain low-fat yogurt
½ teaspoon salt
¼ teaspoon fresh-ground black
   pepper
1 clove garlic, crushed

2 teaspoons paprika
1 teaspoon pure horseradish
1 scallion, diced
2 tablespoons sour cream

1. Combine all ingredients and chill.

Makes about 1 1/4 cups. Serving size is 1 tablespoon.

Per Serving: 12 calories, 1 mg. cholesterol, no dietary fiber, 1 g. fat, 63 mg. sodium.

Vinaigrette Dressing

PREPARATION TIME: 4 MINUTES.

1/2 cup olive oil
2 tablespoons wine vinegar
2 tablespoons lemon juice
1 teaspoon dry mustard

1/2 cup water
Herb Salt to taste (pp. 334–35)
Fresh-ground black pepper to
taste

1. Blend the mustard with a small amount of the vinegar, place all the ingredients in a jar, and shake well.

Makes about 1 1/4 cups. Serving size is 1 tablespoon.

VARIATIONS: Add other herbs or the juice of pressed garlic or onion.

Per Serving: 49 calories, no cholesterol, no dietary fiber, 5 g. fat, 32 mg. sodium (using 1 teaspoon Herb Salt).

No-Cal Salad Dressing

PREPARATION TIME: 4 MINUTES.

½ cup wine vinegar
½ teaspoon Herb Salt (see pp.
  334-35)
1 tablespoon fresh parsley,
  chopped

1 clove garlic, crushed,
  OR ¼ teaspoon garlic
  powder

1. Mix all ingredients well. Store in the refrigerator.

VARIATIONS: Use other vinegars and herbs for variety.
Tarragon is one of our favorite herbs for salad dressing. If
available, try fruit vinegars, such as raspberry and
strawberry. Add water to this recipe if you find it too
vinegary for your taste.

Makes about ½ cup. Serving size is 1 tablespoon.

Per Serving: 2 calories, no cholesterol, no dietary fiber, no fat,
13 mg. sodium.

Italian Dressing

PREPARATION TIME: 5 MINUTES.

⅓ cup water
⅓ cup olive oil
⅓ cup white vinegar
1 tablespoon lemon juice

1 clove garlic, minced
1 teaspoon basil leaves, crushed
¼ teaspoon worcestershire
  sauce

1. Combine all ingredients in a jar, cover and shake until the
   salt dissolves. Store in the refrigerator. Shake before serving.

Makes about 1 cup. Serving size is 1 tablespoon.

Per Serving: 41 calories, no cholesterol, no dietary fiber, 5 g. fat,
12 mg. sodium.

Lime Dressing

PREPARATION TIME: 5 MINUTES.

Try this dressing with the Artichoke-Spinach Salad (p. 85).

¼ cup olive oil
¼ cup water
¼ cup lime juice
1 teaspoon coriander
¼ teaspoon basil

⅛ teaspoon ginger
¼ teaspoon salt
¼ teaspoon fresh-ground black
   pepper

1. Whisk together all ingredients. Store in an airtight container in the refrigerator.

Makes about ¾ cup. Serving size is 1 tablespoon.

Per Serving: 42 calories, no cholesterol, no dietary fiber, 5 g. fat, 45 mg. sodium.

Poppy-Seed Dressing

PREPARATION TIME: 4 TO 5 MINUTES.

This dressing is both sweet and tart. Pour it over fruit salads or a wedge of honeydew or cantaloupe, or on chicken, tuna, or other seafood salads served with fruit or on a bed of lettuce.

1 cup plain low-fat yogurt
2 teaspoons honey
Juice of 1 lime (about 2
   tablespoons)

1 tablespoon poppy seeds

1. Combine all ingredients in a bowl. Serve chilled.

Makes about 1¼ cups. Serving size is 2 tablespoons.

Per Serving: 25 calories, 1 mg. cholesterol, no dietary fiber, 1 g. fat, 16 mg. sodium.

Balsamic Dressing

PREPARATION TIME: 5 MINUTES.

One of the reasons we seem to understand each other and get along so well with our editor, Starling Lawence, at W. W. Norton, is that we share the same love of fine food and physical activity. He plays a mean game of tennis, and, in addition to testing many of our recipes and providing helpful comments, he occasionally shares one of his recipes with us. Balsamic dressing is one of his. Although we have published it before, it has been so popular, we want to publish it again and give him the credit that's due, since we failed to do so the first time.

If you don't have balsamic vinegar, you may substitute another kind. But, if this is the case, start with water and vinegar in equal proportions.

¾ cup water
¼ cup balsamic vinegar
3 teaspoons capers
2 teaspoons Dijon mustard

1½ teaspoon dried basil
1 tablespoon fresh parsley, chopped (optional)

1. Combine the ingredients. Adjust vinegar to taste, since it has a strong flavor. Store in a covered container in the refrigerator.

Makes about 1 cup. Serving size is 1 tablespoon.

Per Serving: 1 calorie, no cholesterol, no dietary fiber, no fat, 7 mg. sodium.

Beef

Beef receives bad marks from some health experts because it is high in saturated fat, and consumption of saturated fat in large amounts appears to be related to a higher incidence of heart disease and certain forms of cancer.

I have a very simple philosophy when it comes to beef: use low-fat cuts in moderation. What's moderation? For me, it's once or twice a week, although I don't feel there is strong evidence against eating low-fat cuts of beef three or four times a week, provided your cholesterol level is normal and there is no history of heart disease in your family.

If you like beef in your diet more than once or twice a week, I think you can help protect yourself against possible ill effects by including plenty of dietary fiber, which will help keep you regular and can help lower cholesterol. That is why I place such a strong emphasis on increasing fruits, vegetables, and whole grains in your diet. In addition, you should include fish at least once a week, preferably twice, since the oil contained in certain fatty fish—tuna, mackerel, sardines, bluefish, rainbow trout, salmon, and herring—also seems to help reduce cholesterol levels. As a general dietary principle, no matter what the source of fat in your diet, I think it's best to stay within the limits of 30 percent total calories from fat.

Choose low-fat cuts of beef: top and bottom round, eye of round, sirloin tip, flank steak and London broil, tenderloin, and, of course, extra-lean hamburger. But, watch out for that hamburger: there is no national standard for fat content in hamburger labeled "lean" or "extra-lean." "Extra-lean" can contain anywhere from five to fifteen percent total fat. That difference amounts to hundreds of extra fat calories per serving.

Trim the fat from other cuts of beef before cooking, not after, as a general rule. If you don't find well-trimmed beef in the market, don't be shy: ask the butcher to trim your meat specially. I recommend that you make friends with your butcher, if you haven't already, and explain what you want and why. I have never met a meat manager in a supermarket who did not want to cooperate with me and I think you will find that to be the case, too. Most supermarkets will go out of their way to keep your business!

Our Oriental recipes are examples of how to use modest amounts of beef, as well as other meats, more as a garnish or condiment accompanying vegetables and other foods than as main courses. My wife, Enid, and I began doing this several years ago, after a visit to San Francisco. We had such memorable Chinese and Indian dinners there that, before returning to Nashville, we purchased some Chinese and Indian cookbooks that appeared to have recipes for some of the dishes we had eaten. To add a pleasant variety to your meals, try using a few Oriental techniques with meat if you aren't already doing so.

Baked Flank Steak

PREPARATION TIME: 12 MINUTES.   COOKING TIME: 30 MINUTES.

1½ pounds flank steak
1 tablespoon vegetable oil
1 cup hot water
1 bay leaf
1 large clove garlic, crushed
1 teaspoon salt

4 tablespoons minced celery
⅛ teaspoon fresh-ground black pepper
2 teaspoons lemon juice
1 medium carrot, diced
¼ medium bell pepper, diced

1. Trim away any visible fat from the steak. Sear the steak in the oil over medium to medium-high heat. Remove the

pan from the heat. Place the steak in a casserole dish.

2. For extra flavoring, pour the water into the cooled skillet you seared the meat in, and stir. Pour this over the meat, then add all the other ingredients.

3. Cook uncovered at 350 degrees for 30 minutes, or longer if you prefer your meat well-done.

LIGHT GRAVY (OPTIONAL): To make the roux, heat 1 tablespoon vegetable oil and stir in 2 tablespoons of whole-wheat flour. Take 1 cup of liquid from the meat and stir into the roux. Stir until thickened, and serve over the meat.

4 servings of 4½ ounces each (cooked weight), plus gravy.

Per Serving (plus gravy): 273 calories, 88 mg. cholesterol, 1 g. dietary fiber, 12 g. fat, 630 mg. sodium.

"Julia Child was cooking coq au vin and tambour parmentier this evening, and during her pommes en belle vue I burned your filet." DRAWING BY BOOTH; © 1979 THE NEW YORKER MAGAZINE, INC.

Eggplant Beef Casserole

PREPARATION TIME: 15 MINUTES.   COOKING TIME: 45 MINUTES.

Serve this with a dinner salad for a complete meal.

2 pounds lean ground beef
1 medium onion, chopped
1 small green pepper, chopped
1 tablespoon whole-wheat flour
½ teaspoon fresh-ground black
  pepper
½ teaspoon salt

1 teaspoon dried oregano
2 cups tomato sauce (try Real
  Italian Tomato Sauce, pp.
  290–91)
1 large eggplant
1½ cups grated part-skim
  mozzarella or cheddar cheese

1. Brown the ground beef. Remove it from the pan, and pour off excess fat, if any, leaving just enough pan-juices to sauté the onion and green pepper.
2. When the onion is translucent, return the ground beef to the pan. Add the flour, spices, and tomato sauce, and let simmer until thick.
3. Meanwhile, slice the eggplant into ½-inch rounds, and layer half of them in a 2-quart casserole. Add half the beef mixture, then half the cheese. Repeat layers.
4. Bake covered in a slow oven, around 325 degrees, for 45 minutes.

12 servings. Serving size is 1 cup.

Per Serving: 227 calories, 61 mg. cholesterol, 2 g. dietary fiber, 15 g. fat, 451 mg. sodium.

Fajitas

PREPARATION TIME: 15 MINUTES.   COOKING TIME: 5 TO 10 MINUTES.

You can prepare this Mexican dish (pronounced fah-hee-tuhs) a day ahead of time by dicing your vegetables, grating the cheese, and so on, after you put the meat in to marinate. Store the prepared ingredients in the refrigerator until the next day. Then cook the meat, slice it on a serving platter, put the prepared vegetables and cheese in individual serving bowls, and let everyone make their own fajitas.

1 pound lean top or bottom round, cut ½-inch thick
Juice of two limes (about ⅓ cup of juice)
2 cloves garlic, minced
½ teaspoon fresh-ground black pepper
¼ teaspoon chili powder
¼ teaspoon cumin
6 Whole-Wheat Tortillas (see pp. 316–17)

¾ cup lettuce, shredded (don't use a food processor or it will not be the right texture)
¾ cup tomato, diced
6 tablespoons scallions, chopped
6 tablespoons grated cheddar cheese

1. Trim any visible fat from the beef. Pound it with a mallet or wooden spoon to about ¼-inch thickness.
2. In a shallow bowl, combine the lime juice, garlic, pepper, chili powder, and cumin. Add the steak, toss lightly, and marinate in the refrigerator overnight or for about 6 or 7 hours, turning the meat occasionally.
3. Broil the steak on a grill over medium-hot coals for about 3 minutes a side, or pan-broil 5 to 10 minutes, turning occasionally. Add some of the marinade if necessary to prevent it from sticking. Meanwhile, warm the tortillas briefly on each side in a dry frying pan or in a warm oven.
4. Slice the beef across the grain into thin slices. Spread lengthwise in the center of each tortilla equal amounts of beef. Then top each serving with 2 tablespoons each of lettuce and tomato, and 1 tablespoon each of onions and cheese. Roll the tortillas up lengthwise and serve.

6 servings. Serving size is 1 tortilla with fillings.

Per Serving: 257 calories, 62 mg. cholesterol, 2 g. dietary fiber, 11 g. fat, 213 mg. sodium.

Zucchini-Stuffed Flank Steak

PREPARATION TIME: 30 TO 45 MINUTES.   COOKING TIME: 1½ HOURS.

This is one of those dishes that takes about 45 minutes to prepare the first time, but which goes much faster once you get the hang of it. It's so good that I'm sure you will want to prepare it many times, with variations. It lends itself to the use of many different sauces and stuffings. There is enough sauce in this version to cover a side of spaghetti; add a salad for a well-rounded meal.

1½ pounds flank steak
2 large cloves garlic
1 tablespoon olive oil
Salt and fresh-ground black pepper to taste
1 medium zucchini, sliced thin
½ cup chopped parsley
½ cup coarse-grated part-skim mozzarella

3 teaspoons fresh Parmesan cheese, grated
2 cans (10 ounces) tomato purée OR Real Italian Tomato Sauce (pp. 290–91)
2 medium yellow crookneck squash, sliced thin
1 tablespoon Mrs. Dash OR Herb Salt (pp. 334–35)

1. Tenderize and thin out the meat by pounding with a flat metal meat pounder until its thickness is reduced by about one half. You can use a small section of two-by-four, a pestle, or the bottom of a small wooden salad bowl for this job, but you must thin it out or it will not roll well. (Cover the meat with a piece of waxed paper to prevent your pounder from sticking, and the meat from splattering.)
2. Crush the garlic in a garlic press and place it on the meat. Add the olive oil and spread the garlic and oil all over the meat.
3. Salt and pepper to taste (it doesn't take much salt because of the other seasonings).
4. Arrange the sliced zucchini down the center (lengthwise) of the meat, and sprinkle with half the parsley.
5. Add the mozzarella and the Parmesan cheeses.

6. Roll up the whole thing, going with the grain of the meat, so that when you slice it you will be going against the grain. Tie it in four or five places with heavy string (if you have trouble holding it together for tying, run a couple of skewers lengthwise through the meat to hold it together, and then use the string; you can remove the skewers at the table before slicing.)

7. Place the rolled steak in a baking dish, pour the sauce or purée over it, add the sliced yellow squash, and sprinkle it with Mrs. Dash or herb seasoning and the remaining parsley.

8. Bake, covered, at 325 degrees for about 1½ hours. Baste two or three times.

9. Remove the roll to a serving dish, with the sauce. Slice, and serve with the sauce.

4 servings of 4½ ounces each (cooked weight), plus sauce.

Per Serving: 404 calories, 97 mg. cholesterol, 6 g. dietary fiber, 15 g. fat, 343 mg. sodium.

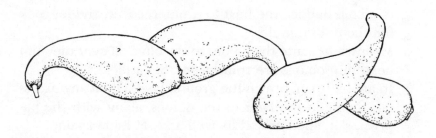

Hungarian Cabbage

PREPARATION TIME: 50 MINUTES.   COOKING TIME: 45 TO 50 MINUTES.

Hungarian cooking is characterized by the use of paprika, and if you can find a true Hungarian paprika, you're in luck. It is more pungent and has a richer flavor than the kind we usually find in the supermarket. Actually, paprika is a type of chili that apparently originated in South America, not Hungary. Wherever it came from, it is delicious in this dish. Serve with a fresh salad or with a dark green or yellow vegetable on the side. Even with low-sodium beef stock, however, this is rather high in sodium.

1¼ cups beef stock
¾ cup brown rice
1 medium onion, chopped
1 tablespoon olive oil
1 pound extra-lean ground beef
2 teaspoons paprika
½ teaspoon salt

2 large cloves garlic, crushed
¾ pound low-fat sausage,
    sliced in ¼-inch-thick slices
1 bag (2 pounds) sauerkraut
½ cup sour cream
½ cup plain low-fat yogurt

1. Bring the beef stock to a boil, add the rice, and bring back to a boil. Reduce the heat to simmer, cover, and let cook for about 45 minutes.
2. Meanwhile, sauté the onions in the olive oil over medium heat until onions are translucent. Set aside.
3. In another pan, brown the ground beef. Drain any excess fat, then add the beef to the onions, along with the paprika, salt, and garlic. Mix well and set aside again.
4. In the same pan you used for the ground beef, quickly brown the sausage slices. Drain the sausage on paper toweling, patting well to remove the fat. Set aside.
5. Pour the sauerkraut into a colander, and rinse with water for several minutes. After rinsing, squeeze well to remove excess water.
6. In a small bowl, combine the sour cream and the yogurt, blending well.

7. In a large 2½ to 3 quart casserole dish, layer half the sauerkraut, half the sausage, and half the ground beef. Top with all of the rice, then add half of the sour cream-yogurt mixture. Repeat the layers of sauerkraut, sausage, ground beef, and the sour cream-yogurt mixture.
8. Bake at 350 degrees for 45 to 50 minutes.

8 servings. Serving size is about 1 ¼ cups.

Per Serving: 401 calories, 79 mg. cholesterol, 3 g. dietary fiber, 27 g. fat, 1295 mg. sodium.

Brisket with Tomato Sauce

PREPARATION TIME: 10 MINUTES.   COOKING TIME: 1½ HOURS.

2 pounds top or bottom round roast
1 clove garlic, crushed
1 teaspoon salt
½ teaspoon fresh-ground black pepper
¼ teaspoon marjoram

1 can (14½ ounces) no-salt-added tomatoes, with juice
1 tablespoon lemon juice
½ cup chopped onion
2 cups sliced carrots

1. Trim all visible fat from the beef. Combine the garlic, salt, pepper, and marjoram, and rub the mixture all over the beef.
2. Pour the juice from the can of tomatoes into your roasting pan or casserole. Add the meat and lemon juice. Arrange the vegetables around the meat.
3. Cover the pan, place it in a cold oven, and turn the heat to 425 degrees. Bake 1½ hours or until done to your taste.
4. Heat the tomatoes in a pan, and serve alongside the roast.

6 servings of 4 ounces each (cooked weight), plus vegetables.

Per Serving: 258 calories, 109 mg. cholesterol, 3 g. dietary fiber, 12 g. fat, 562 mg. sodium.

Beef Taco Salad

PREPARATION TIME: 15 MINUTES.   COOKING TIME: 10 TO 15 MINUTES.

1 medium head iceberg lettuce (or other lettuce)
½ medium cucumber, sliced thin
½ medium bell pepper, sliced or diced
1 large tomato, cut in thin wedges
4 black olives, diced
½ recipe Quick Tortilla Chips (p. 62)
1 pound extra-lean ground beef OR ground turkey
¼ cup water or stock

1 tablespoon chili powder
½ teaspoon cumin
½ teaspoon black pepper
⅛ teaspoon cayenne pepper
¼ teaspoon salt
Dash Tabasco sauce (optional)
1 can (15 ounces) kidney beans, drained
1 or more medium jalapeño peppers, sliced
¼ cup shredded cheddar OR Monterey jack cheese
Herb and Onion Dressing (p. 103) OR other low-cal dressing

1. Tear the lettuce into a large serving bowl. Top with the cucumber, bell pepper, tomato, and olives. Slightly crush the tortilla chips over the salad vegetables.
2. In a large skillet, brown the ground meat. Drain off any excess fat. Add the water, seasonings, and beans, stirring well. Cover and cook for about 10 to 15 minutes, until meat is cooked and beans are heated through.
3. Pour the meat mixture over the salad. Top with sliced jalapeño peppers and the cheese. Serve with dressing on the side, so people can help themselves.

6 servings as a main course. Serving size is about 1½ cups.

Per Serving: 379 calories, 67 mg. cholesterol, 11 g. dietary fiber, 19 g. fat, 603 mg. sodium.

Steak Marinade

PREPARATION TIME: 3 TO 5 MINUTES.

Here are two marinade sauces for flank steak, London broil, or any other lean cut of beef that you might want to use for pan- or oven-broiling, or outdoor grilling. Both the wine and soy sauce have a tenderizing effect, so marinate overnight in the refrigerator, in a large covered bowl or plastic bag. Turn the meat once or twice while it is marinating, to be sure all of it has been well covered.

These amounts will do nicely for 2 pounds of meat.

Basic Marinade

1 tablespoon olive oil
½ cup dry red wine (use white wine for light-colored meats)
¼ teaspoon Herb Salt (pp. 334–35)

1 bay leaf
1 teaspoon chives
1 small onion, minced

Oriental Marinade

1 tablespoon olive oil
¼ cup tamari sauce OR soy sauce
¼ cup dry red wine
4 cloves garlic, minced

4 scallions, minced
6 whole pepper corns
⅛ teaspoon ground coriander
1-inch cube fresh gingerroot, peeled and grated or minced

Olive oil contains approximately 120 calories per tablespoon. The other ingredients provide negligible calories, including the wine, since the alcohol will evaporate and the sugar content is very low. Soy sauce is quite high in sodium, but it is difficult to predict how much will penetrate or adhere to the meat. Our guess is that the sodium content per serving, e.g., 4½ ounces of flank steak, would be moderate, perhaps 500 mg.

Japanese Beef Stir-Fry

PREPARATION TIME: 5 TO 10 MINUTES.   COOKING TIME: 15 TO 20 MINUTES.

Here is an example of Oriental-style cooking in which meat is only part of the "main course." Serve this dish as soon as it's ready. If you are making enough for leftovers, use regular or Chinese cabbage instead of red, as the red cabbage tends to turn other ingredients purple when cooked and stored.

4 beef tenderloin steaks (about 4 ounces each)
1 tablespoon peanut oil
2 packages (6 ounces each) frozen pea pods, thawed
¼ head red cabbage, thinly sliced
¼ inch fresh gingerroot, minced, OR ground ginger to taste
1 tablespoon saké (optional)
Dash tamari sauce OR soy sauce

1. Heat a wok or heavy skillet over medium-high heat for several minutes. Meanwhile, trim the beef of all visible fat and slice the beef into thin slices.
2. Add the oil to the pan, then the beef. Cook, stirring constantly, until browned.
3. Lower the heat to medium, remove the meat from the pan, and set aside.
4. Add the pea pods, cabbage, and gingerroot to the wok, and cook for five minutes, stirring constantly.
5. Return the meat to the wok, and stir in the saké and the soy sauce. Cover, and let simmer for a few more minutes, until the vegetables are just tender and the meat is cooked the way you like it.

4 servings of 3 ounces each (cooked weight), plus vegetables.

Per Serving: 281 calories, 82 mg. cholesterol, 8 g. dietary fiber, 13 g. fat, 81 mg. sodium.

Hungarian Goulash

PREPARATION TIME: 15 TO 20 MINUTES.   COOKING TIME: 15 TO 20 MINUTES.

Serve this with 1 cup of cooked noodles or grain per serving.

3 pounds lean beefsteak
1 cup diced leeks
1 tablespoon olive oil
2 medium carrots, diced
1 can (16 ounces) no-salt-added tomatoes
1 cup beef stock
1 tablespoon paprika

1 teaspoon salt
½ teaspoon black pepper
¼ teaspoon ground cloves (optional)
1 tablespoon cornstarch
¼ cup water
¼ cup sour cream
¼ cup plain low-fat yogurt

1. Trim the beef of all visible fat, and cut the beef into 1-inch chunks. Brown the beef in a skillet, then remove the beef, and drain any excess fat. In the same pan, sauté the leeks in the oil.
2. When the leeks are tender, return the beef to the pan. Add the carrots, tomatoes, stock, paprika, salt, pepper, and cloves.
3. Combine the cornstarch with the water, and stir in with the beef. Cover, and let simmer until meat is tender. Then stir in the sour cream and yogurt and heat through.

8 servings of 4½ ounces each (cooked weight), plus sauce.

Per Serving (meat with sauce): 311 calories, 126 mg. cholesterol, 2 g. dietary fiber, 17 g. fat, 546 mg. sodium.

Cheddar Chili Pie

PREPARATION TIME: 30 MINUTES.   COOKING TIME: 30 MINUTES.

This is a recipe that appeared in *The Rotation Diet*, but it has proven so popular we felt we had to include it in case you missed it before. One look at the ingredients will tell you that it is a very nutritious dish, and your taste buds will carry on from there, so we are sure you will make it frequently. Serve this with a large salad of greens.

1 pound lean ground beef
1 large onion, chopped
2 cloves garlic, chopped fine
1 can (28 ounces) whole tomatoes
1 can (15 ounces) kidney beans, with juice
1¼ cups cornmeal
1 cup grated cheddar cheese
2 tablespoons chili powder

1 teaspoon cumin
¼ teaspoon cayenne pepper
½ teaspoon crushed red pepper
½ teaspoon fresh-ground black pepper
Dash Tabasco sauce
1¼ cups skim milk
2 eggs, lightly beaten
Salt and pepper to taste

1. Sauté the beef, the onion, and the garlic until the meat is browned. Drain off the fat; add the tomatoes, beans, ¾ cup cornmeal, ½ cup cheese, and the seasonings. Cook over low heat, stirring occasionally, for about 15 minutes. Pour into a casserole dish.
2. In the same pan, combine the milk, the rest of the cornmeal, and the salt and pepper to taste. Stir over low heat until it thickens a little. Then add the remaining cheese and the eggs, stirring until smooth. Pour this over the ground-beef mixture. Bake uncovered at 375 degrees for 30 minutes or until the crust is lightly browned.

8 servings. Serving size is 1½ cups.

Per Serving: 366 calories, 121 mg. cholesterol, 7 g. dietary fiber, 15 g. fat, 608 mg. sodium.

Sauerbraten

PREPARATION TIME: 5 TO 10 MINUTES.   COOKING TIME: 2½ TO 3 HOURS.

The traditional German recipe for sauerbraten calls for forty-eight hours of marinating. However, we have found that you can get by with twenty-four hours and still have a tasty dish.

3 pounds top or bottom round
1 teaspoon salt
½ teaspoon black pepper
2 to 3 bay leaves
2 whole peppercorns
4 whole cloves

1 large onion, sliced
1 medium carrot, sliced
1 stalk celery, chopped
1½ cups wine vinegar
2½ cups boiling water
2 tablespoons vegetable oil

1. Trim all visible fat from the beef, and rub the salt and pepper all over the beef. Place the beef in a large pan.
2. Add the remaining ingredients except for the oil and marinate, covered, in the refrigerator for at least 24 hours, turning twice a day.
3. When you're ready to cook the meat, place the oil in a large kettle, add only the meat, and brown over medium heat. Pour in the marinade, cover, and simmer for 2½ to 3 hours, until done.

8 servings of 4½ ounces each (cooked weight).

Per Serving: 289 calories, 123 mg. cholesterol, 1 g. dietary fiber, 17 g. fat, 347 mg. sodium.

Thai Stir-Fry

PREPARATION TIME: 15 MINUTES.   COOKING TIME: 15 TO 20 MINUTES.

Here is an example of how to use nuts or seeds (in this case, sesame) in small amounts as a flavorful garnish. See pages 237–38 for instructions on how to toast them without added fat.

1 pound beef flank steak
¼ cup tamari sauce
  OR soy sauce
3 tablespoons honey
½-inch gingerroot, minced
1 clove garlic, minced or
  crushed
2 tablespoons toasted sesame
  seeds, ground with mortar
  and pestle

1 tablespoon oil (preferably
  peanut)
1 small eggplant, cut in thin
  strips
¼ to ½ teaspoon crushed red
  pepper (optional)
¼ cup stock

1. Cut the beef across the grain into strips about ¼ inch thick. Pound lightly with a meat hammer. Place in a bowl or sealable plastic bag with the tamari, honey, ginger, and garlic.
2. Add the oil to a wok or large frying pan, let it heat through, and add the beef. Cook, stirring constantly, until beef is browned, then remove the beef and reserve.
3. Add the eggplant, the crushed red pepper, and the stock to the pan. Cover, and steam for 5 to 10 minutes, until the eggplant softens, stirring occasionally.
4. Add the beef, cover, and let simmer for several minutes, until done.
5. Sprinkle with sesame seeds and serve.

4 servings of 3 ounces each (cooked weight), plus vegetables.

Per Serving: 313 calories, 82 mg. cholesterol, 5 g. dietary fiber, 15 g. fat, 1037 mg. sodium.

Yukon Stew

PREPARATION TIME: 8 TO 10 MINUTES.   COOKING TIME: 2¼ HOURS.

This recipe originally called for moose or caribou meat. If you have trouble finding these in your local supermarket, substitute beef, as we did! Serve with cooked grain, over whole-wheat noodles, or boiled potatoes, along with a dark green or yellow vegetable, such as steamed carrots.

2 pounds lean top round roast, cut into chunks
3 tablespoons lemon juice
½ teaspoon salt
2 teaspoons chili powder

⅓ cup whole-wheat flour
1 tablespoon vegetable oil
Hot water OR stock to cover
½ cup chopped fresh parsley

1. Sprinkle the meat with the lemon juice. In a shallow bowl, combine the salt, chili powder, and flour, and dredge the meat in flour mixture.
2. Heat a 3-quart saucepan on medium heat. Add the oil, and brown the meat on all sides. Add water or stock to cover. Simmer, covered, for 2 hours, or until the meat is tender. Then remove the cover and let cook for about 15 minutes to thicken the sauce.
3. Add the parsley, stir, and serve.

6 servings of 4 ounces each (cooked weight).

Per Serving: 327 calories, 91 mg. cholesterol, 1 g. dietary fiber, 19 g. fat, 272 mg. sodium.

Easy Beef Stroganoff

PREPARATION TIME: 10 MINUTES.   COOKING TIME: 10 MINUTES.

1 small onion, diced
3 to 4 ounces fresh mushrooms, diced
1 tablespoon vegetable oil
3 cups cooked beef, either ground beef
  OR sliced beefsteak
⅓ cup plain low-fat yogurt

⅓ cup sour cream
¼ cup plus 2 tablespoons dry white wine
½ teaspoon salt
¼ teaspoon fresh-ground black pepper
½ teaspoon nutmeg

1. Sauté the onions and mushrooms in the oil over medium-low heat until the onions are translucent. Stir in the remaining ingredients, and let simmer for 10 minutes, covered, until heated through. Do not boil.

6 servings. Serving size is about ⅞ cup.

Per Serving: 199 calories, 50 mg. cholesterol, 1 g. dietary fiber, 15 g. fat, 233 mg. sodium.

Tarragon Beef

PREPARATION TIME: 15 MINUTES.   COOKING TIME: 3¼ HOURS.

The combination of tarragon and crushed red pepper in this recipe makes for a slightly exotic variation on a standard "meat-and-potatoes" dish. We suggest you try it the first time with the smaller amount of hot pepper, unless you like spicy hot food.

4 pounds of lean beef roast
¾ cup red wine
2 medium onions, quartered
4 medium carrots, cut in chunks
4 medium potatoes, cut in chunks
2 tablespoons dried parsley
2 tablespoons dried tarragon

1 bay leaf
2 cloves garlic, minced or crushed
1 teaspoon salt
1 teaspoon fresh-ground black pepper
¼ to 1 teaspoon crushed dried red pepper

1. Trim any visible fat from the beef, and marinate the beef in all the remaining ingredients in a large roasting pan for at least 2 hours at room temperature.
2. Place the roast in a 450 degree oven for 45 minutes, then lower the temperature to 275 degrees and cook for 2½ hours more.

12 servings of about 4 ounces each (cooked weight).

Per Serving: 352 calories, 91 mg. cholesterol, 2 g. dietary fiber, 17 g. fat, 276 mg. sodium.

Easy Beef and Rice

PREPARATION TIME: 10 MINUTES.   COOKING TIME: 45 TO 50 MINUTES.

With her full schedule as a concert pianist and professor of music at Vanderbilt's Blair School of Music, my wife Enid doesn't often have time for elaborate cooking. Here is one of her many quick-and-easy recipes. Serve with a dinner salad for a complete, tasty meal. You may substitute homemade stock for the bouillon and water if you like.

2 cups brown rice
4 cups water
4 scallions, chopped
4 teaspoons granulated bouillon
  OR 4 bouillon cubes

1 pound extra-lean ground beef
2 cans (10¾ ounces each)
  tomato purée
1 teaspoon Mrs. Dash (or other herb blend)

1. Combine the first 4 ingredients in a 2-quart pot. Bring to a boil, lower the heat, and simmer until tender, about 35 to 40 minutes.
2. In a large frying pan, sauté the ground beef. Drain off any excess fat, then add the purée and seasoning. Add the cooked rice. Heat through, and serve.

8 servings. Serving size is 1 cup.

Per Serving: 275 calories, 38 mg. cholesterol, 3 g. dietary fiber, 9 g. fat, 727 mg. sodium.

Lemon-Pepper Beef

PREPARATION TIME: 5 MINUTES.   COOKING TIME: 18 TO 20 MINUTES.

We first made this dish with ¼ cup of lemon juice (4 table-spoons) and it had a decidedly sharp aftertaste of lemon! So we reduced the amount. Use the lesser amount of lemon juice if you prefer a less intense lemon flavor. Reduce or increase cooking time depending on how you like your meat cooked. This dish goes well with cooked pasta, such as vermicelli, and a dinner salad.

1 pound lean top or bottom round steak, well-trimmed
¼ cup dry red wine
2 to 3 tablespoons lemon juice
½ teaspoon salt

1 bay leaf
2 yellow or red sweet peppers, cut in eighths
Fresh-ground black pepper to taste

1. Combine all ingredients in a large bowl or pan, and marinate overnight, or at least 6 hours in the refrigerator. Turn beef and peppers occasionally.
2. Place beef on broiler pan about 4 inches from heat and broil about 8 minutes. Turn, and add the pepper pieces to the pan. After six minutes or so, turn the peppers over, then broil about 4 minutes more for medium-well-done beef. Slice the beef thinly across the grain, and serve with the peppers.

4 servings of 3 ounces each (cooked weight).

Per Serving: 187 calories, 82 mg. cholesterol, no dietary fiber, 9 g. fat, 316 mg. sodium.

Veal

The best cuts of veal are the loin and round. When well-trimmed, they are 20 to 40 percent lower in calories than similar cuts of mature beef. Our own interest in veal has increased as we became aware of how its delicate flavor makes it such a fine vehicle for carrying the flavors of different sauces. The economy of calories, together with the interest that can be generated by many different blends of herbs and spices, can make veal an excellent alternative to mature beef in your diet.

Look for pale pink-colored flesh and very white fat when you buy veal. If you desire the most tender and exquisitely flavored meat available, select milk-fed veal; it's even more tender than the meat of calves that have been fed solid foods.

We include several recipes for *scaloppines* (very thin, pounded slices of veal) in sauces, plus a variety of other ways to prepare veal, which can be used in meat loaf, meatballs, stew, and as steak.

Perhaps you will notice that many of our veal recipes seem to be of Italian origin. That's because the Italians have perfected the art of preparing delicate sauces to complement the delicacy of veal. In fact, the per-capita consumption of veal in Italy is at least two or three times that of the United States.

Because veal is such a lean and delicate meat, many cooks add an unconscionable amount of butter and oil in its preparation, in the mistaken belief that adding fat is the way to enhance the flavor. From our recipes, you will discover that preparing veal requires very little fat; we find a judicious use of herbs, spices, and wine is the best way to bring out veal's flavor.

Our Herb Salt (pp. 334–35) and Traditional Italian Herb Blend (p. 335) complement veal; keeping some ready-made herb blends on hand for the times when you don't care to start from scratch will save on preparation time.

But veal invites experimentation and every one of the following herbs and spices, alone or in combination, will enhance your pleasure of this delicious meat: rosemary, thyme, sage, bay leaf, chervil, parsley, mustard seed, coriander, tarragon, chives, basil, allspice, or, in place of allspice, a blend of cinnamon, nutmeg, and cloves, which is especially good in meatballs.

Experiment with wine in the sauces: dry sherry, Marsala, Madeira, dry vermouth, and white with the *scaloppine,* and dry red when you want a richer marinade. White wines add little color to the pale meat, while reds, of course, darken it.

When you pound veal to make *scaloppine,* place it on a wooden board and cover it with wax paper to prevent your pounder from sticking and the meat from splattering. I have used everything from a piece of two-by-four to the bottom of a wooden salad bowl to pound meat, but your best implement is a metal pounder made especially for that purpose. I have one that has a flat side for veal and a waffle-edge side for tenderizing tougher cuts of beef. You can find one at a cookware shop.

Brochette of Veal

PREPARATION TIME: 50 MINUTES.   COOKING TIME: 10 MINUTES.

Though we recommend grilling for this recipe, you can also oven-broil.

1½ pounds boneless veal roast, well-trimmed, cut into 1-inch cubes
12 ounces white mushrooms
2 tablespoons olive oil
½ teaspoon salt
Fresh-ground black pepper to taste
2 tablespoons dry red wine

Juice of ½ lemon
¼ teaspoon thyme
1 bay leaf, crushed
1 teaspoon tarragon
3 cloves garlic, minced
2 medium sweet red peppers OR any other sweet peppers, cut into 1-inch pieces

1. Place the cubed veal in a large mixing bowl and add all the remaining ingredients. Cover and marinate in the refrigerator for about 2 hours. Stir the mixture at least twice.
2. About ½ hour before grilling time, prepare a charcoal fire.
3. While the coals are warming, arrange the cubed veal, mushrooms, and peppers, on 6 skewers.
3. When the charcoal fire is hot, place the skewered veal on the grill and cook, turning occasionally, until done (about 10 minutes, depending upon the heat of the grill).

6 servings of 3 ounces each (cooked weight), plus vegetables.

Per Serving: 297 calories, 109 mg. cholesterol, 2 g. dietary fiber, 19 g. fat, 238 mg. sodium.

Lemon Veal *Scaloppine*

PREPARATION TIME: 10 TO 12 MINUTES.   COOKING TIME: 5 TO 10 MINUTES.

1 pound veal, sliced thin (8 slices)
Fresh-ground black pepper to taste
1 tablespoon olive oil
¼ cup dry white wine

¼ cup chicken stock
Juice of 1 lemon (or 1 tablespoon of reconstituted lemon juice)
2 tablespoons chopped fresh parsley

1. Pound the veal to about ½ its original thickness, or as thin as possible without tearing the meat. Sprinkle the meat with pepper.
2. Heat the olive oil in a large nonstick frying pan and, when it is quite hot, brown the veal 1 minute per side.
3. Add the wine, chicken stock, lemon juice, and parsley and continue to cook the veal, occasionally turning the slices, until the sauce has reduced to desired consistency (from 5 to 10 minutes).

4 servings of 3 ounces each (cooked weight), plus sauce.

Per Serving: 218 calories, 109 mg. cholesterol, no dietary fiber, 13 g. fat, 150 mg. sodium.

Roast Veal with Italian Seasoning

PREPARATION TIME: 25 MINUTES.   COOKING TIME: 1¼ HOURS.

1 3-pound boneless veal roast,
  well trimmed
2 cloves garlic, minced
1 teaspoon Traditional Italian
  Herb Blend (p. 335)
½ teaspoon salt
Fresh-ground black pepper to
  taste

2 tablespoons olive oil
4 medium onions, cut into
  quarters
½ cup dry white wine
1½ cups chicken stock
8 medium carrots,
  quartered

1. Preheat the oven to 400 degrees.
2. Place the meat in a shallow roasting pan. Rub the garlic
   and the Herb Blend all over the meat. Sprinkle it with salt
   and pepper and rub it with oil.
3. Place the roasting pan on a low shelf in the oven and
   brown at 400 degrees for about 10 minutes. Pour off all the
   fat from the roasting pan. Place onions around the meat.
   Brown the meat and onions for about 5 minutes.
4. Add the wine and chicken stock, and cover tightly with
   foil. Reduce heat to 350 degrees and bake for about 45
   minutes. Add carrots and bake for an additional 30 minutes, or until a meat thermometer reaches 170 degrees.
   Skim away the fat and serve the meat with its own sauce
   and the vegetables.

8 servings of 4½ ounces each (cooked weight), plus vegetables.

Per Serving: 429 calories, 164 mg. cholesterol, 3 g. dietary fiber,
25 g. fat, 414 mg. sodium.

Veal (or Chicken) Florentine

PREPARATION TIME: 25 MINUTES.   COOKING TIME: 25 MINUTES.

"Florentine" indicates that a dish is made with spinach. It is an
Italian-style of cooking that works well with veal, chicken, or
fish. This is good served with cooked pasta.

1 pound veal cutlets (4 slices)
  OR 4 chicken breasts,
  skinned, boned
¼ teaspoon black pepper
1 package (10 ounces) frozen
  chopped spinach, thawed,
  drained
1 egg OR 2 egg whites

¼ cup part-skim ricotta cheese
2 tablespoons grated Parmesan
  OR sapsago cheese
1 clove garlic, minced or
  crushed
½ teaspoon oregano
2 tablespoons olive oil
1 cup dry white wine

1. Pound the veal or chicken to ¼-inch thickness. Sprinkle
   with the pepper.
2. In a medium bowl, combine the spinach, egg, cheeses,
   garlic, and oregano. Spread this mixture over the veal.
3. Roll the veal, jelly-roll fashion, around the spinach filling,
   securing the rolls with toothpicks or twine.
4. Add the oil and meat to a small skillet, over medium to
   medium-low heat, lightly brown the rolls on all sides.
   Place the rolls in a casserole dish, add the wine, and bake
   at 350 degrees for 25 minutes.

*4 servings (1 roll) of 3 ounces each (cooked weight), plus
vegetables.*

Per Serving (with veal): 319 calories, 184 mg. cholesterol, 2 g.
dietary fiber, 20 g. fat, 201 mg. sodium.

Per Serving (with chicken): 276 calories, 148 mg. cholesterol, 2 g.
dietary fiber, 13 g. fat, 209 mg. sodium.

Veal Stew

PREPARATION TIME: 30 MINUTES.   COOKING TIME (WITHOUT BROWNING): 1¾ HOURS.

Although our Yukon Stew (p. 127) is a delicious exception to the rule, I generally prefer not to brown my meat when I make stews. Skipping the browning step results in a lighter gravy and you save a couple hundred calories of fat content in the total recipe. I also don't normally add any flour or cornstarch to thicken the gravy. It will thicken somewhat during the final minutes of cooking in an uncovered pot.

If you wish to brown the meat (which will take out some of the moisture in the meat, but won't really "seal in" the juices), do it in the same stewpot, using a minimum of oil, say one tablespoon. As for a gravy, if you prefer it thick, make a roux (p. 64) and blend it in during the last 30 minutes of cooking, or simply sprinkle a bit of flour into the stew, about a minute before it finishes cooking, and stir frequently until done.

1 tablespoon oil (optional, for browning)
4 pounds lean veal roast, cut into 1½-inch cubes
3 medium onions, chopped
4 cloves garlic, chopped
½ teaspoon salt
Fresh-ground black pepper to taste
1 bay leaf
½ teaspoon dried thyme
¼ teaspoon rosemary

4 tablespoons chopped fresh parsley
1 cup dry white wine
3 cups chicken stock
4 medium ripe tomatoes, cut into eighths
5 medium carrots
5 small zucchini
4 celery stalks
5 small yellow summer squash
¼ cup chopped fresh parsley for garnish

BROWNING METHOD

1. If you want to brown the meat, heat the oil in a large stewpot or Dutch oven and add veal cubes, turning until brown.
2. Add onions and garlic; heat until translucent. Add all sea-

sonings, wine, stock and tomatoes. Cover and simmer for 30 minutes.

3. As the stew is simmering, cut the carrots, zucchini, celery, and squash into bite-size pieces (about 1 inch long; for the zucchini and squash, halve in the other direction as necessary), add to the pot, cover, and simmer another 45 minutes. Uncover and continue to simmer until the gravy is reduced to the desired consistency.

4. Skim any fat that appears on the surface of the liquid, and serve, garnished with the extra parsley.

TO OMIT BROWNING

1. Prepare the vegetables, and then add all the ingredients to the pot, except for the parsley garnish, cover, and bring to the boiling point. Immediately reduce heat and simmer for about 1½ hours on low heat. Uncover to reduce liquid and skim off the fat. When gravy is of desired consistency, serve with parsley garnish.

10 servings. Serving size is about 2 cups.

Per Serving (without oil): 339 calories, 131 mg. cholesterol, 5 g. dietary fiber, 18 g. fat, 670 mg. sodium. (Oil will add about 10 calories per serving in the form of another gram of fat.)

Veal Roast with Fennel and Leeks

PREPARATION TIME: 15 MINUTES.   COOKING TIME: 1½ TO 2 HOURS.

1 4-pound veal roast, bone in
3 bulbs fennel
4 leeks
16 small new potatoes
½ teaspoon sage
½ teaspoon rosemary

¼ teaspoon coriander
Fresh-ground black pepper to
  taste
1 tablespoon lemon juice
¼ cup white wine or water

1. Trim all visible fat from the roast and place it in a Dutch
   oven or large casserole dish.
2. Trim the tough outer leaves from the fennel. Wash and
   core the bulbs and cut in chunks. Arrange around the veal
   roast.
3. Carefully wash and trim the leeks. Cut the white portion
   in large pieces and add to the roasting pan, along with the
   washed new potatoes.
4. Sprinkle with seasonings, lemon juice, and wine. Cover,
   and bake at 350 degrees for about 1½ to 2 hours.

8 servings of 4½ ounces each (cooked weight), plus vegetables.

Per Serving: 469 calories, 175 mg. cholesterol, 3 g. dietary fiber,
23 g. fat, 97 mg. sodium.

Veal Marsala

PREPARATION TIME: 10 TO 12 MINUTES.   COOKING TIME: 3 MINUTES.

1½ pounds thinly sliced veal
  (12 slices)
¼ teaspoon salt
Fresh-ground black pepper to
  taste

1 tablespoon olive oil
¼ cup Marsala wine
2 tablespoons chopped fresh
  parsley

1. Between wax paper, pound the meat to ¼-inch thickness
   and sprinkle with the salt and pepper.
2. Heat the oil in a large nonstick frying pan. When it is hot,

brown half the veal for 1 minute on each side, and remove to an oven-proof plate warmed in the oven, and hold in reserve. Brown the other half of the veal and then immediately return the meat from the platter to the pan.
3. Add the Marsala and parsley and cook for 3 minutes. Serve at once.

6 servings of 3 ounces each (cooked weight).

Per Serving: 206 calories, 109 mg. cholesterol, no dietary fiber, 12 g. fat, 145 mg. sodium.

Veal-Steak *Milano*

PREPARATION TIME: 10 MINUTES.　　　COOKING TIME: 2 MINUTES.

4 thinly sliced, boneless veal
　steaks (about ½-pound each,
　no more than ½-inch thick)
1 teaspoon Herb Salt (pp.
　334–35)
Fresh-ground black pepper to
　taste

1 tablespoon olive oil
　OR other vegetable oil
2 tablespoons chopped fresh
　parsley
4 lemon wedges

1. Pound the veal with a flat meat mallet until it is about ¼-inch thick.
2. Rub meat on both sides with Herb Salt and pepper, and then brush with oil.
3. Preheat a heavy frying pan until it is hot, then place the meat in it. Sear the meat for about 1 minute on each side, testing for doneness by cutting into the center of a slice with a knife. Cook until done the way you like it.
4. Remove the meat to a warmed serving plate, sprinkle it with parsley, and serve with the lemon wedges.

4 servings of 6 ounces each (cooked weight).

Per Serving: 219 calories, 109 mg. cholesterol, no dietary fiber, 13 g. fat, 590 mg. sodium.

Veal Roast with Mushrooms

PREPARATION TIME: 12 MINUTES.   COOKING TIME: 2½ HOURS.

This recipe can be assembled ahead of time and refrigerated until cooking time, as the lemon juice keeps the potatoes from darkening.

2 pounds veal chuck roast, bone in
2 teaspoons lemon juice
½ cup hot water
1 teaspoon instant chicken bouillon granules
2 large potatoes, cut in large chunks

Ground ginger, Mrs. Dash, and garlic powder to taste
1 medium onion, sliced
1 can (4 ounces) mushrooms, drained

1. Trim the roast of all visible fat and place the roast in a casserole dish.
2. Combine the lemon juice, water, and bouillon granules. Dip the cut potatoes into this mixture, and place them around the roast. Pour the remaining liquid over the roast.
3. Sprinkle with the seasonings, and cover the roast with the onions and mushrooms.
4. Bake covered at 300 degrees for about 2½ hours or until the meat is tender.

4 servings of 4½ ounces each (cooked weight), plus vegetables.

Per Serving: 390 calories, 145 mg. cholesterol, 2 g. dietary fiber, 19 g. fat, 167 mg. sodium.

Veal *Scaloppine*

PREPARATION TIME: 10 TO 12 MINUTES.   COOKING TIME: 15 MINUTES.

1½ pounds veal cutlet, cut into 6 pieces
1 clove garlic, minced
½ teaspoon salt
¼ teaspoon pepper

¼ teaspoon oregano
¼ teaspoon dried basil
½ cup fresh mushrooms, sliced
¼ cup Marsala wine or sherry

1. Pound veal to ¼-inch thickness. In a Teflon-coated or iron skillet, or a skillet sprayed with nonstick vegetable cook-

ing spray, brown the veal on both sides over medium-high heat.
2. Reduce heat to low, and add other ingredients. Cover and cook until veal is tender, about 15 minutes.

6 servings of 3 ounces each (cooked weight), plus sauce.

Per Serving: 202 calories, 109 mg. cholesterol, no dietary fiber, 9 g. fat, 235 mg. sodium.

Veal *Scaloppine* Dijon

PREPARATION TIME: 10 MINUTES.   COOKING TIME: 5 MINUTES.

1½ pounds veal *scaloppine* (about 18 thin pieces)
Fresh-ground black pepper to taste
1 tablespoon olive oil
1 tablespoon butter
4 cloves garlic, minced

2 tablespoons dry white wine
2 tablespoons chicken stock
1 tablespoon Dijon mustard
2 teaspoons Herb Salt (pp. 334–35)
4 tablespoons chopped fresh parsley

1. Pound the meat and then sprinkle with pepper.
2. Heat the oil in a large nonstick frying pan over medium heat, and when it is hot, cover the bottom of the pan with meat. Lightly brown the meat on each side (about 30 seconds), remove it to a warm platter, and continue with the remaining meat until all is done.
3. Remove any remaining fat from the pan and add the butter and garlic. Saute garlic for 30 seconds. Add the wine, chicken stock, mustard, and Herb Salt. As the mixture cooks, scrape the bottom of the pan with a wooden or plastic spatula to blend all ingredients. Return the veal and any liquid to the pan, sprinkle with parsley, and heat for about 1 minute.

6 servings of 3 ounces each (cooked weight; about 3 slices).

Per Serving: 228 calories, 114 mg. cholesterol, no dietary fiber, 14 g. fat, 851 mg. sodium.

Veal Steak with Mushrooms and Mustard

PREPARATION TIME: 5 MINUTES.   COOKING TIME: 10 TO 12 MINUTES.

1 tablespoon fresh ground
  mustard seed or 2 teaspoons
  of Dijon mustard
1 tablespoon olive oil
4 6-ounce veal steaks, about
  ¼-inch thick
½ teaspoon salt
Fresh-ground black pepper to
  taste

1 tablespoon butter
¼ cup chopped scallions
½ pound mushrooms, sliced
  thin
2 tablespoons dry red wine
¼ cup chicken stock
2 tablespoons chopped fresh
  parsley

1. If using mustard seed, grind it with mortar and pestle.
2. Heat the olive oil in a large nonstick frying pan on medi-um-low heat.
3. Sprinkle salt, pepper, and mustard seed on both sides of the veal or spread the Dijon evenly on both sides of each steak.
4. Put the veal in the frying pan and cook for about 3 minutes on each side. Transfer the meat to a serving platter and keep it at serving temperature by covering the platter or placing it in a warm oven.
5. Add the butter to the pan and sauté the scallions and mushrooms until the scallions are translucent.
6. Add the wine and chicken stock to the pan and blend the ingredients well with a spatula. Cook until the liquid is reduced by half. Spoon the sauce over the veal steaks and sprinkle with parsley.

4 servings of 4½ ounces each (cooked weight), plus sauce.

Per Serving: 353 calories, 171 mg. cholesterol, 2 g. dietary fiber, 21 g. fat, 508 mg. sodium.

Pork

Pork, like lamb, is not a regular part of our diet. We have a few favorite recipes for pork as a main course that we occasionally make, and we include three others that illustrate how you can use pork as a condiment in combination with vegetables.

Contrary to what most people believe, pork can be a lean meat! If you serve the lean meat from the butt, blade, or sirloin, it runs only about 55 calories an ounce, and the percent of fat calories is 30 to 35. But be sure to trim the meat well, because the fat content will more than double the calories if you don't.

We calculate the calories in the roast recipes for serving sizes of 4.5 ounces. We slice our meat thinly, averaging three slices of meat per serving of that size. A good-size rib or loin chop, about 1-inch thick before cooking, will have about 2 to 3 ounces of lean meat and contain fewer than 200 calories (eat the fat, and it's more than double).

Normally, the price of pork makes it a bargain compared to other meats and it's just as full of the B vitamins and iron as beef. Trim it well and it's just as lean.

You will rarely see bacon or fatback in our recipes. Bacon, broiled or fried *crisp*, contains about 160 calories an ounce, and of those calories, over 80 percent come from fat! Whenever bacon is called for in your own recipes, try using Canadian bacon (about 80 calories an ounce and about 40 percent fat) or lean ham (about 55 calories an ounce and about 33 percent fat).

Dijon Pork Roast

PREPARATION TIME: 10 MINUTES.   COOKING TIME: 1½ HOURS.

1 pork roast, about 3 pounds
  with bone
2 cups beef stock
½ teaspoon garlic powder
½ teaspoon dry mustard
1 teaspoon thyme
1 medium carrot, sliced into
  ¼-inch rounds
1 medium zucchini, sliced into
  ¼-inch rounds
½ cup chopped leeks
1 stalk celery, sliced
Dijon mustard OR Dijon
  Dressing (p. 298)

1. Trim all visible fat from the roast, and place the roast in a baking pan. Pour the stock over it.
2. Combine the garlic powder, dry mustard, and thyme, and rub the mixture over all sides of the roast. Arrange the chopped vegetables around the roast.
3. Bake at 350 degrees for 1½ hours, or until the roast is cooked through and tender, basting occasionally. Serve each slice of pork with a teaspoon or two of Dijon mustard or Dijon Dressing, plus vegetables.

6 servings of 4.½ ounces each (cooked weight), plus vegetables.

Per Serving: 331 calories, 115 mg. cholesterol, 1 g. dietary fiber, 18 g. fat, 454 mg. sodium.

"You certainly have a peculiar sense of humor." DRAWING BY CHAS. ADDAMS; © 1939, 1967 THE NEW YORKER MAGAZINE, INC.

Pork Loin Stir-Fry

PREPARATION TIME: 12 TO 15 MINUTES.   COOKING TIME: 15 TO 20 MINUTES.

This stir-fry is mild and very good. Serve it over cooked grain or whole-wheat pasta.

2 pounds lean boneless pork loin or shoulder
1 tablespoon peanut oil
1 clove garlic, minced or crushed
½-inch fresh gingerroot, minced, OR 1 teaspoon ground ginger

1 medium onion, cut in chunks
1 medium apple, chopped
1 medium green pepper, sliced in thin strips
4 medium carrots, cut in thin strips, 1-inch long
½ cup water OR stock

1. Trim all visible fat from pork, and cut into strips about 2 inches by ½-inch.
2. Heat the oil in a wok or large frying pan over medium-high heat. Add the pork and brown it, stirring constantly. Remove pork and drain on paper towels.
3. Add the garlic, ginger if using fresh, and onion to the wok, cover, and sauté/steam until onions are translucent.
4. Add the apple, green pepper, carrots, and water. Stir, cover, and reduce the heat to medium low. Cook for about 3 minutes, and return the pork to the pan.
5. If you're using ground ginger, add it to the stir-fry when the apples are just tender. Let sautée/steam for a few more minutes, until pork is cooked through.

6 servings of 4½ ounces each (cooked weight), plus vegetables.

Per Serving: 354 calories, 115 mg. cholesterol, 2 g. dietary fiber, 20 g. fat, 108 mg. sodium.

Pork Chops Parmesan

PREPARATION TIME: 8 TO 10 MINUTES.　　COOKING TIME: 30 MINUTES.

3 tablespoons cornmeal,
　whole-wheat flour, or bread
　crumbs
1 tablespoon grated Parmesan
　cheese
½ teaspoon fresh-ground black
　pepper
½ teaspoon salt

½ teaspoon basil
4 pork-loin rib chops, about ½
　-inch thick
1 tablespoon vegetable oil
3 scallions, chopped
1 clove garlic, minced
¼ teaspoon fennel seeds,
　crushed

1. Combine the cornmeal, Parmesan cheese, pepper, salt, and basil.
2. Trim the pork chops of all visible fat, pat them dry, and dredge in the cornmeal mixture.
3. Heat a skillet over medium heat, and add the oil. When the oil is hot, place the chops in the skillet, and reduce the heat to low.
4. Fry the chops for 10 minutes on each side. Then add the onions, garlic, and fennel, and continue frying for another 10 minutes, turning as necessary to keep from sticking.

4 servings of 2½ ounces each (lean meat only, cooked weight).

Per Serving: 198 calories, 56 mg. cholesterol, 1 g. dietary fiber, 12 g. fat, 340 mg. sodium.

Roast Pork with Vegetables

PREPARATION TIME: 10 MINUTES.　　COOKING TIME: 2 TO 2½ HOURS.

1 pork roast, about 3 pounds,
　with bone
1 teaspoon garlic powder
1 teaspoon fresh gingerroot,
　minced
1 teaspoon sage
2 large potatoes, sliced ½-inch
　thick

1 large onion, sliced
4 ounces fresh mushrooms
1 cup beef OR vegetable stock
2 teaspoons tamari sauce
　OR soy sauce

1. Trim the roast of all visible fat. Place the roast in a baking pan, and rub all sides with the garlic powder, ginger, and sage.
2. Arrange the vegetables around the roast. Combine the stock and the tamari sauce, and pour over the roast and vegetables.
3. Bake at 375 degrees for 30 minutes then reduce the heat to 350, and bake an additional 1½ to 2 hours, or until pork is cooked, and appears gray throughout. Baste every 40 minutes.

6 servings of 4½ ounces each (cooked weight), plus vegetables.

Per Serving: 397 calories, 115 mg. cholesterol, 3 g. dietary fiber, 18 g. fat, 283 mg. sodium.

Baked Pork Chops

PREPARATION TIME: 5 TO 10 MINUTES.   COOKING TIME: 1 HOUR.

4 pork chops, 4–6 ounces each
⅛ teaspoon garlic powder
¼ teaspoon Traditional Italian Herb Blend (p. 335)
Dash of salt and black pepper
1 can (16 ounces) unsalted tomatoes

4 ounces fresh mushrooms, sliced
¼ cup grated cheese (Swiss is good)

1. Trim the chops of all visible fat and place them in a roasting pan. Sprinkle with the herbs.
2. Drain the juice from the tomatoes into the pan, over the pork chops. Reserve the tomatoes.
3. Bake the chops at 375 degrees for 30 minutes.
4. Cover the chops with the mushrooms, the reserved tomatoes, and the cheese, and bake an additional 30 minutes.

4 servings of 2½ ounces each (lean meat only, cooked weight), plus vegetables

Per Serving: 229 calories, 61 mg. cholesterol, 2 g. dietary fiber, 11 g. fat, 324 mg. sodium.

Oriental Pork Chops

PREPARATION TIME: 5 MINUTES. COOKING TIME: 35 MINUTES.

Serve this with cooked grain or a baked potato, and a vegetable stir-fry, such as Chinese Cabbage Stir-Fry (p. 280).

4 lean pork chops, 4–6 ounces each
1 tablespoon tamari sauce OR soy sauce
½ teaspoon salt
½ teaspoon black pepper
1 slice fresh gingerroot, about ¼-inch thick, minced
3 tablespoons white wine
¼ cup beef stock

1. Trim the chops of all visible fat and place them in a baking pan.
2. Combine the remaining ingredients, except for the stock, in a small bowl. Brush the sauce mixture over each chop, reserving any remaining sauce.
3. Bake the chops at 350 degrees for 20 minutes.
4. Pour the stock over the chops, along with any remaining sauce. Bake an additional 10 to 15 minutes, basting occasionally, until chops are cooked (gray all the way through the center).

4 servings of 2½ ounces each (lean meat only, cooked weight), plus sauce.

Per Serving: 177 calories, 55 mg. cholesterol, no dietary fiber, 9 g. fat, 629 mg. sodium.

Jambalaya

PREPARATION TIME: 25 MINUTES. COOKING TIME: 20 MINUTES.

Jambalaya is good served hot over brown rice or other cooked grain for a complete meal. Check your supermarket for specially marked packages of *lean* ham and low-fat sausage. We use Eckrich's "Lean Supreme" sausage; there are no doubt other good brands as well. However, the computer program we used to analyze recipes does not list low-fat sausage, so the analysis we give at the end of this recipe has somewhat higher values than you would get if you used the low-fat sausage.

10 ounces cooked lean ham, diced

½ pound smoked low-fat sausage, cut into ¼-inch-thick slices

2 medium onions, diced

1 large clove garlic, crushed

1 teaspoon vegetable oil (optional)

2 cans (16 ounces each) unsalted tomatoes

1 can (4 ounces) oysters, plus their liquid, OR 4 ounces fresh oysters

1 tablespoon whole-wheat flour

2 packages (6 ounces each) mini-shrimp

1. Brown the ham and the sausage in a skillet. Drain off any fat, and place the meat on paper towels, patting dry to remove excess fat.
2. In the same pan, sauté the onions and garlic, adding a teaspoon of vegetable oil if necessary to keep them from sticking.
3. In a large pot, heat the tomatoes, cutting the larger ones in half. When the tomatoes are hot, add the onions and garlic, ham and sausage, and simmer over low heat.
4. Drain the oysters, reserving their juice. Mix the flour with a little bit of the juice to make a thick roux. Add this to the pot, stirring well.
5. Add the oysters and the shrimp, and let simmer for 20 minutes.

8 servings. Serving size is about 1½ cups.

Per Serving (using regular sausage): 248 calories, 107 mg. cholesterol, 2 g. dietary fiber, 13 g. fat, 1149 mg. sodium.

Pork Chops à la Grecque

PREPARATION TIME: 15 MINUTES.   COOKING TIME: 35 MINUTES.

4 lean pork chops, 4–6 ounces each

½ teaspoon salt

2 medium onions, sliced

1 tablespoon olive oil
OR vegetable oil

4 ounces fresh mushrooms, sliced

¼ cup unsweetened orange juice

¼ cup water or beef stock

¼ cup Greek OR other black olives, diced

1 tablespoon lemon juice

¼ teaspoon black pepper

1. Trim all visible fat from the chops. Place the chops in a baking pan and sprinkle with the salt.
2. Bake at 350 degrees for 20 minutes.
3. While the chops are baking, prepare the sauce by sautée-ing the onions in the oil. When onions are translucent, add the mushrooms, cover, and cook two to three minutes more. Add the remaining ingredients, and heat through.
4. Spoon the sauce over the chops. Bake another 10 to 15 minutes or longer, depending on the thickness of the chops. Baste occasionally, until the chops are cooked through.

4 servings of 2½ ounces each (lean only, cooked weight), plus sauce.

Per Serving: 255 calories, 55 mg. cholesterol, 2 g. dietary fiber, 16 g. fat, 435 mg. sodium.

Stir-Fry Pork with Pea Pods

PREPARATION TIME: 10 MINUTES.   COOKING TIME: 30 MINUTES.

4 pork chops, 4–6 ounces each
1 tablespoon peanut oil
  OR vegetable oil
¼ teaspoon black pepper
1 tablespoon tamari sauce
  OR soy sauce
1 clove garlic, crushed
1 slice fresh gingerroot, about

½-inch thick, minced
2 teaspoons sesame seeds
⅓ cup water
¼ cup scallions
  OR leeks, diced
1 6-ounce package frozen pea
  pods

1. Trim all visible fat from the chops, and slice the meat into thin strips, about ¼-inch thick, and ½- to 1-inch wide.
2. Heat the oil in a wok or large skillet over medium heat, then add the pork and brown, stirring often.
3. Mix together the pepper, tamari sauce, garlic, ginger, sesame seeds, and water, and add to the browned meat. Add the onions.
4. Cover, reduce heat, and let simmer for about 30 minutes, until the pork is cooked through, stirring occasionally. Add more water if necessary to prevent sticking.
5. Meanwhile, cook the pea pods according to package directions, without adding salt. Add the cooked pea pods to the pork, stir, and serve.

4 servings of 2½ ounces each (lean meat only, cooked weight), plus vegetables.

Per Serving: 237 calories, 55 mg. cholesterol, 2 g. dietary fiber, 14 g. fat, 316 mg. sodium.

Lamb

Although I have never had much of a preference for fatty meats in general and have never regretted the close trimming of any other meat, lamb is an exception. I can remember, as a child, gnawing and sucking every gram of meat, fat, and marrow from my serving of two little ribs of broiled lamb chops. I could never get enough of them, nor could the rest of the family. Always expensive, they were served only when we decided that it was time for a treat.

Indeed, the source of a never-to-be-forgotten memory is the first night I brought my future wife, Enid, to meet my parents.

As my mother approached the dinner table with a platter laden with luscious double-thick chops, my brother and father rose from their chairs to a near-standing position to spear a chop before the platter could be set upon the table. Enid, the slowest eater of the group, was still at work carefully cutting and trimming her second chop after everyone else had finished and cleaned their bones. About half-way through, Enid made the fatal error of pausing and putting her fork down. Before Enid's hand could come to rest, my Mother reached across the table and speared the remainder of the meat. As she stabbed the plump little chop, Mother said to Enid, "You don't want this?" It was more a statement than a question.

Whenever lamb chops were served at my family's dinner table, Enid rightly felt she had to be on guard.

Like most Americans, we do not eat lamb on a regular basis.

In fact, in the United States, lamb runs a poor fourth in consumption to beef, pork, and veal. In the eastern and western regions of the country, where consumption is high, good-quality lamb is easier to come by than in others parts of the United States. There is a big difference between young lamb, under six months old, and that which has reached six months to a year. We are fortunate to have one store in Nashville (the Green Hills Market) which has always had the very best lamb.

Most of our lamb recipes, such as Lamb Shanks and Lentils, one of our most special entrées, have their origin in Middle Eastern cooking, where lamb is a preferred meat. We guarantee both Sesame-Ginger Lamb Chops and Surprise Lamb Chops are two dishes worth keeping in your "special dinner" category.

But, yes, lamb is truly a fat meat. The chops that I trimmed to the bone with my teeth as an overweight child averaged 423 calories for just 3½ ounces! But lamb doesn't have to be that fatty. If you thoroughly trim your roast or chops before eating, you can still enjoy the wonderful flavors in our recipes, and end up with lamb at 55 to 65 calories per ounce. So, don't pass up the recipes in this chapter.

Lamb Roast with Savory Tomato Sauce

PREPARATION TIME: 10 MINUTES.   COOKING TIME: 2 HOURS.

1 boneless leg of lamb, about 3
  pounds
1 medium white onion,
  chopped in chunks
2 medium tomatoes, cut in
  quarters
1 medium bell pepper, cut in
  chunks

2 cloves garlic, crushed
1/3 cup dry red wine
1 can (6 ounces) tomato paste
Fresh-ground black pepper to
  taste
1 teaspoon dried thyme
1/2 teaspoon dried savory
1 bay leaf

1. Trim all visible fat from the leg of lamb. Place it in a large
   roasting pan or Dutch oven. Arrange the cut-up vegetables around the lamb. Spread the crushed garlic on top of
   the meat.
2. Pour the wine over the lamb, then top with tomato paste,
   black pepper, thyme, and savory. Float the bay leaf in the
   bottom of the pan.
3. Cover and bake at 325 degrees for about 2 hours, basting
   occasionally.

8 servings of 4 1/2 ounces each (cooked weight).

Per Serving: 390 calories, 156 mg. cholesterol, 1 g. dietary fiber,
19 g. fat, 114 mg. sodium.

Lamb Shanks and Lentils

PREPARATION TIME: 55 MINUTES TO 1 HOUR.   COOKING TIME: 40
                                                         MINUTES.

1 1/2 cups lentils
1 medium onion, stuck with 2
  whole cloves
1 bay leaf
3 cups beef stock
4 lamb shanks

1/4 to 1/3 cup whole-wheat flour
2 cloves garlic, chopped
1 tablespoon vegetable oil
1/2 cup beef stock
1/2 cup white wine

The following to taste: ground ginger, dry mustard, oregano,
  tarragon, salt, pepper

1. Overnight, soak the lentils, the onion stuck with the cloves, and the bay leaf in the 3 cups of stock. (Add a little more stock or water if necessary to completely cover the lentils.)
2. Next day, bring this mixture to a boil, then reduce heat and simmer until the lentils are tender, about 35 to 40 minutes. Remove from the heat and let cool.
3. Dust the lamb shanks with the flour (we shake them together in a bag). Set aside.
4. In a skillet, brown the garlic in the oil. Remove the garlic, then brown the lamb shanks in the same pan. Sprinkle them with ginger, mustard, oregano, and tarragon as they brown. Then pour in the ½ cup beef stock and the wine and sprinkle in a little salt and pepper. Simmer, covered, until tender.
5. With a slotted spoon, remove the lentils from their broth, and put them in a large baking dish. Remove the cloves from the onion and discard; also discard the bay leaf.
6. Chop the cooked onion, and mix in with the lentils. Place the lamb shanks on top, and pour in the juice from the lamb. Then pour in the broth from the lentils until it just comes to the top of the lentils.
7. Bake at 375 degrees for 40 minutes.

4 servings of 1 lamb shank each, plus about 1 cup lentils.

Per Serving: 405 calories, 115 mg. cholesterol, 5 g. dietary fiber, 15 g. fat, 917 mg. sodium.

Sweet-Pepper Lamb

PREPARATION TIME: 10 MINUTES.   COOKING TIME: 1¼ HOURS.

If you can't find the red peppers that make this dish so attractive, try the yellow variety. Green or purple peppers are fine, too.

2½ pounds lean lamb meat—
  (leg roast preferred)
2 cups beef OR vegetable stock
2 large cloves garlic, minced or
  crushed
⅛ cup dried parsley

2 teaspoons rosemary
1 teaspoon sage
Salt and fresh-ground black
  pepper to taste
2 whole fresh red peppers, cut
  into strips

1. Preheat oven to 350 degrees.
2. Trim the visible fat from the lamb, and place the lamb in a roasting pan. Pour the stock over the lamb, and add the spices. Arrange the strips of red pepper on top of the meat.
3. Cover and bake for 1 hour and 15 minutes.

8 servings of 4 ounces each (cooked weight), plus peppers.

Per Serving: 309 calories, 130 mg. cholesterol, no dietary fiber, 16 g. fat, 487 mg. sodium.

Cubed Lamb

PREPARATION TIME: 8 TO 10 MINUTES.   COOKING TIME: 1½ HOURS.

This goes well with a side dish of pasta, and fresh cooked spinach or other greens, such as kale, collards, mustard, or turnip greens.

1 pound lean lamb, cubed
1 tablespoon vegetable oil
  OR olive oil
1 medium tomato, diced
1 tablespoon parsley

1 teaspoon oregano
2 to 3 scallions, diced
1 tablespoon lemon juice
1 teaspoon salt

1. Trim the lamb of all visible fat, and brown the lamb in the oil in a large saucepan or skillet.
2. Add the remaining ingredients, stirring well. Cover, and reduce heat to low. Simmer for at least 1½ hours, stirring occasionally.

4 servings of 3 ounces each (cooked weight), plus sauce.

Per Serving: 230 calories, 80 mg. cholesterol, 1 g. dietary fiber, 12 g. fat, 609 mg. sodium.

Rolled Lamb Roast

PREPARATION TIME: 10 MINUTES.   COOKING TIME: 45 TO 60 MINUTES.

For a simple and delicious treat, have your butcher bone and trim a leg of lamb and tie a rolled roast for you. I think the roast is most tender when cooked in a slow oven, around 300 degrees, until my meat thermometer reaches 170 degrees. If you don't have a meat thermometer, figure 15 minutes per pound.

1 3-pound rolled lamb roast
1 teaspoon each of rosemary, thyme, sage, marjoram, ground ginger and fresh-ground black pepper

1 to 2 cloves garlic, crushed
½ teaspoon salt
1 tablespoon olive oil
1 tablespoon soy sauce

1. Use the tip of a sharp knife to make gashes about an inch apart in the meat.
2. In a bowl or cup, mix together the remaining ingredients to make a paste. Rub the paste well into the roast, covering all exposed meat and pushing it into the gashes you have made.
3. Place in a 300 degree oven for about 45 minutes to 1 hour, until the roast is cooked the way you like it.

8 servings of 4½ ounces each (cooked weight).

Per Serving: 265 calories, 114 mg. cholesterol, no dietary fiber, 12 g. fat, 349 mg. sodium.

Curried Lamb with Vegetables

PREPARATION TIME: 20 MINUTES.   COOKING TIME: 40 MINUTES.

In countries where curries are popular, every great cook creates a curry powder out of a variety of spices, such as the ones in this recipe. Even if you've never liked curry, you'll probably like this—it's quite mild.

4 lamb loin OR shoulder chops, about ¾-inch thick (4–6 ounces each)
2 cloves garlic, minced
1 tablespoon vegetable oil
1 cup water OR stock
1 teaspoon cumin
½ teaspoon ground ginger
¼ teaspoon ground coriander
¼ teaspoon cayenne pepper
½ teaspoon turmeric
1 medium zucchini, cut in chunks
2 medium carrots, sliced
1 medium onion, cut in chunks
Fresh-ground black pepper to taste
1 package (10 ounces) frozen green peas

1. Trim any visible fat from the chops, and brown them with the garlic in the vegetable oil in a large skillet.
2. Remove the lamb, and add the remaining ingredients except the peas. Cover and bring to a boil. Reduce heat to simmer, and put the lamb back in the pan. Cover, and simmer for 30 minutes.
3. Add the peas, and simmer another 10 minutes, until the vegetables are tender and the lamb is cooked.

4 servings of 2½ ounces each (lean only, cooked weight), plus vegetables.

Per Serving: 223 calories, 60 mg. cholesterol, 10 g. dietary fiber, 10 g. fat, 120 mg. sodium.

Moroccan Stew

PREPARATION TIME: 20 MINUTES.   COOKING TIME: 2½ HOURS.

Serve this stew over cooked semolina, the grain often used in Moroccan couscous, or any other of your favorite cooked grains. Or serve it alone as a soup.

3 cups water
1 leg of lamb, about 3 pounds
1 can (16 ounces) tomatoes,
    with juice
2 medium onions, sliced or
    quartered
2 cups carrots, sliced about
    ¼-inch thick
1 piece fresh gingerroot, about
    ½-inch thick

2 cinnamon sticks
3 whole cloves
½ teaspoon saffron
1 teaspoon salt
½ teaspoon black pepper
½ teaspoon ground coriander
1 cup cooked garbanzo beans
1 medium zucchini, diced
¼ cup raisins

1. Bring the water to a boil in a large pot. Meanwhile, trim the lamb of any visible fat. Add the lamb to the boiling water, along with the tomatoes and their juice, the onions, and the carrots. Bring to a boil again. Reduce the heat to low, cover, and let simmer, turning the meat and basting it occasionally to cook evenly.

2. Put the ginger, cinnamon sticks, and cloves in a cheese-cloth bag and add to the stew. (You can add these without the bag, but the bag makes them easier to remove.)

3. Combine the saffron, salt, pepper, and coriander, and add to the stew after it has been simmering for about 1½ hours.

4. Add the garbanzos, zucchini, and raisins, and continue cooking for another hour.

5. Remove the cheesecloth spice bag or individual spices, and serve.

8 servings of 4½ ounces of meat (cooked weight), plus vegetables.

Per Serving: 337 calories, 114 mg. cholesterol, 4 g. dietary fiber, 11 g. fat, 476 mg. sodium.

Sesame-Ginger Lamb Chops

PREPARATION TIME: 5 TO 10 MINUTES.   COOKING TIME: 23 TO 26 MINUTES.

Prepare the marinade early in the morning (before work, for example) or the night before. Then almost all that remains to be done to prepare this main dish for dinner is to broil it. See pages 237–38 for instructions on how to toast seeds.

4 lamb chops, 4–6 ounces each
3 tablespoons tamari sauce
  OR soy sauce
¼ cup water
1 teaspoon lemon juice
1 teaspoon honey

1 slice fresh gingerroot, ½-inch thick, minced
4 teaspoons toasted sesame seeds, crushed with mortar and pestle

1. Trim the chops of all visible fat. Arrange the chops in a shallow pan.
2. In a small bowl, combine the tamari, water, lemon juice, honey, and ginger. Pour this mixture over the lamb and cover. Marinate in the refrigerator overnight or for about 8 hours.
3. When you're ready to cook the meal, remove the chops from the marinade, and arrange on a broiler pan. Broil about 5 inches from the heat at your oven's lowest broiler setting for 10 minutes. Turn and broil another 8 minutes.
4. Sprinkle the chops with the sesame seeds, and broil 5 to 8 minutes more.

4 servings of 2½ ounces each (lean meat only, cooked weight).

Per Serving: 175 calories, 60 mg. cholesterol, no dietary fiber, 8 g. fat, 827 mg. sodium.

Roast Herbed Leg of Lamb

PREPARATION TIME: 15 MINUTES.   COOKING TIME: 3½ HOURS.

1 leg of lamb, 4 pounds
Salt and pepper to taste

4 cloves garlic, cut in slivers
1 teaspoon dried thyme

1 teaspoon dried rosemary
Juice of 2 lemons
2 tablespoons olive oil
6 small whole onions, peeled
12 small new potatoes, washed

2 pounds yellow squash
1 cup water (optional)
2 teaspoons cornstarch
  (optional)
2 tablespoons water (optional)

1. Trim the lamb of all visible fat. Lightly sprinkle the lamb with salt and pepper. Cut small slits in the meat, and insert the garlic slivers. Sprinkle the herbs over the meat. Place the lamb in a roasting pan.
2. In a small bowl, combine the lemon juice and olive oil. Pour this mixture over the meat.
3. Bake at 325 degrees for about 2½ hours.
4. Arrange the vegetables around the roast, cutting the larger squash in half. Return the roast to the oven for another hour.
5. (Optional) To make a gravy, remove the completely cooked lamb and vegetables to a large serving platter. Skim off any fat in the pan. Add the cup of water to the pan, and stir constantly on the stovetop over low heat. Dissolve the cornstarch in the 2 tablespoons of water, and add to the gravy to thicken, if desired.

6 servings of 4½ ounces each (cooked weight), plus vegetables.

Per Serving: 333 calories, 114 mg. cholesterol, 4 g. dietary fiber, 15 g. fat, 114 mg. sodium.

Surprise Lamb Chops

PREPARATION TIME: 12 TO 15 MINUTES.   COOKING TIME: 1 HOUR.

This recipe is so-named because each serving comes wrapped in its own foil "surprise package."

4 lamb shoulder chops, 4–6
  ounces each
1 teaspoon salt
½ teaspoon pepper
1 teaspoon oregano
3 small potatoes, sliced ¼-inch
  thick
1 large carrot, sliced ¼-inch
  thick

½ medium zucchini, sliced
4 fresh mushrooms, sliced
4 teaspoons crumbled feta
  cheese (or other cheese of
  choice)
2 teaspoons lemon juice
Aluminum foil

1. Trim the chops of all visible fat. Place each chop on a *doubled over* piece of foil (or use heavy-duty foil) large enough to fold over the chop and vegetables.
2. Combine the salt, pepper, and oregano, and sprinkle each chop with one-quarter of the mixture. Then cover each chop with a layer of each different vegetable, a teaspoon of cheese, and a sprinkling of lemon juice.
3. Bring the longest edges of the foil together and roll down until it fits well across the top of the chop and vegetables, sealing them. Roll up the ends securely so that you have a neat package.
4. Place the 4 packages in a baking pan, in order to catch any juices. Bake at 350 degrees for 1 hour.
5. Serve in the package if you like; just be careful when unwrapping—it will be hot!

4 servings of 2½ ounces each (lean only, cooked weight), plus vegetables.

Per Serving: 261 calories, 66 mg. cholesterol, 5 g. dietary fiber, 8 g. fat, 728 mg. sodium.

Poultry

Chicken in one form or another is about the most frequent main course for dinner in my home and in Terri's. One reason is that it is so simple to prepare. Buy extra and freeze it, if you like. If you forget to defrost the night's dinner before you leave the house in the morning, and you have a microwave oven, a cut-up fryer will defrost in just a few minutes in the microwave when you get home. Then you can pop it in the oven with very little fuss. Look, for example, at the variations of Baked Chicken (pp. 164–66) or, for a spicy treat, our Oven-Fried Chicken (p. 168). Talk about ease of preparation!

In comparison with red meats, chicken is a low-fat source of protein. We knew there was a difference between the fat levels of beef and chicken, but it was not until we had to look up some information about the relative nutrient content of both that we became fully aware of some incredible differences. A half breast of chicken—about 3 ounces of white meat without skin—might contain 140 or so calories, with only about 20 percent of its nutrient weight, or 27 calories, in fat. A *small* rib-eye steak—about 3½ ounces cooked, and not well trimmed—might contain 440 calories, with about 80 percent, or 360 calories, in fat!

While we still like our chicken prepared as a main course according to the recipes we include in this chapter, we have also begun using chicken as a condiment in combination with other foods. Check out our various chicken combination dishes, such as Chicken with Broccoli and Carrot (p. 169), with

Cashews and Broccoli (p. 176), and with Leeks and Mushrooms (p. 171). Remember to save the carcass from roasted chicken to make soups and stock.

Our nutritional analyses assume half white meat, half dark, when whole chickens are called for. White meat contains about 25 percent less fat and calories than dark meat. When our recipes call for chicken breasts, we mean split breasts; that is, 4 chicken breasts equal 4 half breasts unless otherwise specified.

Neither Terri nor I has ever made a duck! The thought of all the fat is a turn off. So you can imagine our surprise when Chef Sylvain Le Coguic at Julian's, which is one of Nashville's most noted restaurants, responded to our request to illustrate a dish that he might serve to someone interested in keeping fat and calories low, with a recipe for duck! It isn't, of course, possible to prepare duck so that it ends up containing as few calories as the white meat of chicken, but Julian's Grilled Breast of Duck ends up at only 60 calories an ounce. The entire main course, prepared as directed, is only 400 calories. If you like duck and thought you might have to deprive yourself because it's so high in fat, try preparing it this way. It's a pleasure to look at, as well as to eat.

Baked Chicken

PREPARATION TIME: 5 TO 10 MINUTES.   COOKING TIME: 25 MINUTES.

For days when you really want a low-calorie entree or need something quick to throw in the oven, baked chicken is a simple yet delicious solution.

Try the following seasoning combinations for variety:

VARIATION 1: Sprinkle liberally with onion and garlic powder, and Herb Salt (pp. 334–35). Or make your own selection of herbs, using one or more of the following: marjoram, oregano, rosemary leaves, tarragon, or thyme leaves. Add fresh-ground black pepper.

VARIATION 2: Sprinkle liberally with chili powder, paprika, and a dash of cayenne pepper. Add salt at the table after tasting.

VARIATION 3: Calories are significantly reduced if the chicken is skinned *before* baking. But skinning prior to cooking creates a problem since the meat is likely to dry out. You can prevent this by coating the skinned chicken with a basting sauce made from ½ cup catsup, 2 tablespoons of tamari sauce or low-sodium soy sauce, and 2 ounces of sherry. Then sprinkle with herbs of your choice. (Additional salt is not needed because of the soy sauce.) Loosely cover the chicken with a piece of aluminum foil for about half the cooking time and it will stay moist.

Here are the basic directions for baking chicken.

1 small frying chicken, about 3 to 3½ pounds cut-up   **Your favorite seasonings**
Aluminum foil

1. Line a baking pan with foil and lay out the pieces of the fryer. Season as desired and bake at 400 degrees for approximately 25 minutes. Skin before eating. (Much of the flavor of the seasonings will have penetrated to the flesh of the chicken during baking; however, add more at the table, if desired.)

6 servings of about 3 ounces each (cooked weight).

Per Serving (half light, half dark meat): 155 calories, 72 mg. cholesterol, no dietary fiber, 3 g. fat, 63 mg. sodium.

White meat without skin is about 45 calories an ounce, while dark meat is almost 60 because it contains more fat. Simply multiply the number of ounces per serving times the number of calories per ounce, and you will get the total calories per serving. On 600/900 rotations, serving size is 3 ounces cooked (135 and 150 calories for white and dark meat). On 1200-calorie rotations, serving size is 4½ ounces (208 and 270 calories for white and dark meat). On 1500 and 1800 rotations, serving size is 6 ounces (270 and 360 calories for white and dark meat). Basting sauce will add between 15 and 30 calories per serving, depending on size.

Barbecued Chicken

PREPARATION TIME: 5 MINUTES.   COOKING TIME: 45 TO 50 MINUTES.

You can use this recipe with our Barbecue Sauce (p. 290) or your own variation. Or substitute store-bought sauce if you wish. Look for the one lowest in sugar and salt.

2½ pounds chicken pieces   1 cup barbecue sauce

1. Preheat oven to 350 degrees.
2. Skin the chicken. Place the pieces "skin" side down in a large, shallow baking pan. (You may wish to line the pan with foil for easy cleaning.)
3. Baste the chicken liberally with barbecue sauce, and place in the oven.
4. Bake 20 minutes, basting halfway through. Then turn the chicken over and bake another 25 to 30 minutes, or until chicken is tender, basting occasionally.

6 servings of about 3½ ounces each (cooked weight), plus sauce.

Per Serving: 174 calories, 78 mg. cholesterol, 1 g. dietary fiber, 5 g. fat, 86 mg. sodium.

Patti's Roast Chicken

PREPARATION TIME: 10 MINUTES.

COOKING TIME: 1 HOUR AND 50 MINUTES.

Patti Bereyso is one of the video producers and writers at Scene Three, Inc. of Nashville, who helped produce *The Rotation Diet Home Companion* video. Ever energetic, she cheerfully handed us this recipe as soon as she heard we were writing a cookbook.

Prepare this a day in advance, then discard the fat, reheat, and serve with its own rich-tasting gravy over cooked grain.

4 chicken breasts, skinned (about 6 ounces each)
¾ cup water
¼ cup tamari sauce OR soy sauce

1 teaspoon garlic powder
1 teaspoon dried rosemary
1 bay leaf

1. Preheat the oven to 375 degrees. Wash the chicken with cold water and pat dry with paper towels.
2. Place the chicken in a roasting pan. Pour ¾ cup water into the bottom of the pan. Pour the tamari sauce or soy sauce over the chicken, then sprinkle with garlic and rosemary. Float the bay leaf in water in the bottom of the pan.
3. Bake at 375 degrees for 1½ hours, basting frequently, until chicken is tender and well-browned. Add more water (and soy sauce, if you like) as needed.
4. Cool and refrigerate overnight. The fat will harden when chilled. Carefully spoon out the fat, leaving the jelled water-soy mixture in the pan. Place the pan in a 325-degree oven for about 20 minutes, or until thoroughly heated.

4 servings of 3½ ounces each (cooked weight).

Per Serving: 157 calories, 73 mg. cholesterol, no dietary fiber, 3 g. fat, 1093 mg. sodium.

Oven-Fried Chicken

PREPARATION TIME: 15 MINUTES.　　　COOKING TIME: 1 HOUR.

1 tablespoon vegetable oil
1 teaspoon lemon juice
3 pounds chicken pieces,
　skinned
About ⅓ cup skim
　OR low-fat milk
　OR buttermilk
½ cup flour (all-purpose,
　whole-wheat, or combination)

1½ teaspoons paprika
¼ teaspoon salt
¼ teaspoon black pepper
¼ teaspoon onion powder
¼ teaspoon garlic powder
⅛ teaspoon cayenne pepper
¼ teaspoon marjoram
¼ teaspoon oregano

1. Combine the oil and lemon juice, and brush each piece of skinned chicken with the mixture.
2. Place the milk in a shallow bowl, and set aside. Combine the flour(s) and seasonings in another bowl, mixing well.
3. Dip the chicken into the milk, coating all sides. Then coat with the flour mixture.
4. Place the chicken "skin"-side-down in a foil-covered baking pan. Cover loosely with foil, and bake at 350 degrees for 30 minutes. Turn the chicken pieces over, and bake 30 minutes more, or until cooked through.

6 servings of 3½ ounces each (cooked weight).

Per Serving: 221 calories, 78 mg. cholesterol, no dietary fiber, 7 g. fat, 168 mg. sodium.

Chicken with Broccoli and Carrot

PREPARATION TIME: 12 MINUTES.   COOKING TIME: 10 MINUTES.

Here we try to replicate one of Chef Wang Chia Hsin's creations from Nashville's Peking Garden restaurant. It was the first dish in which we ever used the Chinese technique of dipping the cut-up chicken in egg white and sprinkling with cornstarch before stir-frying. It's a technique worth using.

2 chicken breasts, skinned, boned, and cut into 1-inch pieces, about 4½–5 ounces each
1 egg white
½ teaspoon cornstarch
1 large stalk fresh broccoli

1 small carrot
2 teaspoons vegetable oil
½ cup chicken stock
¼ teaspoon cornstarch, dissolved in a small amount of water

1. Dip the chicken pieces in the egg white, and place them on a dish. Sprinkle with the ½ teaspoon of cornstarch.
2. Cut the broccoli and carrot into bite-size pieces and steam over hot water until tender.
3. While the vegetables are cooking, heat a wok or large skillet until hot, add the oil and the chicken. Cook for about 3 minutes on high heat, or until nearly done, stirring frequently. Reduce heat to medium.
4. Remove the broccoli and carrot from the steamer and add to the wok or skillet.
5. Add the chicken stock and the dissolved cornstarch. Bring to a boil, stirring constantly. Reduce heat and continue to stir, cooking only until sauce is just slightly thickened. Then immediately remove from the heat and serve.

2 servings of 1 cut up breast each, plus vegetables.

Per Serving: 176 calories, 42 mg. cholesterol, 3 g. dietary fiber, 9 g. fat, 84 mg. sodium.

Happy Heart Chicken

PREPARATION TIME: 10 MINUTES.   COOKING TIME: 1 HOUR.

The layer of vegetables in this recipe helps keep the skinned chicken moist. Notice that no oil is necessary!

3 pounds chicken pieces,
  skinned
2 teaspoons dried basil
3 tablespoons lemon juice
4 green scallions, chopped

1 can (14 ounces) hearts of palm
  OR artichoke hearts
1 large zucchini
2 medium carrots

1. Arrange the chicken in a large casserole dish. Sprinkle with the basil and lemon juice. Chop the onions and spread over the chicken.
2. Scrub the zucchini and carrots clean—do not peel—then cut each vegetable in half. Quarter them lengthwise to make 8 pieces out of each vegetable. Arrange the vegetables in an alternating pattern on top of the chicken, along with the hearts of palm.
3. Cover and bake at 350 degrees for 1 hour, or until the carrots are just tender.

8 servings of 3½ ounces each (cooked weight), plus vegetables.

Per Serving: 191 calories, 59 mg. cholesterol, 4 g. dietary fiber, 8 g. fat, 334 mg. sodium.

Greek Chicken

PREPARATION TIME: 4 MINUTES.   COOKING TIME: 35 MINUTES.

Try serving this with warmed whole-grain pita bread, rice, or Tabbouli (p. 98) and Greek Salad (pp. 94–95).

4 chicken breasts
  OR 8 thighs, skinned
Juice of 2 lemons
1 tablespoon olive oil

3 cloves garlic, crushed
1 teaspoon oregano
Salt and pepper to taste

1. Place the chicken in a shallow pan. Combine all remaining ingredients, and pour over the chicken. Cover and refrigerate at least 3 hours, preferably overnight.
2. Place the chicken on a broiler pan, barbecue grill, or on a rack in a baking pan in a 450-degree oven, and cook for about 35 minutes.

4 servings of 3½ ounces of meat (cooked weight).

Per Servings: 180 calories, 73 mg. cholesterol, no dietary fiber, 6 g. fat, 198 mg. sodium. (Analysis is for chicken breasts. Thighs will contain about 50 calories more than breasts, with a total of about 11 grams of fat.)

Chicken with Leeks and Mushrooms

PREPARATION TIME: 10 MINUTES.   COOKING TIME: 1½ HOURS.

Mild and tasty, and easy to prepare.

2 cups stock
1 cup brown rice
4 chicken breasts, skinned, about 6 ounces each

6 ounces fresh mushrooms, quartered
2 whole leeks
Mrs. Dash to taste

1. Put the stock and the rice in a large casserole dish, and place the chicken breasts on top. Spread the mushrooms over the chicken.
2. Wash the leeks thoroughly, separating the leaves to get all the dirt out. Then slice the leeks in 1-inch pieces, and place on top of the chicken and mushrooms. Sprinkle with Mrs. Dash.
3. Bake at 325 degrees for 1½ hours.

4 servings of 3½ ounces meat (cooked weight), plus vegetables and rice.

Per Serving: 341 calories, 74 mg. cholesterol, 5 g. dietary fiber, 5 g. fat, 808 mg. sodium.

Chicken Divan

PREPARATION TIME: 30 MINUTES.   COOKING TIME: 20 MINUTES.

If you wish, you may substitute ¾ cup of canned evaporated skim milk for the regular skim milk and nonfat dry milk combination in this recipe. The sapsago cheese is a hard cheese, low in fat, which is similar to Parmesan.

6 chicken breasts, boned and skinned, 5 ounces each
1½ cups chicken stock
4 tablespoons whole-wheat flour
¾ cup skim OR low-fat milk
¼ cup nonfat dry milk
¼ cup white wine
¼ teaspoon pepper
1 large bunch fresh broccoli
  OR 2 packages (10 ounces each) frozen broccoli spears
1 tablespoon fresh parsley, chopped
½ cup sapsago cheese
  OR Parmesan, grated

1. Wrap the chicken breasts in aluminum foil and bake at 350 degrees for 30 minutes.
2. Meanwhile, bring the chicken stock to a boil.
3. In another pan over low heat, combine ¼ cup of the boiling broth and the flour. Cook and stir until smooth. Gradually add the rest of the broth, stirring until thickened. Remove from heat.
4. Combine the skim and nonfat dry milk, and add to the broth, along with the wine and pepper.
5. Place the broccoli spears in a shallow baking dish. Top with half the sauce. Arrange the cooked chicken breasts on top of the broccoli. Combine half the cheese with the rest of the sauce, and pour over the chicken. Sprinkle with parsley and the remaining cheese, and bake at 350 degrees for 20 minutes.

6 servings of 1 breast, plus vegetables.

Per Serving: 247 calories, 79 mg. cholesterol, 4 g. dietary fiber, 6 g. fat, 438 mg. sodium.

Baked Lemon Chicken with Vegetables

PREPARATION TIME: 8 MINUTES.   COOKING TIME: 30 MINUTES.

It seems every low-fat cookbook has a recipe for lemon-baked chicken. In fact, both *Beyond Diet* and *The Rotation Diet* have slightly different versions of it, so this time we were going to leave it out, and substitute our Lime-Light Chicken (p. 174). But this variation is so good, we gave in to tradition. It is excellent served with brown rice or any other cooked whole grain.

4 chicken breasts, skinned and
  boned, about 4½–5 ounces
  each
1 clove garlic, crushed
½ teaspoon oregano
Dash of salt (optional)
Fresh-ground black pepper to
  taste

2 medium zucchinis, sliced
1 medium green pepper, sliced
  in strips
½ cup chicken stock
3 tablespoons lemon juice
1 tablespoon white wine

1. Place the chicken in a casserole dish. Top with the garlic, the other seasonings, and the vegetables. Pour in the stock, lemon juice, and wine.
2. Cover tightly and bake at 350 degrees for 30 minutes or until chicken is cooked through.

4 servings of about 3.5 ounces meat (cooked weight), plus vegetables.

Per Serving: 164 calories, 73 mg. cholesterol, 1 g. dietary fiber, 3 g. fat, 162 mg. sodium.

Lime-Light Chicken

PREPARATION TIME: 5 MINUTES.   COOKING TIME: 50 TO 55 MINUTES.

This is good hot, and for some reason, even better cold. Make it ahead of time for a picnic lunch: chill it in the refrigerator for several hours or overnight, then skim off any fat that has risen to the top. Add a small amount of salt at the table if you like.

4 chicken breasts, skinned
  (about 6 ounces each)
1 bay leaf
1 tablespoon vegetable oil
1 tablespoon white vinegar
1 tablespoon lime juice

1 teaspoon dried thyme
1/4 teaspoon ground coriander
Fresh-ground black pepper to
  taste
1 lime, cut into thin rounds

1. Preheat the oven to 325 degrees. Place the chicken breasts and the bay leaf in a casserole dish. Pour the vegetable oil, vinegar, and lime juice over the top.
2. Sprinkle with the seasonings, cover, and bake in the oven for 45 minutes.
3. Remove the chicken from the oven, and arrange the lime slices on top of the chicken. Return the chicken to the oven and bake uncovered for another 5 to 10 minutes, until chicken is cooked through.

4 servings of 3 1/2 ounces each (cooked weight).

Per Serving: 180 calories, 73 mg. cholesterol, no dietary fiber, 6 g. fat, 64 mg. sodium.

Easy Indian Chicken Stir-fry

PREPARATION TIME: 12 MINUTES.   COOKING TIME: 20 MINUTES.

We tried this with chicken, but it would do just as well with any leftover cooked meat, or even as a vegetarian stir-fry. It's also a great way to use up any extra raw or cooked vegetables you may have on hand. Use any vegetables you like, to make 2 cups, and always remember to start cooking the ones which take the most time first, adding the others as you go along. If you use cooked vegetables, they will need only a quick warming up.

For a "make-ahead" dish, simply dice the meat and vegetables the night before or in the morning, and store in the refrigerator.

Have ready:

1 tablespoon peanut oil
1 clove garlic, crushed
2 scallions, diced
1 medium zucchini, thinly sliced
8 ounces mushrooms, sliced

1 tomato, diced
2 cups cooked chicken, skinned, diced
2 tablespoons tamari sauce OR soy sauce

Spices:

½ teaspoon cumin
½ teaspoon fresh gingerroot, minced
¼ teaspoon ground coriander
¼ teaspoon cayenne pepper
½ teaspoon turmeric

¼ teaspoon fresh-ground black pepper
(Or substitute 2¼ teaspoons of Indian Spice Blend, p. 334, for these spices.)

1. Heat the oil in a wok or large skillet over medium heat. Add the garlic and onions, and cook for 2 to 3 minutes, stirring constantly. Add the zucchini, and stir-fry for about 6 or 7 minutes. Add the mushrooms and tomato, and stir-fry until zucchini is almost tender.
2. Add the chicken, and heat through, still stirring. Then add the tamari sauce and the spices, mix well, and serve.

4 servings. Serving size is 1 cup.

Per Serving: 255 calories, 96 mg. cholesterol, 3 g. dietary fiber, 8 g. fat, 605 mg. sodium.

Chicken with Cashews and Broccoli

PREPARATION TIME: 15 MINUTES.   COOKING TIME: 10 TO 15 MINUTES.

Assemble all of your ingredients ahead of time, so you can follow the steps of this Oriental dish quickly and easily. Serve with steaming-hot brown rice.

1 tablespoon cornstarch
1 cup chicken stock
3 tablespoons dry sherry
2 tablespoons tamari sauce
  OR soy sauce
½ teaspoon Tabasco sauce
1 tablespoon peanut oil
3 whole chicken breasts,
  skinned, boned, and cut in
  1-inch chunks
2 slices fresh gingerroot,
  ¼-inch thick each

3 cups broccoli flowerets
1 medium sweet red pepper,
  cut in 1-inch squares
½ pound fresh mushrooms,
  sliced
1 bunch scallions (about 5 or 6),
  slivered
1 clove garlic, crushed or
  minced
⅓ cup roasted unsalted
  cashews OR peanuts

1. Combine the cornstarch, chicken stock, sherry, tamari sauce, and Tabasco in a small bowl.
2. Heat the oil in a hot skillet or wok. When the oil is very hot, add the chicken and ginger. Cook, stirring constantly, until chicken turns white. Remove the ginger and push the chicken aside.
3. Place the broccoli, red pepper, mushrooms, scallions, and garlic in the skillet or center of the wok. Cook 3 minutes, stirring constantly.
4. Combine the broth mixture with the vegetables and continue stirring until the sauce thickens slightly. Stir in the chicken from the sides of the wok.
5. Sprinkle with nuts and serve immediately.

6 servings of ½ breast each (about 3½ ounces of meat, cooked weight), plus vegetables.

Per Serving: 260 calories, 73 mg. cholesterol, 5 g. dietary fiber, 9 g. fat, 548 mg. sodium.

White-Wine Worcestershire Chicken

PREPARATION TIME: 15 MINUTES.   COOKING TIME: 45 TO 60 MINUTES.

This very easy recipe uses Lea and Perrins White Wine Worcestershire sauce, which, along with a dry white wine, is the primary seasoning. Check your supermarket for this fine Worcestershire sauce.

3 pounds chicken pieces, skinned
3 medium potatoes, cut in chunks
2 medium onions, cut in chunks

4 ounces mushrooms, whole
1 pint cherry tomatoes, whole
½ cup white wine
2 tablespoons White Wine Worcestershire sauce
1 bay leaf

1. Place the skinned chicken in a casserole dish and cover with the vegetables. Pour in the wine and the Worcestershire sauce, and float the bay leaf in the bottom of the dish.
2. Bake, covered, at 350 degrees for 45 minutes to 1 hour, until the chicken is cooked through and tender.

6 servings of 3½ ounces each (cooked weight), plus vegetables and sauce.

Per Serving: 262 calories, 78 mg. cholesterol, 5 g. dietary fiber, 5 g. fat, 176 mg. sodium.

Quick Chicken Stir-Fry with Bulgur Wheat

PREPARATION TIME: 12 MINUTES.   COOKING TIME: 10 TO 15 MINUTES.

¾ cup bulgur wheat, uncooked
Water to cover
1 tablespoon peanut oil
2 scallions, minced
1 clove garlic, crushed or
  minced
¼ green bell pepper, diced
1 stalk celery, diced
6 fresh mushrooms, sliced

2 cups cooked chicken, diced
½ teaspoon fresh-ground black
  pepper
¼ teaspoon salt
¼ cup unsalted, dry roasted
  peanuts
¼ cup plain low-fat yogurt
1 tablespoon tamari sauce
  OR soy sauce

1. Soak the bulgur in water to cover for 3 to 4 hours. When
   the bulgur is ready—puffy and chewable—drain off any
   remaining water.
2. Heat the oil in a large skillet or wok over medium heat.
   Add the onions, garlic, bell pepper, and celery, and stir-fry
   for 2 minutes. Add the mushrooms, and stir-fry until vegetables are tender.
3. Add the chicken and seasonings, and stir-fry until chicken
   is heated through.
4. Stir in the peanuts, yogurt, and tamari sauce, mixing well.
   Serve over the bulgur.

8 servings of about 1 cup each.

Per Serving: 204 calories, 49 mg. cholesterol, 2 g. dietary fiber,
6 g. fat, 269 mg. sodium.

New-Style Creamed Chicken and Vegetables

PREPARATION TIME: 20 MINUTES.   COOKING TIME: 35 TO 40 MINUTES.

This recipe is based on an old Shaker recipe—a traditional
American dish with a "new-style" lower calorie twist that provides another complete meal-in-one when served with cornbread as suggested below.

1 large diced potato
1 cup green peas
  OR green beans
1 large diced carrot
Water
1 tablespoon butter
  OR margarine
1 large onion, chopped
2 stalks celery, chopped
6 tablespoons whole-wheat
  flour

½ teaspoon salt
2 teaspoons marjoram
½ teaspoon-fresh ground black
  pepper
Up to 1 cup water
  OR stock
2 cups low-fat milk
3 cups cooked chicken,
  chopped and skinned
⅓ cup chopped fresh parsley
½ teaspoon dried rosemary

1. Place the potato, peas, and carrot in a steamer over water, and steam until just tender. Reserve the liquid used for steaming.
2. Meanwhile, melt the butter in a large saucepan and sauté the onion and celery in it until the onion is translucent. Remove from the heat and stir in the flour, 5 tablespoons of the reserved liquid, the salt, marjoram, and pepper. Blend until smooth.
3. Return to the stove on medium heat. Add enough water or stock to the remaining reserved liquid to make one cup, and gradually stir the liquid and the milk into the flour-onion mixture. Bring to a slow boil over medium heat, stirring frequently.
4. Add the chicken, steamed vegetables, parsley, and rosemary. Heat through, and serve over warm Buttermilk Cornbread (p. 312).

6 servings. Serving size is about 1¾ cups.

Per Serving (not including cornbread): 380 calories, 109 mg. cholesterol, 7 g. dietary fiber, 8 g. fat, 379 mg. sodium.

Chicken Italian Style

PREPARATION TIME: 25 MINUTES.   COOKING TIME: 25 MINUTES.

1 tablespoon olive oil
2 large tomatoes, diced
1 clove garlic, crushed
½ teaspoon salt
¼ teaspoon pepper
½ teaspoon dried parsley
½ teaspoon basil
1 egg, beaten

¼ cup skim milk
4 chicken breasts, skinned and
  boned, about 4½ to 5 ounces
  each
About 1 teaspoon olive oil
1 cup Whole-Wheat Bread
  Crumbs (pp. 307–8)

1. Heat the tablespoon of oil in a skillet over medium heat, then add the tomatoes, garlic, and other seasonings. Simmer on low for 10 minutes, stirring occasionally. Set aside.
2. Beat together the egg and milk. Pound the chicken breasts between wax paper until thin.
3. Brush another skillet with the 1 teaspoon of olive oil. Turn heat on to medium. Dip the chicken in the egg batter and then in the bread crumbs. Saute a couple of minutes on each side until lightly browned.
4. Place the chicken in a baking dish, and top with the tomato sauce. Bake at 350 degrees for 25 minutes.

4 servings of 1 breast each, plus sauce.

Per Serving: 336 calories, 143 mg. cholesterol, 4 g. dietary fiber, 11 g. fat, 552 mg. sodium.

Indian Tandoori Chicken

PREPARATION TIME: 40 MINUTES.　　　COOKING TIME: 40 MINUTES.

This simple version of Tandoori Chicken should be prepared a day in advance, as it must marinate for twenty-four hours before cooking. Serve with cooked grain and curried vegetables.

4 chicken breasts, skinned
　(about 6 ounces each)
1½ teaspoons chili powder
3 tablespoons lemon juice
1 cup plain low-fat yogurt
5 cloves garlic, roughly
　chopped
1 tablespoon raisins

1 slice gingerroot, 1½ inches
　thick, roughly chopped
½ teaspoon ground cumin
1 teaspoon ground coriander
½ teaspoon crushed red
　pepper
¼ teaspoon salt

1. Place the chicken in a large shallow pan. Slash each chicken breast a few times. Mix together the chili powder and lemon juice, and brush over the chicken breasts with a pastry brush. Let stand 30 minutes.
2. Combine all other ingredients in a blender or food processor, and purée until smooth. Pour over the chicken, cover, and refrigerate for 24 hours.
3. Bake the chicken at 450 degrees for about 40 minutes.

4 servings of about 3½ ounces each (cooked weight).

Per Serving: 202 calories, 77 mg. cholesterol, no dietary fiber, 4 g. fat, 248 mg. sodium.

Baked Horseradish Chicken

PREPARATION TIME: 7 MINUTES.   COOKING TIME: 50 T60 MINUTES.

½ cup white wine
4 chicken breasts, skin removed,
    about 6 ounces each
1 tablespoon vegetable oil
2 tablespoons plain horseradish
1¼ teaspoons mustard seed

½ teaspoon onion powder
½ teaspoon garlic powder
¼ teaspoon dried thyme
2 tablespoons fresh parsley,
    chopped fine

1. Pour the wine into a casserole dish, then add the chicken breasts.
2. Using a pastry brush, baste each piece of chicken with the oil. Spread ½ tablespoon of horseradish on each breast.
3. Bake covered at 350 degrees for about 30 minutes. While chicken is baking, grind the mustard seed and combine it with the remaining ingredients.
4. After 30 minutes, baste the chicken with the wine sauce in the pan. Then pour the mustard seed mixture over the chicken, and bake uncovered another 20 to 30 minutes, until chicken is tender.

4 servings of about 3½ ounces each (cooked weight).

Per Serving: 178 calories, 73 mg. cholesterol, no dietary fiber, 6 g. fat, 72 mg. sodium.

Almond Chicken

PREPARATION TIME: 10 MINUTES.   COOKING TIME: 20 TO 25 MINUTES.

⅓ cup tamari sauce
    OR soy sauce
1 teaspoon ground ginger
1 teaspoon garlic powder
3 pounds chicken, skinned and
    boned

½ cup whole-wheat flour
½ cup finely ground almonds
½ teaspoon salt
½ teaspoon black pepper
2 tablespoons peanut oil

1. In a large bowl, combine the tamari sauce, ginger, and garlic powder. Cut the chicken into bite-size chunks, and

marinate it in the tamari-sauce mixture while preparing the other ingredients.

2. In another bowl, combine the flour, almonds, salt, and pepper.
3. Heat the oil in a wok or large saucepan on high heat. When the oil is hot, coat the chicken pieces with the flour mixture, and add to the wok. Reduce the heat to medium.
4. Cover and cook, stirring often, until the chicken is done, about 20 minutes.

8 Servings of 4½ ounces each (cooked weight).

Per Serving: 325 calories, 108 mg. cholesterol, 2 g. dietary fiber, 12 g. fat, 909 mg. sodium.

Grilled Duck Breast (Julian's)

PREPARATION TIME: 10 MINUTES.   COOKING TIME : 30 TO 40 MINUTES.

1 ounce wild rice
Herbs to taste
1 duck breast
½ fresh tomato
2 ounces fresh spinach

½ ounce clarified unsalted
  butter
Pinch nutmeg
1 bunch watercress

1. Cook the wild rice in water along with your favorite herb or herbs.
2. Grill the duck breast, skin side down, until medium-well-done. At the same time, grill the half tomato. When cooked, peel the skin off the tomato if desired.
3. Just before the duck breast is ready to serve, thoroughly wash the spinach. Heat the butter in a sauté pan, add the spinach and nutmeg, and toss until tender.
4. Remove the skin from the duck breast, and slice the breast. Arrange the slices on a platter with the tomato and the rice. Garnish with watercress.

1 serving of 3½ ounces of meat (cooked weight).

Per Serving: 400 calories, 107 mg. cholesterol, 6 g. dietary fiber, 22 g. fat, 118 mg. sodium.

Chicken À L'Orange

PREPARATION TIME: 15 MINUTES.   COOKING TIME: 45 TO 50 MINUTES.

2 ½ pounds chicken pieces,
  skinned
1 cup orange juice
½ cup white wine
Paprika to taste
Traditional Italian Herb Blend
  (p. 335) to taste

1 teaspoon peanut oil
1 medium onion, diced
1 large tomato, diced
4 ounces fresh mushrooms,
  diced

1. Preheat oven to 375 degrees. Place chicken pieces in a shallow baking pan. Combine the orange juice and white wine and pour them over the chicken.
2. Sprinkle seasonings over chicken.
3. Bake at 375 degrees for 35 minutes.
4. While chicken is baking, prepare the sauce by brushing a skillet with the peanut oil and heating over medium-high heat. Add the onions, tomato, and mushrooms, and sauté, stirring constantly.
5. When onions are translucent, spoon the sauce over the chicken and bake an additional 10 to 15 minutes.

6 servings at 3½ ounces each (cooked weight), plus sauce.

Per Serving: 190 calories, 78 mg. cholesterol, 1 g. dietary fiber, 6 g. fat, 163 mg. sodium.

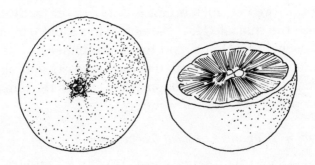

Rock Cornish Game Hens with Orange–Wild Rice Stuffing

PREPARATION TIME: 20 MINUTES.   COOKING TIME: 1 TO 1¼ HOURS.

Although some persons might think this will end up a very fatty dish, it doesn't; even if you leave the skins on, only 30 percent of the total calories will come from fat. You can reduce that by removing the skin before eating. Use lesser amounts of seasonings if you prefer a milder flavor.

4 game hens, about 22 ounces each	10 mushrooms, diced
1 tablespoon vegetable oil	½ medium green pepper, diced
2 to 3 teaspoons garlic powder	2 small oranges
1 to 2 teaspoons marjoram	1 teaspoon dried parsley
1 box (7 ounces) wild rice	¼ teaspoon salt
	Paprika

1. Brush the hens with the oil, then rub all sides with the garlic powder and marjoram.
2. Cook the rice according to package directions. Meanwhile, prepare the vegetables. To make an especially delicate orange flavor, peel the oranges, and remove all seeds, membranes, and skin. Chop the inner fruit into small pieces. When the rice is cooked, add the parsley, salt, mushrooms, green pepper, and oranges, and mix thoroughly.
3. Fill the cavity in the hens with the wild rice mixture, and seal the opening with a small metal or wooden skewer. Place the hens on a rack in a shallow pan.
4. Bake at 350 degrees for 50 minutes, basting occasionally. Sprinkle paprika on the hens, and bake an additional 10 to 15 minutes until nicely browned. Turn the hens over, sprinkle with paprika, and brown the other side.

4 servings.

Per Serving: 390 calories, 118 mg. cholesterol, 4 g. dietary fiber, 11 g. fat, 244 mg. sodium.

Turkey Meatballs with Tomato Sauce

PREPARATION TIME: 12 TO 15 MINUTES.   COOKING TIME: 15 TO
                                                        20 MINUTES.

Many meatball recipes start out with raw ground meat, to
which you then add your other ingredients. In this recipe,
however, you brown and drain the meat first, thereby reducing the cooking time of the meatballs. If you want to use homemade tomato sauce, try Fresh Tomato Sauce with White Wine
(pp. 298–99) or Real Italian Tomato Sauce (pp. 290–91).

1 pound lean ground turkey,
  cooked
½ cup bread crumbs
1 tablespoon olive oil
1 medium onion, minced
2 garlic cloves, minced
1 large egg, lightly beaten
½ cup chicken stock

1 teaspoon dried basil
¼ teaspoon salt
Fresh-ground black pepper to
  taste
1 can (15 ounces) tomato sauce
  OR 2 cups homemade tomato
  sauce
¼ cup chopped fresh parsley

1. Combine the turkey and bread crumbs in a mixing bowl.
2. In a frying pan, sauté the onion and garlic in the olive oil
   until translucent.
3. Keeping the fat, carefully remove the onions and garlic
   from the pan, and blend them, together with the egg,
   stock, basil, salt, and pepper in the mixing bowl with the
   turkey and bread crumbs.
4. Shape the mixture into approximately 24 little meatballs.
5. Place the meatballs in the frying pan and brown evenly
   over medium heat (about 5 minutes). Drain whatever fat
   remains visible at this time. Add the tomato sauce to the
   pan and bring to a simmer. Sprinkle with fresh parsley and
   serve.

6 servings of 4 meatballs each, plus sauce.

Per Serving: 267 calories, 110 mg. cholesterol, 2 g. dietary fiber,
14 g. fat, 803 mg. sodium.

Turkey-Apple Stir-Fry

PREPARATION TIME: 15 MINUTES.   COOKING TIME: 15 MINUTES.

This may sound like an odd combination at first, but the apple in this recipe won't taste too sweet, and it will blend well with the onion and celery. A great way to use up leftover cooked turkey.

As always when stir-frying, be sure to have all your vegetables and the turkey chopped and ready to toss in the pan.

1 tablespoon peanut
  OR vegetable oil
1 medium apple, chopped
1 small onion, chopped
1 clove garlic, minced or
  crushed
½ cup green pepper, diced
2 stalks celery, chopped
1 tablespoon butter
  OR margarine

1 tablespoon whole-wheat flour
1 cup chicken stock
¼ teaspoon curry powder (try
  Indian Spice Blend, p. 334)
½ teaspoon lime juice
¼ teaspoon minced fresh
  gingerroot
2 cups cooked turkey, diced
½ teaspoon salt

1. Heat the oil in a wok or medium-sized skillet over medium heat. Add the apple, onion, and garlic, and cook, stirring often, until tender.
2. Add the green pepper and celery and stir-fry 2 minutes more. Remove from the heat and set aside.
3. In another large skillet, melt the butter or margarine, and stir in the flour. Cook, stirring, for a minute or two, until the flour is golden brown.
4. Slowly stir in the chicken stock, curry powder, lime juice, and ginger. Then add the apple mixture and the turkey, and simmer until heated through. Stir in the salt, and serve.

4 servings. Serving size is about 1 ½ cups.

Per Serving: 206 calories, 57 mg. cholesterol, 2 g. dietary fiber, 9 g. fat, 554 mg. sodium.

Australian Shepherd's Pie

PREPARATION TIME: 45 MINUTES.   COOKING TIME: 1 HOUR AND
                                                     5 MINUTES.

The original Australian recipe calls for beef, but we have substituted ground turkey with the same delicious results. This is
another "meal-in-one" recipe.

Nonstick vegetable cooking
  spray
2 pounds ground turkey
  OR extra-lean ground beef
1 tablespoon olive oil
  OR other vegetable oil
1 medium onion, chopped
2 leeks OR 4 scallions, chopped
  fine
1 large carrot, chopped
2 stalks celery, chopped fine
6 medium potatoes, cut in
  chunks

Water for boiling
1 teaspoon thyme
½ teaspoon salt
Fresh-ground black pepper to
  taste
1 tablespoon Worcestershire
  sauce
¾ cup tomato purée
¾ cup chicken stock
½ cup skim milk OR plain
  low-fat yogurt
Dash salt, pepper (optional)
¾ cup frozen green peas

1. Spray a skillet with cooking spray and brown the meat
   over medium heat. Pour off any fat.
2. In another large skillet, heat the oil. Add the chopped
   vegetables. Turn the heat to low, and simmer, covered, for
   20 minutes, stirring occasionally.
3. Meanwhile, boil the potatoes in water until tender.
4. Add the meat, thyme, salt, pepper, Worcestershire sauce,
   tomato puree, and stock to the cooked vegetables, and stir
   well. Pour into a casserole dish.
5. Cover and bake at 350 degrees for 20 minutes.
6. Meanwhile, mash the cooked potatoes with the milk or
   yogurt to make stiff mashed potatoes. Add a little more salt
   and pepper if you wish.
7. Stir the peas into the meat mixture. Spread the mashed
   potatoes on top. Make a crisscross pattern with a fork for
   decoration.

8. Bake at 375 degrees for 45 minutes or until brown and bubbly on top.

4 servings of 6 ounces meat (cooked weight), plus vegetables.

Per Serving: 590 calories, 110 mg. cholesterol, 11 g. dietary fiber, 21 g. fat, 653 mg. sodium.

South American Turkey Stew

PREPARATION TIME: 15 MINUTES.   COOKING TIME: 1 HOUR AND 20 MINUTES.

¼ cup red wine vinegar
2 cloves garlic, crushed or minced
½ teaspoon salt
½ teaspoon black pepper
2 turkey drumsticks
1 tablespoon olive oil
  OR corn oil
1 can (10¾ ounces) tomato purée
1 green bell pepper, sliced
Water
2 tablespoons capers
3 medium potatoes, sliced
¼ cup black olives, sliced
½ cup frozen green peas

1. Combine the vinegar, garlic, salt, and pepper. Marinate the turkey in the mixture for 1 hour.
2. Heat the oil in a heavy pot, and brown the turkey. Add the tomato purée, bell pepper, and water to cover. Simmer, covered, over medium-low heat for 1 hour.
3. Add the capers, potatoes, and olives, and simmer for 20 more minutes. Add the peas, and simmer another 15 minutes.
4. Remove the turkey and cut the meat off the bones. Chop into chunks, and return the meat to the stew. Heat thoroughly and serve.

4 servings 3½ ounces meat each (cooked weight), plus vegetables.

Per Serving: 363 calories, 74 mg. cholesterol, 7 g. dietary fiber, 10 g. fat, 388 mg. sodium.

Golden Turkey Breast

PREPARATION TIME: 5 MINUTES.   COOKING TIME: 2 HOURS.

We usually omit sugar whenever it is called for in sauces or meats that simply don't require it. However, this recipe is so good with the sugar that we are leaving in the option of using a little.

1 turkey breast, about 3 pounds   1 tablespoon sugar (optional)
1 cup chicken stock   1 medium onion, sliced
½ cup white wine   ⅓ cup golden raisins
1 tablespoon lime juice

1. Place the turkey breast in a shallow baking pan. Pour the chicken stock, wine, and lime juice over it. Sprinkle the sugar, if you're using it, over the turkey and into the liquid. Arrange the onion slices around the turkey.
2. Bake at 375 degrees for 2 hours, or until the turkey is tender, basting every ½ hour. Add the raisins for the last 10 minutes of cooking. Remove the skin before serving.

8 servings of 4½ ounces each (cooked weight), plus sauce.

Per Serving (with sugar): 229 calories, 89 mg. cholesterol, 1 g. dietary fiber, 4 g. fat, 180 mg. sodium.

Turkey Loaf

PREPARATION TIME: 10 MINUTES.   COOKING TIME: 1 HOUR.

Ground turkey is becoming increasingly accepted as a substitute for ground beef in loaves and meatballs. Here we have used it alone, but you can blend it with other meats, such as veal. In this recipe we get a bit more elaborate than absolutely necessary by sautéeing our mushrooms, onions, and garlic before blending with the other ingredients, but you can whip up a quick version, with different herbs, such as we illustrate in Quick Turkey Loaf (p. 191). If you are really in a hurry, do this one with canned mushrooms, and use onion and garlic powder instead of the fresh onion and garlic cloves.

1 tablespoon butter
  OR margarine
½ pound mushrooms, sliced
1 medium onion, chopped
2 garlic cloves, chopped
1½ pounds lean ground turkey
1 tablespoon soy sauce

Fresh-ground black pepper to
  taste
¾ cup dry bread crumbs
¼ cup chicken OR turkey stock
4 tablespoons chopped fresh
  parsley OR 2 teaspoons dried
1 large egg, lightly beaten

1. Preheat the oven to 350 degrees.
2. Melt the butter in a frying pan and sauté the mushrooms, onion, and garlic until the onions are translucent.
3. Transfer the mixture to a bowl and combine with the turkey, soy sauce, pepper, bread crumbs, stock, parsley, and eggs. Blend thoroughly.
4. Bake uncovered in a 9 × 5 × 3-inch loaf pan for 1 hour. Let stand for 10 minutes before serving.

6 servings, 1½-inch slices each.

Per Serving: 288 calories, 124 mg. cholesterol, 1 g. dietary fiber, 15 g. fat, 458 mg. sodium.

Quick Turkey Loaf

PREPARATION TIME: 5 MINUTES.   COOKING TIME: 1 HOUR.

1½ pounds lean ground turkey
¾ cup dry bread crumbs
1 tablespoon soy sauce
¼ cup chicken
  OR turkey stock
1 teaspoon Worcestershire sauce

Fresh-ground black pepper to
  taste
½ teaspoon each thyme,
  marjoram, and basil
1 teaspoon dried parsley
1 large egg, lightly beaten

1. Preheat the oven to 350 degrees.
2. Blend all the ingredients thoroughly in a mixing bowl and bake uncovered in a 9 × 5 × 3-inch loaf pan for 1 hour. Let stand for 10 minutes before serving.

6 servings, 1½-inch thick slices.

Per Serving: 259 calories, 118 mg. cholesterol, 1 g. dietary fiber, 13 g. fat, 436 mg. sodium.

Sage Sausage or Meatballs

PREPARATION TIME: 12 MINUTES.

COOKING TIME:
SAUSAGE—8 TO 10 MINUTES.
MEATBALLS—55 MINUTES.

The sage and fennel seeds conjure up the taste of Italian sausage. In the form of meatballs, this dish goes well with spaghetti.

1 pound ground turkey
½ cup rolled oats
1 egg
1 medium onion, chopped fine
1 or 2 cloves garlic, minced or
  crushed
2 tablespoons fresh parsley,
  chopped

½ teaspoon sage
1 teaspoon ground thyme
½ teaspoon fresh-ground black
  pepper
1 teaspoon fennel seeds,
  crushed
¼ teaspoon salt (optional)

1. In a large bowl, combine all ingredients, blending well.
2. For sausage patties, shape into a dozen rounds, flattening them with your palms. Place the patties on a nonstick baking sheet, or cover a baking sheet with foil and spray with nonstick cooking spray. Broil at about 3 inches from heat source for 5 minutes or until lightly browned. Then turn and broil 3 minutes more.
3. For meatballs, shape into a dozen balls and brown lightly in a pan heated over medium-high heat, with no added fat. Then add to your favorite tomato sauce, and let cook in the sauce for about 45 minutes.

6 servings (2 sausage rounds or 2 meatballs, each).

Per Serving: 174 calories, 94 mg. cholesterol, 2 g. dietary fiber, 9 g. fat, 80 mg. sodium.

Fish

Fish is not only an excellent, low-calorie source of protein, but there are certain fatty acids in fish, called Omega III fatty acids, that can reduce the risk of heart disease. One of these, eicosapentanoic acid (EPA), has been shown to lower serum cholesterol and triglycerides, and to increase high-density lipo-proteins (HDL). Higher HDL levels, like lower total choles-terol, are associated with a reduction in the risk of cardiovascu-lar disease. EPA also brings about some changes in the red blood cells and the platelets in the blood stream that are re-sponsible for clotting, so that the risk of blood clots and stroke is reduced.

The best sources of Omega III fatty acids are fatty fish such as salmon, mackerel, pollock (blue fish), albacore tuna, and herring. Halibut, red snapper, swordfish, and shellfish have medium amounts, and cod, monkfish, and orange roughy (a newcomer to American fish markets) a little less.

I eat fish at least twice a week when I am in Nashville, and when I travel, I tend to search out restaurants that feature seafood. I probably eat fish three or four times a week on the road, and much prefer it to meat.

I didn't always enjoy fish and my consumption went up from almost zero to the present high level when my wife, Enid, and I learned how to prepare it! Up until about a dozen years ago, all of our efforts at cooking fish seemed to turn out badly. Then, on a trip to Miami, a relative introduced us to a former commo-dore of the New York Yacht Club, Jim Foster. As he drove us back to our relative's home after a sightseeing trip to the Everglades, the conversation turned to plans for dinner. I commented on our poor luck preparing fish. Jim snorted and said, "Well, I think I can take care of that!" Without further comment, he made a heart-stopping U-turn in order to head for his favorite fish market. He bought three different varieties of fish, which he prepared by tossing together into a large covered baking dish and poaching to perfection in a broth containing sliced fresh tomatoes, onions, and a fifty-fifty mixture of water and dry white wine. Along with one of the best dinners we had ever eaten, we had a lesson in how to prepare fish. Here are the rules we learned.

The first rule is: DO NOT OVERCOOK FISH. Follow cooking times closely.

Second, to keep your interest and appetite at a high level, learn to use many different ways of preparing fish: broil, steam, bake, and grill, as well as poach.

Third, learn to use herbs and spices appropriately, together with various sauces. Fish is mild flavored and at its best when fresh. As with veal, this mildness permits a creative, delicate approach to seasoning. Fresh fish is firm to the touch, does not have a strong, unpleasant odor, and, if you are buying the whole fish rather than fillets, has bulging eyes and reddish gills.

Of course, buy fresh fish whenever possible and cook it the same day. But if you happen to find a bargain, then purchase an extra, wrap it well in freezer paper so it won't suffer "freezer burn," and store it for special occasions. We have kept whole salmons frozen for six months or more, and they were still excellent when defrosted and either wrapped in foil and baked in a court bouillon or grilled over a charcoal fire. Remember: if you want to freeze fresh fish and have it hold up well, your freezer *must* be kept at 0 degrees Fahrenheit or lower, and the fish must be wrapped in airtight freezer paper. (This applies to fresh meat, too.) When we know at the time of purchase that meat or fish is to go in our freezer, we ask the meat or fish manager at our grocery to wrap it for us especially for freezing. The market has the equipment for double wrapping and heat sealing the meat or fish in plastic.

If we had to pick just a few recipes that we think can make you as enthusiastic about fish as we are, we advise starting with Royal Indian Salmon (p. 202). I published this recipe of Terri's before, but it is SO good, and such a fine example of how to broil fish steaks in general, that we could not think of omitting it from this cookbook. Then, give Steamed Trout (pp. 196–97) a try, using any other fish fillets if trout is not available or if you feel inadequate to do the difficult job of filleting a trout. This Oriental preparation method was demonstrated for us by Chef Wang Chia Hsin at the Peking Gardens in Nashville, and once you try it, we think you, too, will adopt this way of preparing fish as part of your stock in trade. Finally, there's Arthur's Court Bouillon, designed for poaching halibut steaks (pp. 198–99) as part of a five-course, 600-calorie gourmet dinner. It can become your standard for poaching.

Court Bouillon (Arthur's)

This is the Court Bouillon used at Arthur's, one of Nashville's finest restaurants, and recommended especially for the Poached Halibut (pp. 198–99) as well as other fish fillets and steaks.

1 quart water
¼ cup wine vinegar
  OR lemon juice
1 small onion, sliced
1 stalk celery, sliced
1 medium carrot, sliced

2 teaspoons salt
6 whole peppercorns, crushed
1 bay leaf
Pinch of thyme
3 to 4 fresh parsley sprigs

1. Combine all ingredients in a stock pot or saucepot and bring to a boil. Reduce the heat and simmer 30 minutes. Strain and cool. (It is not possible to compute the caloric value of the strained bouillon, but it is very low.)

Steamed Trout

PREPARATION TIME: 10 TO 15 MINUTES.   COOKING TIME: 10 MINUTES.

You can steam just about any fish, and fillets of various kinds are perfect for the style of preparation we present here.

In order to preserve the sauce that develops as you cook the fish, this recipe is served on the dish or platter that you will use for steaming, so prepare your dishes and pans in advance. You can invert one dish in the bottom of a pan, put enough water in it to just cover that dish, and place the fish platter on top. The pan or pot must be deep enough so that it can be covered. The first time I prepared fillets this way, I used a roasting pan with a rack inside, and fashioned a platter from heavy-duty aluminum foil by folding up the sides. I heated it on top of the stove over low heat, after bringing the water to a boil, and it worked perfectly.

¼ cup dried black mushrooms (or white, if you cannot find black in the international or Oriental food section of your market

1 pound rainbow trout, filleted as well as possible (it's quite impossible to bone a trout perfectly)

Dash of salt
2 scallions
2 inches fresh gingerroot
Fresh-ground black pepper to taste
1 teaspoon rice wine OR dry white wine
1 teaspoon vegetable oil

1. Soak the black mushrooms for about 30 minutes in warm water.
2. Score the trout with a sharp knive every inch or so on the back side. Sprinkle this side with salt and place the fish back-side down on the platter you will use for steaming and serving.
3. Use only the bottom 4 inches of the scallions and cut these pieces in half. Peel the ginger. Remove the mushrooms from the water and pat dry with a paper towel. Remove the stems from the mushrooms and discard. Then, slice the scallions and ginger lengthwise, julienne style, and do

the same in the longest direction with the mushrooms. The closer you get to matchstick thinness the better, but it will taste fine even if your matchsticks are pretty thick.

4. Spread the scallions, ginger, and mushrooms evenly over the fish. Sprinkle the pepper, wine, and oil evenly over the fish.
5. Place in the steamer and bring the water to a boil. Cover, reduce the heat, and steam for 10 minutes. Carefully remove the platter so as not to lose the sauce, and serve.

VARIATIONS: Add 1 carrot and/or 1 ounce boiled ham, sliced julienne style.

2 servings of about 6 ounces each (cooked weight).

Per Serving: 144 calories, 67 mg. cholesterol, no dietary fiber, 3 g. fat, 155 mg. sodium.

Baked Bass with Lemon-Wine Bouillon

PREPARATION TIME: 5 MINUTES. COOKING TIME: 30 MINUTES.

4 bass fillets, about 1½ pounds raw
½ teaspoon dried chives
¼ teaspoon dried chervil
  OR dried parsley
¼ teaspoon dried tarragon
1 tablespoon lemon juice (fresh is best!)

½ cup dry white wine
½ cup whole-wheat Bread Crumbs (pp. 307–8)
1 tablespoon butter
  OR margarine

1. Place the fillets in a shallow baking dish. Sprinkle with seasonings and lemon juice. Pour the wine over the fish.
2. Bake at 400 degrees for 15 minutes. Then sprinkle the bread crumbs on top, and dot with butter. Bake 15 minutes more, or until fish flakes easily with a fork.

4 servings of 4½ ounces each (cooked weight).

Per Serving: 327 calories, 102 mg. cholesterol, 1 g. dietary fiber, 9 g. fat, 201 mg. sodium.

"Fish, without complications." DRAWING BY W. B. PARK; ©
1986 THE NEW YORKER MAGAZINE, INC.

Poached Halibut in Court Bouillon (Arthur's)

PREPARATION TIME: 5 MINUTES.   COOKING TIME: 5 MINUTES.

Poaching the fish in the wonderful Court Bouillon is seasoning
enough and no additional sauce is necessary. Serve the fish
with Poached Vegetables with Shallots (p. 278).

1 teaspoon butter
1 or 2 chopped shallots
6 ounces halibut (or other fish
    fillets or steaks such as sole,

turbot, haddock, cod, pike,
    perch, or salmon)
Court Bouillon to cover (p. 195)

1. Lightly butter the bottom of a pan with low sloping sides, such as a pie pan. Sprinkle with chopped shallots. Place fish on top in a single layer, and cover with the court bouillon.
2. Cover and place in a preheated, 350-degree oven. This takes just a few minutes to cook—no more than 5. Remove from the heat and place on a serving plate.

1 serving of 4 1/2 ounces (cooked weight)

Per Serving: 207 calories, 104 mg. cholesterol, no dietary fiber, 9 g. fat, 229 mg. sodium.

Vegetable-Simmered Fish Steaks

PREPARATION TIME: 10 MINUTES.   COOKING TIME: 15 TO 20 MINUTES.

1 medium onion, chopped
1 clove garlic, chopped
1 tablespoon butter
  OR margarine
4 small tomatoes, cut into
  eighths
8 ounces fresh mushrooms,
  thickly sliced

8 fresh basil leaves, coarsely
  shredded OR 1/2 teaspoon
  dried basil
1/4 teaspoon salt
Fresh-ground black pepper to
  taste
1 1/2 pounds fish steaks, cut into
  4 servings

1. Sauté the onion and garlic in the butter, covered, over low heat, until golden. Add the tomatoes and simmer, covered, until the tomatoes soften. Add the mushrooms and seasonings, and simmer for about 3 minutes.
2. Add the fish, spoon some sauce over each portion, and simmer, covered, for 5 to 10 minutes, until fish flakes easily with a fork.

4 servings of 4 1/2 ounces each (cooked weight), plus vegetable sauce.

Per Serving: 331 calories, 98 mg. cholesterol, 4 g. dietary fiber, 12 g. fat, 320 mg. sodium.

Simple Salmon

PREPARATION TIME: 5 MINUTES.   COOKING TIME: 10 TO 12 MINUTES.

Most recipes for poached fish are simple to prepare and this one is no exception.

4 salmon steaks, 1-inch thick
(about 6 ounces each)
½ cup white wine
½ cup lemon juice
1 bay leaf

1 medium onion, sliced into
rounds
Fresh-ground black pepper to
taste
Water

1. Place steaks in a large shallow saucepan, preferably one you can use to cook in later. Add remaining ingredients except the water, and marinate, covered, in the refrigerator, for 1 hour or more.
2. Remove from refrigerator and add enough water to cover the steaks. Heat on medium-high heat until just under a boil, then turn to low and poach (simmer) for about 10 minutes, until fish flakes easily with a fork.

4 servings of about 4½ ounces each (cooked weight).

Per Serving: 268 calories, 90 mg. cholesterol, no dietary fiber, 8 g. fat, 144 mg. sodium.

Teriyaki Salmon

PREPARATION TIME: 4 MINUTES.   COOKING TIME: 14 TO 20 MINUTES.

This dish vies with Royal Indian Salmon for ease of preparation and elegant taste.

Nonstick vegetable cooking
spray
1½ pounds salmon fillets
OR 4 steaks, about 6 ounces
each

1 tablespoon tamari sauce
OR soy sauce
1 tablespoon honey
¼ teaspoon ground ginger
⅛ teaspoon mace (optional)

1. Spray a foil-lined broiler pan with nonstick cooking spray.
2. Arrange the salmon on the pan. In a small bowl, combine the remaining ingredients to make a teriyaki sauce.
3. Brush the salmon with the teriyaki sauce. Broil about 7 to 10 minutes a side, basting frequently with the sauce.

4 servings of 4½ ounces each (cooked weight).

Per Serving: 230 calories, 90 mg. cholesterol, no dietary fiber, 8 g. fat, 340 mg. sodium.

Poached Sweet-Pepper Salmon

PREPARATION TIME: 7 MINUTES.   COOKING TIME: 7 TO 8 MINUTES.

The sweet, or bell, pepper is a mild-mannered relative of the hot chili pepper. You can use green, yellow, red, or purple bell peppers interchangeably in almost any recipe, to add color and flavor. Here, they enhance the already marvelous taste of salmon, in another "serve-hot-or-cold" recipe.

⅓ cup dry white wine
1½ pounds salmon fillets
  OR steaks
1 bell pepper, diced fine

½ teaspoon salt
2 teaspoons dried parsley
2 teaspoons lime juice

1. Pour the wine into a large skillet, and add the fish fillets.
2. Sprinkle the fillets evenly with the remaining ingredients.
3. Cover and bring almost to a boil, then reduce heat to low. Let cook for about 7 to 8 minutes, until fish flakes easily with a fork.

4 servings of 4½ ounces each (cooked weight).

Per Serving: 259 calories, 90 mg. cholesterol, no dietary fiber, 8 g. fat, 409 mg. sodium.

Royal Indian Salmon

PREPARATION TIME: 5 MINUTES.   COOKING TIME: 16 TO 20 MINUTES.

We couldn't resist including this recipe, which first appeared in the original *Rotation Diet* book. It is one of our all-time favorites, delicately flavored and very easy to prepare.

4 salmon steaks, 1-inch thick
(about 6 ounces each)
¼ cup chicken
OR vegetable stock
2 tablespoons lemon juice
½ teaspoon fennel seeds,
crushed

¼ teaspoon cumin
¼ teaspoon ground coriander
Dash of salt and fresh-ground
black pepper

1. Place the steaks in a shallow baking pan. Pour the stock and the lemon juice over the steaks. Add the seasonings. Marinate, covered, in the refrigerator for at least two hours, turning the steaks occasionally.
2. To cook, place the steaks on a foil-covered broiling pan. Spoon 2 teaspoons of the marinade on top of each steak. Place under the broiler on low broil for 8 to 10 minutes, or until slightly brown on the edges. Turn steaks over, spoon on the remaining marinade, and broil for an additional 8 to 10 minutes.

4 servings of about 4½ ounces each (cooked weight).

Per Serving: 215 calories, 90 mg. cholesterol, no dietary fiber, 8 g. fat, 198 mg. sodium.

Broiled Cod with Shallots

PREPARATION TIME: 10 MINUTES.   COOKING TIME: 10 MINUTES.

2 pounds cod fillets
Nonstick vegetable spray
2 teaspoons butter
OR vegetable oil

3 shallots, chopped
1 clove garlic, minced
1 tablespoon lemon juice
1 teaspoon dried dillweed

| 3 tablespoons fresh parsley, minced | Salt and fresh-ground black pepper to taste |

1. Place fillets on foil-covered broiler pan that has been sprayed lightly with vegetable spray.
2. Heat saucepan over medium heat, add butter or oil, and shallots. Cover and let cook, stirring occasionally, for about a minute, then add garlic, lemon juice, dillweed, and parsley. Let cook until onions are translucent.
3. Spread shallot mixture over fish. Add salt and pepper to taste.
4. Broil for about 5 minutes, turn, baste, and broil for an additional 5 minutes, or until fish flakes easily with a fork.

6 servings of 4 ounces each (cooked weight).

Per Serving: 185 calories, 80 mg. cholesterol, no dietary fiber, 6 g. fat, 243 mg. sodium.

Easy Mushroom and Shrimp Dinner

PREPARATION TIME: 5 MINUTES.   COOKING TIME: 15 MINUTES.

Try this dish over cooked grain (½ cup of grain per serving). It's especially good with brown rice or bulgur wheat.

2 teaspoons peanut oil	2 tablespoons white wine
8 ounces mushrooms, sliced	½ teaspoon Traditional Italian
2 scallions, diced	Herb Blend (p. 335)
¼ green or red pepper, diced	
2 packages (6 ounces each) mini-shrimp	

1. Heat the oil in a skillet on medium heat. Add the mushrooms, scallions, and green pepper. Sauté 5 to 7 minutes, stirring constantly.
2. Add the shrimp, wine, and Herb Blend. Reduce heat to low, cover, and simmer for 5 minutes.

4 servings. Serving size is about ¾ cup.

Per Serving: 133 calories, 126 mg. cholesterol, 2 g. dietary fiber, 4 g. fat, 156 mg. sodium.

Curried Shrimp

PREPARATION TIME: 7 MINUTES.   COOKING TIME: 12 TO 15 MINUTES.

Serve this over cooked grain, whole-grain English muffins, or toast.

1 teaspoon vegetable oil
½ medium red onion, diced
1 small apple, diced
1 tablespoon butter
  OR margarine
1 tablespoon whole-wheat flour
1 cup chicken stock
3 tablespoons skim OR low-fat
  milk stock

½ teaspoon salt
Fresh-ground black pepper to
  taste
½ teaspoon Indian Spice Blend
  (p. 334) OR other curry
  powder
¼ teaspoon ground ginger
2 packages (6 ounces each)
  mini-shrimp

1. Brush a skillet with the 1 teaspoon of oil, and heat over medium-low heat. Add the diced onions and apples, and sauté, covered, until onions are translucent. Add a little water if necessary to prevent sticking.
2. In another small pan, melt the butter or margarine over medium heat. Stir in the flour. Cook, stirring constantly, until nicely browned. Stir in the chicken stock, and cook a couple more minutes.
3. Add the chicken-stock mixture to the onion-apple mixture, along with the remaining ingredients. Blend well. Cover and let simmer until thickened and heated through.

4 servings. Serving size is about 1 cup.

Per Serving: 150 calories, 122 mg. cholesterol, 1 g. dietary fiber, 6 g. fat, 636 mg. sodium.

Crab Quiche with Crumb Topping

PREPARATION TIME: 8 TO 10 MINUTES.   COOKING TIME: 45 MINUTES.

You can halve this recipe and make only one quiche, but we usually make two and freeze one for another time.

2 packages frozen crabmeat, thawed, drained
2 cups skim milk
2 cups grated cheddar cheese
6 eggs, beaten
2 teaspoons dried parsley
1/2 teaspoon salt
1/4 teaspoon pepper
1/4 teaspoon marjoram
1/4 teaspoon garlic powder
1/4 teaspoon nutmeg
2 cups Pepperidge Farm seasoned bread crumbs
1/2 tablespoon butter
OR margarine

1. Layer the crab on the bottom of two empty pie pans.
2. Combine all other ingredients except the bread crumbs and butter, and pour half of the mixture into each pie pan.
3. Bake at 350 degrees for 30 minutes. Then top each quiche with 1 cup of bread crumbs and dot with 1/4 tablespoon of butter. Bake 15 minutes more.
4. Remove from the oven and let stand for about 3 to 5 minutes.
5. Cut each quiche into quarters and serve.

8 servings. Serving size is 1/4 quiche.

Per Serving: 395 calories, 352 mg. cholesterol, 1 g. dietary fiber, 18 g. fat, 1507 mg. sodium.

Oriental Shark Steaks

PREPARATION TIME: 8 MINUTES.   COOKING TIME: 20 MINUTES.

3 scallions, minced
3 tablespoons tamari sauce
  OR soy sauce
3 tablespoons orange juice
1 tablespoon vegetable oil
1 tablespoon honey

½ teaspoon ground ginger
½ teaspoon fresh-ground black
  pepper
2 pounds shark steaks
1 medium orange, cut in thin
  rounds

1. Combine all the ingredients except the shark steaks and orange slices. Cut the steaks into 6 individual portions, and place in a shallow baking dish.
2. Baste the steaks with about half the sauce, and broil for 10 minutes. Turn the fish over and cover with the remaining sauce. Top with orange slices and broil for another 10 minutes, or until fish flakes easily with a fork.

6 servings of 4½ ounces each (cooked weight).

Per Serving: 252 calories, 68 mg. cholesterol, 1 g. dietary fiber, 9 g. fat, 668 mg. sodium.

Steamed Fish Fillets Oriental

PREPARATION TIME: 5 MINUTES.   COOKING TIME: 4 TO 5 MINUTES.

Remember one of the basic tricks to Oriental cooking: have everything chopped and ready to go, because the food cooks quickly.

1 pound fish fillets
5 tablespoons scallions,
  chopped fine
1 small clove garlic, minced

1 slice gingerroot, ¼-inch thick,
  minced
2 tablespoons tamari sauce
  OR soy sauce

1. Place the fish on a steamer rack over boiling water, and sprinkle with the onions.
2. Combine the garlic, ginger, and tamari sauce in a small

bowl, and spread all of the mixture over the fish.

3. Steam, covered, for about 4 to 5 minutes, or until fish flakes easily with a fork.

4 servings of 3 ounces each (cooked weight).

Per Serving: 90 calories, 45 mg. cholesterol, no dietary fiber, 1 g. fat, 618 mg. sodium.

Fillet of Roughy Espagnole

PREPARATION TIME: 10 MINUTES.   COOKING TIME: 15 TO 20 MINUTES.

For a complete meal, serve this over cooked grain with a salad on the side.

2 medium onions, chopped	1 teaspoon dried basil
1 tablespoon butter	¼ teaspoon crushed red
OR margarine	pepper
1 large clove garlic, chopped	¼ teaspoon dried thyme
3 stalks celery, sliced	1 tablespoon dried parsley
1 green pepper, chopped	1 can (15 ounces) tomato sauce
1 teaspoon dried cilantro	1½ pounds orange roughy
OR tarragon	OR other thick fish fillets

1. Sauté the onions in the butter or margarine until translucent. Add the next 8 ingredients and sauté a few moments more.
2. Add the tomato sauce and simmer until the vegetables are tender. Add the fish, and simmer just until fish flakes easily with a fork, about 5 to 10 minutes.

4 servings of 4½ ounces each (cooked weight), plus sauce.

Per Serving: 294 calories, 101 mg. cholesterol, 3 g. dietary fiber, 12 g. fat, 854 mg. sodium.

Seafood Stove-Top Casserole

PREPARATION TIME: 12 MINUTES.   COOKING TIME: 15 TO 20 MINUTES.

You can serve this over brown rice, or pour it into a baking dish, bake for 10 minutes or so in a 350-degree oven, and serve as is.

2 cups stock
1 cup dry white wine OR 1 cup
  low-fat milk
1 bay leaf
1 cup sliced fresh mushrooms
2 red peppers, sliced into strips
1 tablespoon dried parsley
  OR ⅓ cup fresh, minced
Fresh-ground black pepper to
  taste

4 cups cooked lobster, crab,
  scallops OR monkfish, cut
  into chunks
2 eggs
2 teaspoons cayenne pepper
1 tablespoon dry mustard
4 pimiento strips (optional)

1. Bring the stock and wine to a boil in a large saucepan. (If you're using milk instead of wine, add the milk to the eggs later; just boil the stock now.)
2. Add the bay leaf, mushrooms, sliced peppers, parsley, and black pepper to the stock, reduce the heat, and let simmer for about 5 to 10 minutes, until the vegetables are just tender. Add the seafood, and simmer 5 minutes more.
3. In the meantime, blend the egg, milk if used instead of wine, cayenne pepper, and mustard together. Add to the seafood, and let simmer for a couple more minutes. Garnish with pimiento strips, if desired.

8 servings. Serving size is about 1 ¼ cups.

Per Serving (with milk): 149 calories, 157 mg. cholesterol, 1 g. dietary fiber, 4 g. fat, 253 mg. sodium.

Per Serving (with wine): 128 calories, 154 mg. cholesterol, 1 g. dietary fiber, 3 g. fat, 238 mg. sodium.

Mexican Red Snapper

PREPARATION TIME: 10 MINUTES.   COOKING TIME: 25 MINUTES.

The fresh coriander in this recipe is available in most Oriental or international markets, and really makes this dish special. If you absolutely can't find it, you may substitute an equal amount of fresh parsley, or 1 or 2 tablespoons of dried cilantro.

2 medium onions, sliced
2 pounds red snapper fillets
¼ teaspoon salt
¼ teaspoon pepper
⅓ cup lime
   OR lemon juice

3 jalapeños, chopped
1 bunch fresh coriander, leaves
   only (about 1 cup)

1. In an oblong casserole or baking dish, layer half the sliced onions, followed by the fish, then the rest of the onions. Sprinkle with salt and pepper. Pour the lime juice over the fish, and let sit for 1 to 2 hours.
2. Top the fish dish with the jalapeños and the coriander.
3. Cover and bake at 350 degrees for 25 minutes, or until tender.

4 servings of 6 ounces each (cooked weight), plus vegetables.

Per Serving: 210 calories, 103 mg. cholesterol, 1 g. dietary fiber, 2 g. fat, 230 mg. sodium.

Fish Fillets *Veronique*

PREPARATION TIME: 15 TO 20 MINUTES.   COOKING TIME: 7 MINUTES.

1 cup seedless grapes
2 tablespoons white wine
1 tablespoon lemon juice
2 pounds fish fillets (flounder, sole, or snapper)
1 teaspoon grated lemon peel
1 tablespoon lime juice
1 tablespoon fresh gingerroot, julienned in small strips
1/2 medium bell pepper, julienned
1/4 teaspoon salt
Fresh-ground black pepper to taste
Fresh parsley OR coriander for garnish
Lemon and/or lime wedges for garnish

1. Slice the grapes in half, and place them in a bowl with the wine and the lemon juice, tossing gently.
2. Line a broiling pan with foil, and arrange the fish in the pan. Sprinkle the lemon peel and lime juice over the fish. Top with the ginger, bell pepper, and seasoning, except for the garnish.
3. Broil the fish for about 5 minutes, until the fillets begin to turn golden. Pour the grape-wine mixture over the fish, arranging the grapes cut-side down. Broil a couple more minutes, until fish flakes easily with a fork. Serve with garnishes.

6 servings of 4 ounces each (cooked weight), plus grapes and vegetables.

Per Serving: 160 calories, 103 mg. cholesterol, 1 g. dietary fiber, 2 g. fat, 272 mg. sodium.

Fish Florentine

PREPARATION TIME: 8 MINUTES.   COOKING TIME: 15 TO 20 MINUTES.

This Italian style of cooking (with spinach) works as well with fish as it does with veal and chicken.

1 pound fish fillets (try flounder or sole)

1 package (8 ounces) frozen chopped spinach, thawed and drained

10 whole-wheat crackers, crushed

2 tablespoons wheat germ

3 tablespoons Parmesan OR sapsago cheese

1. Arrange the fillets in the bottom of a shallow baking dish.
2. Cover the fish with the well-drained spinach.
3. Combine the cracker crumbs, wheat germ, and cheese, and pour over the fish and spinach.
4. Bake, uncovered, at 400 degrees for 15 to 20 minutes.

4 servings of 3 ounces each (cooked weight), plus spinach.

Per Serving: 165 calories, 62 mg. cholesterol, 2 g. dietary fiber, 4 g. fat, 296 mg. sodium.

Shrimp Skimpy

PREPARATION TIME: 5 MINUTES.   COOKING TIME: 4 MINUTES.

2 tablespoons tamari sauce OR soy sauce

2 tablespoons lemon juice

2 tablespoons oil

2 cloves garlic, finely chopped

Bay seasoning OR seasonings of your choice, to taste

1½ pounds shelled, uncooked shrimp

1. Combine all the ingredients, except the shrimp, in a bowl and mix well. Add the shrimp and marinate for an hour or so, stirring occasionally.
2. Broil in a shallow pan for about 4 minutes, turning pieces midway during cooking.

4 servings of 4½ ounces each (cooked weight).

Per Serving: 225 calories, 226 mg. cholesterol, no dietary fiber, 9 g. fat, 789 mg. sodium.

Mock Crabmeat and Pasta

PREPARATION TIME: 20 MINUTES.   COOKING TIME: 10 MINUTES.

Mock or imitation crabmeat is often made from bluefish, and presents a cheaper alternative to the real crab. Of course you may substitute frozen or canned crabmeat.

1 medium onion, diced
4 cloves garlic, minced
1 medium green pepper, diced
2 stalks celery, sliced thin
1 tablespoon butter
   OR margarine
1 tablespoon water
6 ounces fresh mushrooms,
   sliced
½ teaspoon marjoram
½ teaspoon thyme

¼ teaspoon salt
¼ teaspoon black pepper
2 carrots, diced
6 ounces fresh mushrooms,
   quartered
2 cups low-fat milk
1 pound imitation crabmeat,
   diced
8 ounces vermicelli, cooked
   and drained

1. Sauté/steam the onion, garlic, green pepper, and celery in the combined butter and water, covered, over medium-low heat, until the celery and green pepper are tender. Stir occasionally.
2. Add the sliced mushrooms and the seasonings. Remove from the heat, and set aside.
3. In a small amount of water, cook the carrots and the quartered mushrooms until the carrots are tender. Drain, and purée in a blender or food processor. Combine with the milk, and add to the sautéed vegetables, along with the imitation crab.
4. Combine the cooked pasta and the crab mixture. Place in a casserole dish, and bake at 350 degrees for about 10 minutes, or until heated through.

8 servings. Serving size is about 1½ cups.

Per Serving: 157 calories, 38 mg. cholesterol, 3 g. dietary fiber, 4 g. fat, 208 mg. sodium.

Lime-Steamed Fish Fillets

PREPARATION TIME: 3 TO 5 MINUTES.   COOKING TIME: 5 MINUTES.

If you have a wok, you may have a metal or bamboo steamer rack that came with it. If not, use any other steamer or rack you have on hand, or use the "plate" method, as described in the recipe for Steamed Trout (pp. 196–97).

1½ pounds fish fillets (try flounder or sole)
Juice of 1 lime

¼ cup shallots, minced
Fresh-ground black pepper to taste

1. Arrange fillets in foil or on a plate, and place on a steamer rack over boiling water.
2. Squeeze the lime juice over the fish, and top with shallots and pepper.
3. Cover and steam for about 5 minutes, until fish flakes easily with a fork.

4 servings of 4½ ounces each (cooked weight).

Per Serving: 124 calories, 66 mg. cholesterol, no dietary fiber, 2 g. fat, 155 mg. sodium.

Blackened Fish

PREPARATION TIME: 5 MINUTES.   COOKING TIME: 5 MINUTES.

The recent rise in popularity of this spicy, Cajun-style dish in restaurants is a testimonial to what spices can do to disguise the flavor of less palatable (and often cheaper!) varieties of fish. At home, you can start out with any kind of firm-fleshed fish you want.

1 teaspoon salt
1 tablespoon garlic powder
2 teaspoons thyme
1 tablespoon dried parsley
   flakes
1 tablespoon basil
1 to 2 teaspoons cayenne
   pepper

¼ teaspoon black pepper
4 fillets of redfish, red snapper,
   OR other firm fish, about 1½
   pounds raw
1 tablespoon olive oil
   OR corn oil

1. Combine the spices on a flat plate. Press the fish fillets firmly into the spices, coating both sides.
2. Heat the oil to almost smoking in a heavy skillet. Cook the fish about 2½ minutes on each side, for fillets not more than ¾-inch thick. Serve immediately.

4 servings of 4½ ounces each (cooked weight).

Per Serving: 199 calories, 77 mg. cholesterol, 1 g. dietary fiber, 7 g. fat, 602 mg. sodium.

Oyster Stew

PREPARATION TIME: 15 MINUTES.   COOKING TIME: 10 MINUTES.

4 cups low-fat milk
1 large potato, unpeeled, diced
   fine
1 tablespoon butter
   OR margarine
2 leeks, washed, trimmed, and
   diced

1 pint fresh oysters, undrained
½ teaspoon salt
⅛ to ¼ teaspoon cayenne
   pepper

1. Heat the milk along with the potatoes in a double boiler

over medium heat. Do not boil.

2. In a large saucepan or kettle, melt the butter over medium heat. Add the leeks and sauté, covered, stirring often.
3. Add the oysters, and sauté, covered, until the edges of the oysters begin to curl.
4. Pour the hot milk and potatoes into the saucepan with the oysters. Add the salt and cayenne.

8 servings. Serving size is about 1 cup.

Per Serving: 144 calories, 45 mg. cholesterol, 1 g. dietary fiber, 5 g. fat, 254 mg. sodium.

Halibut Steaks

PREPARATION TIME: 15 MINUTES.   COOKING TIME: 15 TO 20 MINUTES.

This dish is good hot or cold.

1 tablespoon olive oil
1 small onion, diced
½ medium bell pepper (green, red, purple, or yellow), diced
8 fresh mushrooms, chopped fine
2 pounds halibut steaks, 1-inch thick

½ teaspoon salt
½ teaspoon fresh-ground black pepper
½ teaspoon dried marjoram
1 medium tomato, sliced as thinly as possible

1. Preheat oven to 400 degrees.
2. Heat oil in skillet on medium heat, and sauté onions, bell pepper, and mushrooms, covered, stirring occasionally, until onions are translucent.
3. Place steaks in baking dish, and season with salt, pepper, and marjoram. Spread sautéed vegetables over the top.
4. Bake at 400 degrees for 10 minutes, then cover with a layer of tomato slices. Bake an additional 5 minutes, or until fish flakes easily with a fork.

6 servings of 4½ ounces each (cooked weight).

Per Serving: 244 calories, 93 mg. cholesterol, 2 g. dietary fiber, 11 g. fat, 337 mg. sodium.

Poached Grouper with Clams

PREPARATION TIME: 15 MINUTES.   COOKING TIME: 20 MINUTES.

The bouillon in this recipe is so good that the first time we made it, we couldn't resist eating our main course out of bowls, as a soup. Try it that way—it's delicious!

1 medium onion, thinly sliced
1 clove garlic, minced
1 tablespoon butter
  OR margarine
1½ pounds grouper fillets
1 large tomato, thinly sliced
3 thin slices lemon

2 cans (6½ ounces each)
  minced clams, with juice
4 ounces dry white wine
1 teaspoon dried basil
Dash of salt and fresh-ground
  black pepper

1. Lightly sauté the onions and garlic in the butter in a large frying pan, until onions are translucent. Place fish fillets on top; then layer tomatoes, lemon slices, clams and clam juice, and wine on top of the fish. Sprinkle with basil, salt, and pepper.
2. Cover the pan, bring to a boil, then turn down the heat and simmer for about 20 minutes, or until fish flakes easily with a fork. Serve in bowls with the bouillon.

4 servings of 4½ ounces each (cooked weight).

Per Serving: 220 calories, 143 mg. cholesterol, 2 g. dietary fiber, 11 g. fat, 322 mg. sodium.

Monkfish Italian Style

PREPARATION TIME: 8 MINUTES.

COOKING TIME: 15 TO 20 MINUTES.

1 medium onion, sliced
½ pound mushrooms, sliced
1 medium green pepper, diced
1 tablespoon vegetable oil
½ cup dry white wine
2 cloves garlic, minced or
    crushed

1 can (10¾ ounces) tomato
    purée
2 teaspoons dried basil
2 pounds monkfish fillets

1. Sauté the onions, mushrooms, and green pepper in the oil over medium-low heat, covered, until the onions are translucent.
2. Add the remaining ingredients, cover, and let simmer for about 12 to 15 minutes, or until fish flakes easily with a fork.

VARIATION: For a quick version of this recipe, you can use our Real Italian Tomato Sauce, (pp. 290–91), if you have any pre-made. Pour two and a half cups of sauce into a saucepan on medium heat, add the fish, and cook until done.

6 servings of 4 ounces each (cooked weight), plus sauce.

Per Serving: 246 calories, 82 mg. cholesterol, 2 g. dietary fiber, 11 g. fat, 150 mg. sodium.

Really Orange Roughy

PREPARATION TIME: 25 MINUTES. COOKING TIME: 25 TO 30 MINUTES.

Nonstick vegetable cooking
  spray
1 pound orange roughy fillets
1 onion, chopped
1 green pepper, chopped
1 clove garlic, minced
1 tablespoon butter
  OR margarine

2 medium carrots, diced
1 cup plain low-fat yogurt
Grated rind and juice of ½
  orange
1 teaspoon Dijon mustard
¼ teaspoon tarragon
Salt and pepper to taste

1. Spray a casserole dish with nonstick cooking spray. Place the fish in the casserole.
2. Sauté the onion, green pepper, and garlic in the butter until onion is slightly golden in color. Spoon this mixture on top of the fillets.
3. Meanwhile, lightly steam the carrots in another pan.
4. In a blender or food processor, blend the yogurt, cooked carrots, orange rind and juice, mustard, tarragon, salt, and pepper. Pour over the fish.
4. Bake at 350 degrees for 25 to 30 minutes until bubbly around the edges and fish flakes easily with a fork.

4 servings of 3 ounces each (cooked weight), plus vegetables.

Per Serving: 177 calories, 85 mg. cholesterol, 2 g. dietary fiber, 5 g. fat, 337 mg. sodium.

Pasta

Pasta used to be considered fattening, along with bread and potatoes, but now that carbohydrates are getting "better press" and people are realizing their healthful attributes, we find a surge of interest in new and attractive pasta dishes. There are some restaurants that serve only pasta: pasta salads, pasta entrées, and even pasta desserts. (No one has gone so far as to process pasta into a beverage—yet!)

Pasta can be made from wheat, soy, rice, corn, buckwheat, other grains, or a wide variety of other ingredients, including legumes and even seaweed. Pastas come in many colors: you can sometimes even find black or brown noodles; green noodles are colored with spinach. The kind most of us in America are used to is an egg noodle made from durum-wheat semolina that is often enriched to provide extra nutrients. One cup of cooked egg noodles contains about 50 milligrams of cholesterol; we normally use pasta made from enriched semolina that contains no eggs or cholesterol.

Look in health-food stores or international markets for more exotic noodles. Oriental noodles, such as soba noodles, are especially delicate in texture and flavor. Whole-wheat pasta is higher in fiber, but has a somewhat stronger flavor than egg noodles or regular semolina, so you may want to combine it with other kinds of pasta until you get used to it or as a way to add color.

One cup of cooked spaghetti contains about 200 calories. With a low-calorie sauce, a fresh garden salad, a beverage, and a fruit for dessert, you have a complete meal. Although spaghetti is mentioned here, pasta comes in dozens of shapes and sizes, from shells and corkscrews (fusilli) to the wide noodles used in fettucine and lasagna. One of the delights of discovering pasta is determining by experiment which pasta forms go best with your favorite sauces.

In addition to serving our tomato sauces with pasta, be sure to try our delicious meatball recipes as well. (Turkey Meatballs with Tomato Sauce, p. 186, and Sage Sausage or Meatballs, p. 192). Also see our tofu section for several more pasta recipes that use tofu as a principal ingredient.

As you experiment with cooking different types of pasta, keep in mind the amount of time you'll need to cook your pasta *al dente*—that is, it should be slightly firm, not mushy, when you bite into it. Although we have never used one, a multicooker/steamer, sometimes called simply a "pasta cooker," can be very handy if you make a lot of pasta. An 8-quart stockpot will contain a 6-quart colander insert that automatically drains your pasta when you remove it. The gadget is also useful for cooking clams, shrimp, or anything else that requires draining. There is also a shallow insert for steaming.

Pasta with Garlic-and-Clam Sauce

PREPARATION TIME: 8 MINUTES.   COOKING TIME: 15 MINUTES.

This unusual but very tasty garlic-and-clam sauce combines vegetables with the clams so that a large serving can use less spaghetti or linguine and more sauce, with fewer calories per portion.

½ cup chopped onion
½ cup chopped green peppers
4 cloves garlic, minced
2 tablespoons olive oil
½ pound mushrooms, sliced
2 cans (6 or 7 ounces each) minced clams, plus their liquid
1½ teaspoons dried thyme leaves

Salt and fresh-ground black pepper to taste
2 tablespoons chopped fresh parsley
Dash of cayenne pepper
4 cups cooked spaghetti OR linguine (about 8 ounces uncooked)
Parmesan cheese (optional)

1. Sauté the onion, green peppers, and garlic in the olive oil until onions are translucent. Add a little water and cover if necessary to prevent sticking. Add the mushrooms and continue heating in the covered saucepan for about 3 minutes.
2. Add the remaining ingredients except for the cheese, and heat until hot in the covered saucepan. Serve with pasta and sprinkle with Parmesan cheese if desired.

4 servings. Serving size is 1 cup pasta, plus 1 cup sauce.

Per Serving: 326 calories, 54 mg. cholesterol, 3 g. dietary fiber, 14 g. fat, 175 mg. sodium.

Per Serving (with 1 tablespoon grated Parmesan cheese): 349 calories, 58 mg. cholesterol, 3 g. dietary fiber, 15 g. fat, 270 mg. sodium.

"Once in a while couldn't we just have some pasta?" *THE FAR SIDE.* COURTESY CHRONICLE FEATURES, SAN FRANCISCO.

Spinach Roll-Ups

PREPARATION TIME: 30 MINUTES. COOKING TIME: 30 MINUTES.

6 lasagne noodle strips
1 package (10 ounces) frozen chopped spinach
4 ounces fresh mushrooms, diced
2 tablespoons water
2 eggs, slightly beaten
1 cup low-fat cottage cheese
1/8 teaspoon garlic powder
1/8 teaspoon onion powder
Fresh-ground black pepper to taste

1 tablespoon butter OR margarine
2 tablespoons whole-wheat flour
1 cup low-fat milk
1/8 teaspoon salt
2 tablespoons grated Parmesan cheese
Nonstick vegetable cooking spray

1. Cook the lasagne noodles according to the package directions. Then place them in cool water until ready to use.

2. Cook the frozen spinach and mushrooms in the 2 table-spoons of water until the spinach is completely defrosted and the mushrooms are just beginning to look cooked. Drain well.

3. In a medium to large bowl, combine the eggs, cottage cheese, garlic and onion powders, pepper, and spinach and mushrooms, mixing well.

4. In a saucepan, melt the butter slowly over medium-low heat. Stir in the flour, mixing until it is thoroughly moistened. Add the milk slowly, stirring constantly. Add the salt and the Parmesan cheese, and cook over very low heat, stirring frequently, until the sauce just begins to thicken. Remove from the heat and cover.

5. Spray a casserole dish with the cooking spray. On a plate, cut each lasagne strip in half. Place about a tablespoonful of the spinach mixture on each strip and fold the ends over, leaving the sides open. Place the roll-ups folded-side down in the casserole dish. Fill in the empty spaces in the dish with any leftover spinach mixture. Cover with the cheese sauce.

6. Bake at 325 degrees for about 30 minutes, or until bubbly.

4 servings of 3 roll-ups each.

Per Serving: 280 calories, 157 mg. cholesterol, 4 g. dietary fiber, 9 g. fat, 497 mg. sodium.

Linguine al frutti di mare
(Linguine with Shellfish)

PREPARATION TIME: 30 TO 40 MINUTES.   COOKING TIME: 15 MINUTES.

Here is another fine recipe from the Villa Romano, again with reduced oil. Though you may use canned or frozen shellfish and squid that are already cleaned and ready for cooking, use fresh if you can; directions follow on how to clean it, and the extra trouble is worth it if you have time.

Clams in the shell: Scrub and wash in several bowls of water or under running water to remove as much sand as possible. Soak them in a large pot filled with 1 gallon of water and ⅓ cup of salt. Throw out any clams that have broken shells or that float. Shells should be tightly closed or should close at a touch if barely open. The shells will open as they cook. It's very difficult to get all the sand out; some people even wash the clams in cold running water once they're cooked.

Mussels in the shell: Throw out any mussels with broken shells. Again, the shells should be tightly closed. If a mussel is open, put it in a freezer for a couple of minutes. The shell should close; if it won't, throw it out. If the two sides of the shell can be slid back and forth against each other, discard it—it may be more mud than mussel. Clean as for clams. Clip the "beard" off the mussel before cooking.

Squid: Be sure the squid is dead! A strong blow to the head is a good precautionary measure. Then firmly hold the head section just underneath the eyes and pull the outer portion of the tail and fin section away. You will find the gray ink sac, which should be removed and discarded. (Though some recipes use the ink from the sac for coloring and flavoring sauces, this recipe does not.) Cut away the tentacles just above the eyes. Throw out the eye section, innards, and the small roundish cartilage at the base of the tentacles (this should be easy to remove with your fingers). Throw away the cuttlebone inside the tail, then rub off the red membrane covering most of the squid. If the squid is over 8 inches long, pound well with a mallet to tenderize. Now the tentacles, arms, and body meat are ready for slicing.

1 tablespoon olive oil
2 to 3 shallots, chopped
4 to 5 cloves garlic, minced
1 dozen littleneck clams, washed and scrubbed
2 dozen mussels, washed and scrubbed
¾ pound squid, cleaned and sliced in rings ¼ to ½ inch-thick (you'll end up with about 2 cups squid)
¼ cup white wine
2 cups Basil-Tomato Sauce (pp.296–97)
¼ teaspoon crushed red pepper
Pinch of saffron
Chopped fresh parsley to taste
Dash of salt and black pepper if needed
12 large fresh shrimp, shelled and deveined
8 ounces linguine, cooked and drained

1. Heat olive oil over medium heat. Add the shallots and garlic. Sauté until soft, being careful not to burn.
2. Add the clams and stir, cooking for about 1 minute. Add the mussels and squid. Cook, stirring constantly, over medium-high heat for 1 more minute. Add the wine, basil-tomato sauce, and the rest of the spices. Cover and cook 4 to 5 minutes, until the clams and mussels have fully opened.
3. Add the shrimp. Cover and cook for 1 to 1½ minutes, just until the shrimp is pink. Serve in flat soup bowls or plates over cooked linguine. Chef Ramovic suggests another way to serve this dish: arrange the pasta, topped with the shrimp and sauce, in the middle of the plate and put the other shellfish around the pasta.

4 servings. Serving size is 1 cup pasta, plus sauce.

Per Serving: 499 calories, 319 mg. cholesterol, 5 g. dietary fiber, 13 g. fat, 294 mg. sodium.

Sunflower Pasta Salad

PREPARATION TIME: 20 MINUTES. REFRIGERATION TIME: 1 HOUR.

Although slightly different in taste, black and white pepper may be used interchangeably, as in this recipe. White pepper is actually the fully ripened pepper berry with the dark outer shell removed. Black pepper is underripe, and is fermented and dried in the sun before grinding. Often, cooks choose one or the other depending on color preference for a given recipe —white pepper is used in white sauces, for example.

For variety, try one or more of the following herbs in this salad: parsley, rosemary, thyme, oregano, or chives. Or choose your own favorite herbs. As always, fresh is best, but dried is often easier to obtain for those of us who don't grow our own herbs.

4 ounces bow-tie
  OR twist pasta
2 tablespoons lemon juice
2 tablespoons sunflower, olive,
  OR safflower oil
1 clove garlic, crushed
1/4 teaspoon salt
Fresh-ground black
  OR white pepper to taste
1 cup cherry tomatoes
  OR tomato wedges

1/4 cup black olives (Greek
  olives are best), pitted and
  sliced
1/2 medium cucumber, thinly
  sliced
4 radishes, thinly sliced
1/4 cup dry-roasted, unsalted
  sunflower seeds
1 tablespoon fresh
  OR 1 teaspoon dried of your
  favorite herb combination

1. Cook the pasta according to the package directions, without added salt.
2. Meanwhile, combine the lemon juice, oil, garlic, salt, and pepper in a jar. Cover and shake.
3. Combine all the other ingredients, including the cooked, drained pasta, in a large bowl. Add the dressing, and toss.
4. Refrigerate, covered, for at least 1 hour before serving.

2 servings as a main course. Serving size is about 2 cups.

Per Serving: 359 calories, no cholesterol, 4 g. dietary fiber, 27 g. fat, 418 mg. sodium.

Spinach Lasagne

PREPARATION TIME: 30 MINUTES.   COOKING TIME: 30 MINUTES.

2 pounds fresh spinach
4 tablespoons grated Parmesan cheese
1 cup part-skim ricotta cheese
¼ teaspoon nutmeg
¼ teaspoon salt
Fresh-ground black pepper to taste
1 tablespoon vegetable oil OR olive oil

2 cloves garlic, crushed
½ cup chopped onion
½ cup chopped bell pepper
2 cups tomato sauce
½ teaspoon basil
½ teaspoon oregano
½ teaspoon thyme
½ pound lasagne noodles

1. Wash the spinach carefully to remove grit, then steam until just limp, about 1 or 2 minutes. Chop the spinach, and mix with 2 tablespoons of the Parmesan, the ricotta, nutmeg, salt, and pepper.
2. Heat the oil in a large saucepan, and sauté the garlic, onions, and bell pepper until the onions are translucent. Stir in the tomato sauce, basil, oregano, and thyme. Cover and let simmer until ready to use.
3. Cook the noodles according to the package directions.
4. Preheat the oven to 350 degrees.
5. Layer the noodles alternately with the cheese-spinach mixture and the tomato sauce in an 8 × 13-inch baking dish. Sprinkle the top with the remaining Parmesan.
6. Bake at 350 degrees for 30 minutes, until bubbly.

8 servings. Serving size is about 1½ cups.

Per Serving: 387 calories, 41 mg. cholesterol, 6 g. dietary fiber, 17 g. fat, 871 mg. sodium.

Triple-Cheese Manicotti

PREPARATION TIME: 25 MINUTES.   COOKING TIME: 25 MINUTES.

8 manicotti shells
1 tablespoon vegetable oil
  OR olive oil
½ cup chopped onions
2 cloves garlic, crushed
½ cup chopped bell pepper
2 cups tomato sauce
½ teaspoon basil
½ teaspoon oregano

½ teaspoon thyme
¼ teaspoon salt
¼ teaspoon black pepper
1½ cups shredded part-skim
  mozzarella cheese
1 cup low-fat cottage cheese
⅓ cup grated Parmesan cheese
2 eggs, beaten

1. Cook the manicotti shells according to the package directions, and drain. While they are cooking, heat the oil in a large saucepan, and sauté the onions, garlic, and bell pepper until the onions are translucent. Stir in the tomato sauce, basil, oregano, thyme, salt, and pepper. Cover and let simmer until needed, stirring occasionally.
2. Combine 1 cup of the mozzarella cheese with the cottage cheese, Parmesan, and beaten eggs. Stir gently.
3. Stuff the cheese mixture into the cooked, drained shells, using about ¼ cup per shell.
4. Pour ½ cup of the tomato sauce mixture into a shallow 2-quart casserole dish. Arrange the stuffed manicotti shells on top, then pour the remaining sauce over them. Sprinkle with the remaining ½ cup of mozzarella cheese.
5. Bake uncovered at 350 degrees for 25 minutes, or until sauce is bubbly and cheese is melted.

4 servings. Serving size is 2 shells each, plus sauce.

Per Serving: 354 calories, 169 mg. cholesterol, 3 g. dietary fiber, 17 g. fat, 1491 mg. sodium.

Mock Lasagne

PREPARATION TIME: 25 MINUTES.   COOKING TIME: 45 MINUTES.

This can be prepared early in the day and refrigerated. It may take a little more cooking time if you put it in the oven cold. Serve with a spinach salad or other fresh greens on the side.

4 cups elbow macaroni, uncooked
Nonstick vegetable cooking spray
1½ pounds extra-lean ground beef, ground turkey, OR ground veal
2 cloves garlic, minced
½ teaspoon ground ginger

3 cups canned tomato sauce OR Real Italian Tomato Sauce (pp. 290–91)
1 pound low-fat cottage cheese
1 pound Neufchatel cheese
½ cup plain low-fat yogurt
1 medium bell pepper, chopped
1 bunch scallions, chopped
½ teaspoon oregano

1. Cook the macaroni in water according to the package directions. Drain.
2. Spray a 4-quart casserole dish with the cooking spray. Put in half the cooked macaroni.
3. In a skillet, brown the ground meat and remove it from the pan with a slotted spoon. Sauté the garlic in the skillet, then return the meat to the pan. Sprinkle in the ginger, and stir in the tomato sauce. Remove from the heat.
4. In a bowl, combine the cottage cheese, Neufchatel, yogurt, bell pepper, and scallions. Spread this mixture over the macaroni in the casserole dish. Add the remaining macaroni, spreading evenly. Spread the meat-tomato sauce over the top, and sprinkle with the oregano.
5. Bake at 375 degrees for 45 minutes.

12 servings. Serving size is about 1⅓ cups.

Per Serving: 343 calories, 70 mg. cholesterol, 2 g. dietary fiber, 18 g. fat, 717 mg. sodium.

Capellini di angelo al filetto di pomodoro (Angel-Hair Pasta with Basil-Tomato Sauce)

PREPARATION TIME: 15 MINUTES.   COOKING TIME: 15 TO 20 MINUTES.

The original recipe for this dish from the Villa Romano restaurant in Nashville calls for four times the amount of olive oil used here. Olive oil has about 135 calories per tablespoon, so this version has 405 fewer calories.

The basil-tomato sauce given here is a basic sauce used in other recipes, including *Linguine al frutti di mare*. (The sauce recipe alone appears in the sauce section, on pp. 296–97.) Though tomato skins contain fiber, vitamins, and minerals, more elegant recipes, such as this one, generally say to remove them. If you wish to remove the skins, drop the tomatoes in boiling water for about 1 minute. Remove them from the pot and run them under cold water; the skins should now peel off easily. Fresh basil will give the richest flavor, but the dried herb can be substituted.

Villa Romano's proprietor and chef, Kem Ramovic, suggests serving this delicate pasta as an appetizer or as a light main course. In restaurants that prepare pasta fresh when ordered, as is the case at the Villa Romano, you should ask for a low-fat version of your favorite sauce. Most chefs can cut the quantity of fat on request.

1 tablespoon olive oil
  (extra-virgin if available)
4 to 5 cloves garlic, minced
1 large shallot, minced
1 can (28 ounces) Italian plum
  tomatoes, quartered, OR 3
  large ripe tomatoes, skinned,
  seeded, and chopped

Salt and coarse fresh-ground
  black pepper to taste
¼ cup fresh basil, chopped
  OR 4 teaspoons dried basil
8 ounces angel-hair pasta
3 quarts water
4 tablespoons grated Parmesan
  cheese

1. Heat the oil over medium heat. Add the garlic and shallot, and sauté until the garlic is golden and the shallot wilted. Add the tomatoes. Season with salt, pepper, and basil.
2. Meanwhile, cook the pasta in an uncovered pot in rapidly

boiling water for about 1 to 2 minutes. Test it after 1 minute for *al dente* ("firm to the bite") texture.

3. Drain the pasta, reserving 2 tablespoons of the water it was cooked in. Add the pasta and the reserved water to the tomato sauce. Stir gently to coat the pasta with the sauce. Remove to a serving platter, sprinkle with the Parmesan cheese, and serve immediately.

4 servings. Serving size is about 1 cup pasta with ½ cup sauce.

Per Serving: 246 calories, 4 mg. cholesterol, 4 g. dietary fiber, 6 g. fat, 240 mg. sodium.

Tuna-Pasta Salad

PREPARATION TIME: 20 TO 25 MINUTES

Combine whole-wheat and regular egg macaroni for a pleasing color and taste combination, and do try the caraway seeds.

1 package (8 ounces) macaroni	1 tablespoon prepared mustard
1 package (10 ounces) frozen peas	1 teaspoon garlic powder
2 small cans (6½ ounces each) water-packed tuna, drained	Fresh-ground black pepper to taste
1 to 2 scallions, minced	1 teaspoon caraway seeds (optional)
2 tablespoons mayonnaise	½ teaspoon salt
¾ cup plain low-fat yogurt	

1. Cook the macaroni according to the package directions, without added salt. Drain and reserve.
2. In another saucepan, cook peas according to directions.
3. In a large bowl, combine remaining ingredients. Add drained macaroni and drained peas, and mix lightly. Chill.

8 servings. Serving size is about 1 cup.

Per Serving: 239 calories, 29 mg. cholesterol, 4 g. dietary fiber, 4 g. fat, 477 mg. sodium.

Macaroni Shells with Crab

PREPARATION TIME: 25 MINUTES.　　　COOKING TIME: 30 MINUTES.

You may substitute frozen crab for canned.

1 package (12 ounces) jumbo
  macaroni shells
2 cans (6½ ounces each)
  crabmeat, drained
1¼ cups low-fat cottage
  OR ricotta cheese
¼ teaspoon dried marjoram

¼ teaspoon dried rosemary
½ teaspoon garlic powder
¼ cup fresh parsley, minced
3 cups Real Italian Tomato
  Sauce (pp. 290–91)
  OR other tomato sauce

1. Cook the shells according to the package directions but without the salt. Drain, and spread the shells in a single layer on foil to prevent them from sticking together.
2. In a medium bowl, combine the crab, cheese, and seasonings, blending well. Then fill each shell with about 1 tablespoon of the crab-cheese mixture.
3. Pour half the tomato sauce into the bottom of a 9 × 13-inch baking pan. Place the shells, open-side down, in a single layer on top of the sauce. Cover with the remaining sauce.
4. Bake covered at 350 degrees for about 25 minutes. Remove the cover and bake about 5 minutes longer, until bubbly.

8 servings. Serving size is about 1½ cups.

Per Serving: 279 calories, 58 mg. cholesterol, 2 g. dietary fiber, 6 g. fat, 675 mg. sodium.

Meatless Main Courses

For those of you who are used to centering every meal around a main course of meat, it may be a surprise to learn that most Americans eat twice as much protein each day as necessary to meet the body's daily protein needs. Much of this protein comes from meat.

Yet there is a wide variety of protein sources in the plant world: beans and other legumes, grains, and seeds provide endless possibilities for tasty, protein-filled dishes.

I recommend that you try at least one meatless day a week. Begin to think of meat as a seasoning or special condiment to your main recipe ingredients from the plant world, which are generally lower in fat, cholesterol, chemical additives, and cost, than meat.

If you think going a whole day without meat is next to impossible for you, try one meatless meal first. As you realize you won't go hungry or be bored with a vegetarian meal, you'll see how easy it is to go for a whole day, or several days if you like, without meat.

Most people in the Orient eat very little meat. They survive primarily on what is known as "complementary protein," from combinations of legumes, grains, and seeds. This provides the same nutritional benefit as protein from meat.

To help you understand what protein is, think of mechanical gears meshing: one gear can't turn without at least one other. Likewise with complete proteins, which are made up of "gears" called amino acids. There are twenty-two amino acids we need our bodies can manufacture fourteen of them. The other eight amino acids must come from the foods we eat.

We need larger amounts of some amino acids than we do of others in order to utilize the protein effectively. You might think of amino acids, then, as *different-sized* gears, all moving together to keep our bodies moving.

Fish, poultry, meat, eggs, and dairy products provide essentially complete, *usable* protein: all the amino acids are present in these foods in levels our bodies can use.

But did you know that soy flour has twice as much protein in it as some meat products? And that legumes, such as dried beans and peas, lentils, and peanuts have about the same amount of protein as meat? Yet these foods are limited in their protein *usability* because one or more of those eight essential amino acids are missing, or are present in limited amounts.

So we come to the concept of "complementary protein." To complement means "to make complete or perfect." In order for the amino acid "gears" from plant foods to mesh and be completely usable, we must combine two or more different kinds of plant foods.

Here is one simplified example: wheat flour is low in lysine, while beans are high in lysine. Put them together in a bean burrito and you have complementary protein because the beans supply what the wheat flour lacks.

You can also use small amounts of dairy products and/or meat products to boost the usability of your plant proteins. To make it easy for you to experiment on your own with complementary protein combinations, here are the basic guidelines. Use:

—grains with legumes (for example, rice and beans)
—seeds with legumes (sesame with beans)
—grains with dairy products (macaroni and cheese)
—grains with sesame or sunflower seeds (breads with seeds)
—dairy products with sesame (sprinkle sesame on cheesy casseroles)
—dairy products with some legumes (cheese on chili with beans)

LEGUMES, SPROUTS, GRAINS, NUTS, AND SEEDS

These are the basic non-animal sources for protein and they are valuable sources of other nutrients including dietary fiber. We'd like to provide a few tips for combining and cooking these healthful foods so that you will use them more frequently.

LEGUMES

First, all beans are legumes, but not all legumes are beans. Any plant that has seeds growing in a pod is considered a legume; these include peas, string beans, other beans, and even peanuts, which are usually mistakenly thought of as nuts.

Among the many varieties of legumes in the world are the flavorful black bean, black-eyed peas, garbanzos (chickpeas), kidney beans, navy beans, lentils, pinto beans, split peas, and white beans. Soybeans, highest in protein of all the beans, are most bland in flavor, but you can use them in any recipe calling for beans.

Beans seem to require more salt to bring out their flavor than many foods, and you will find our bean recipes contain more salt than our other recipes. However, as always, we combine salt with herbs, stock, and other seasoning agents.

Before cooking, rinse dried beans and discard any small stones that may have gotten mixed in with them.

Different-sized beans require different cooking times, as we illustrate in recipes calling for several varieties of beans. They also expand in size, as do grains, when cooked. On average, 1 cup of dried beans will provide anywhere from 2½ to 3½ cups of cooked beans.

Though we generally use the slow method of bean cookery, which involves soaking them overnight first, there is a quick method if you forget to soak them the night before.

Cover the beans well with water or stock, bring to a boil, and cook for 2 minutes. Remove from heat, cover, and let stand for 1 hour. Add more liquid if necessary. Then cook as you would if you had soaked them overnight.

Canned beans are fine, but not as tasty or pleasant in texture as those made from scratch.

SPROUTS

Sprouts from beans and seeds are high in nutrients and low in calories. You can grow your own fairly easily (there are many books that can tell you how), or look for them "ready-made" in the produce section of your local supermarket. They are especially suitable for use in salads and sandwiches, or as a garnish.

GRAINS

Generally, when cooking grains, you'll need almost twice as much liquid (stock or water) as grain. Some of the larger grains need more water, the smaller ones, less.

Stirring is not necessary when cooking grains, and in fact, seems to interfere with the even cooking and the final texture of the grain.

The best combination for brown rice seems to be about 1 3/4 cups of liquid to 1 cup rice. Bring the liquid to a boil, add the grain, and bring back to a boil. Then cover, reduce heat, and let simmer until tender and fluffy. Long-grain brown rice takes about 40 to 45 minutes. Long-grain brown rice stays separated better and is fluffier than the medium- or short-grain brown rice; experiment until you find the one you like the best. Short-grain brown rice is good for casseroles and stuffings, since it does tend to stick together.

The tiny kernels of millet take less cooking time, while larger grains, such as whole wheat and barley, take about the same time as rice or a few minutes longer.

Millet and brown rice cooked together in vegetable or chicken stock make a delicious combination. Experiment with combining one or more grains: long-, medium-, or short-grain brown rice; wild rice, which isn't a rice at all but the seed of an aquatic grass; barley; millet; oats; wheat; bulgur wheat; buckwheat; wheat berries; rye; triticale, which is a cross between rye and wheat; amaranth; and so on.

Though some purists say that when combining grains for a dish you should cook them separately, Terri often throws them in a pot together, sacrificing perhaps a small amount of delicate consistency in exchange for ease of preparation and shorter clean-up time.

NUTS AND SEEDS

Nuts and seeds are good sources of protein, but unfortunately they contain a high proportion of fat as well. We use them sparingly as a protein booster in meatless cooking and as a garnish (for example, Thai Stir-Fry, p. 126, uses sesame seeds in this way).

Toasting your own seeds and nuts means you can control the amount of fat and salt added—you don't really need to add any, especially when the final product will be used in another recipe. You can sometimes find dry-roasted, unsalted nuts and seeds in a supermarket; a better bet for finding raw nuts and seeds is health-food stores.

To toast your own, use one of the following methods:
Oven-Toasting—Spread the nuts or seeds in a single

layer on a baking sheet and place in a 375- to 400-degree oven. Let bake, stirring occasionally, until golden brown, which could take anywhere from 3 to 10 minutes depending on the type of nut or seed. A general rule of thumb is the smaller the nut or seed, the shorter the roasting time. Try a small amount first so you can monitor the time and heat.

Pan-Toasting—Place the nuts or seeds in a hot, dry skillet, and toast over medium heat, stirring often, until golden brown.

By the way, toasted pumpkin and squash seeds are delicious. We do them in the oven and they are among our favorite snacks.

Now we are ready to go on to some of our favorite meatless main dish recipes, and we hope to get you started on the road to at least one meatless day each week.

Classic Steamed Veggies and Rice

PREPARATION TIME: 10 MINUTES.   COOKING TIME: 40 MINUTES.

This is a standard vegetarian recipe, easy to prepare, with complementary protein provided by the brown rice and the cheese. Our favorite vegetable combination for this recipe is broccoli, carrots, onions, yellow squash, and mushrooms. We start cooking the broccoli and carrots first, because they take longer. Then we add the other veggies as we go along.

We also like chunks of red cabbage, zucchini, tomatoes, green beans, cauliflower—well, just put in your favorite vegetables, and enjoy!

1½ cups water
  OR Vegetable Stock (p. 66)
1 cup brown rice

2 cups mixed vegetables of
  choice, cut in chunks

Water for steaming   **Dash tamari sauce**
4 ounces grated cheddar cheese   **OR soy sauce (optional)**

1. Pour the water or vegetable stock into a saucepan, cover, and bring to a boil. Pour in the brown rice, cover, and reduce heat to simmer. Do not stir.
2. After rice has been cooking for about 20 minutes, start steaming your vegetables (see directions for steaming, p. 265).
3. When all veggies are just tender, ladle them over the rice, and top with the cheese. Let everyone add their own bit of tamari sauce if they desire.

4 servings. Serving size is ½ cup rice, ½ cup veggies, 1 ounce cheese.

Per Serving: 251 calories, 30 mg. cholesterol, 4 g. dietary fiber, 10 g. fat, 180 mg. sodium.

"Joey says he's not used to cold stuffed zucchini boats." © 1986 *GOURMET* MAGAZINE. REPRINTED BY PERMISSION OF DONALD REILLY.

Eggplant Parmesan

PREPARATION TIME: 35 MINUTES.   COOKING TIME: 40 MINUTES.

Eggplant is known for its ability to absorb huge quantities of oil. This "no-fry" version of a delectable Italian dish eliminates almost all of the oil, and therefore, several hundred calories. Protein in this recipe comes from the egg, milk, and cheese, along with the wheat germ and whole-wheat bread crumbs.

1 medium eggplant (about 1 pound)
1 egg
  OR 2 egg whites
2 tablespoons skim milk
¼ cup wheat germ
½ cup Whole-Wheat Bread Crumbs (pp. 307–8)
1 tablespoon Parmesan cheese
Nonstick vegetable cooking spray
2 cups Real Italian Tomato Sauce (pp. 290–91)
¾ cup part-skim mozzarella

1. Slice the eggplant into 8 slices, ½-inch thick.
2. Beat together the egg and milk in a small, shallow bowl.
3. In another bowl, combine the wheat germ, bread crumbs, and Parmesan cheese.
4. Spray a foil-lined baking sheet with cooking spray. Dip the eggplant slices into the egg mixture, coating well. Then dip them into the bread crumb mixture. Place the slices on the baking sheet, and bake at 350 degrees for 15 minutes. Turn the slices over, and bake for 10 more minutes. Remove from oven.
5. Make a layer of eggplant in a casserole dish, top with tomato sauce, then mozzarella cheese. Repeat the layers until no ingredients remain.
6. Bake covered at 350 degrees for 25 minutes, then uncover and bake 15 minutes more.

4 servings. Serving size is 2 slices each, plus sauce.

Per Serving: 256 calories, 81 mg. cholesterol, 9 g. dietary fiber, 8 g. fat, 438 mg. sodium.

Basic Beans

PREPARATION TIME: 15 MINUTES.   COOKING TIME: 4½ HOURS.

Here's a basic bean recipe that you can use with virtually any dried bean. Serve over grain to provide complementary protein for your main course or as a side dish. Add the optional crushed red pepper if you like spicy food.

2 cups dried beans
Water
½ bulb garlic (about 4 to 5
    cloves), minced
2 teaspoons salt

1 tablespoon olive oil
2 medium onions, cut in
    chunks
1 to 1½ teaspoons crushed red
    pepper (optional)

1. Rinse the beans thoroughly in water to remove dirt. Pick over to remove any small stones that may have gotten mixed in with the beans. Soak the beans overnight in a large kettle, in 5 cups of water. (Before cooking the beans, some people will change the water. Since we are more likely to use the recipe for Basic Better Beans (below), which calls for soaking beans in stock, we don't discard the liquid.)
2. The next day, bring the beans to a boil. Turn to simmer, and add the remaining ingredients. Let simmer about 4 hours, until most or all of the water is gone, stirring occasionally.

8 servings. Serving size is about ½ cup.

Per Serving: 133 calories, no cholesterol, 7 g. dietary fiber, 2 g. fat, 542 mg. sodium.

Basic Better Beans

PREPARATION TIME: 15 MINUTES.   COOKING TIME: 1 HOUR.

The use of stock—along with a whole onion stuck with whole cloves—instead of water for soaking and cooking, makes beans even more flavorful.

2 cups dried beans
  OR lentils
4 cups chicken stock
2 large onions

6 whole cloves
2 tablespoons olive oil
Dash of salt and pepper

1. Place the beans in a pot with the stock. Peel the onions, stick the whole cloves in them, and place in the pot with the beans. Soak overnight.
2. Remove the onions and cloves, bring the beans to a boil, then reduce heat and cook, covered, until just tender, about 3 hours.
3. Discard the cloves, chop the onions, and sauté in the oil until translucent.
4. Place all ingredients in a large casserole dish and bake for 1 hour at 325 degrees.

8 servings. Serving size is about ¹/₂ cup.

Per Serving: 181 calories, no cholesterol, 6 g. dietary fiber, 5 g. fat, 438 mg. sodium.

Swiss-Mozzarella Bake

PREPARATION TIME: 10 MINUTES, PLUS 30 TO 45 MINUTES STANDING
TIME.   COOKING TIME: 1 HOUR.

This is a very good and simple dish that's especially handy if you have some leftover bread that's beginning to get stale. Fresh bread works wonderfully too. This dish is like a soufflé or pudding, and is baked by setting the pan in a larger pan of hot water in the oven. This helps keep the consistency moist and light.

We like to use whole mustard seed and crush it ourselves with a mortar and pestle, but if you prefer, you can substitute ground dry mustard. As always, you can leave out the tamari sauce if you wish to cut back on salt.

1 cup grated Swiss cheese
2 cups grated part-skim
   mozzarella cheese
5 slices whole-grain bread
1½ cups low-fat milk
2 eggs
½ cup plain low-fat yogurt
¾ teaspoon dried thyme

½ teaspoon crushed mustard
   seed OR ground dry mustard
½ teaspoon fresh-ground black
   pepper
1 teaspoon dried parsley
½ teaspoon tamari sauce
   OR soy sauce (optional)

1. Combine the two cheeses. Then, in an 8-inch square baking dish, alternate layers of bread and cheese until used up.
2. Combine the remaining ingredients and pour over the bread and cheese. Let stand for 30 to 45 minutes, until the bread soaks up the liquid.
3. Place the casserole in a larger pan of hot water, and bake at 350 degrees for 1 hour.

6 servings. Serving size is about 1 cup.

Per Serving: 309 calories, 137 mg. cholesterol, 3 g. dietary fiber, 16 g. fat, 477 mg. sodium.

Terrific Tater Toppers

A hot, freshly baked potato can be the foundation for a complete, delicious meal. We hope the following ideas and recipes will tantalize your tastebuds, and trigger your imagination to create your own delectable, low-calorie tater-topping alternatives to sour cream and butter. Here are some ideas for toppings; use them singly or in combination. The majority of these Tater Toppers are meatless, but we include a few that do have meat in order to show you the wide variety that is possible.

(*Note:* Tater Toppers cooking times do not include time for baking the potatoes.)

Mix-and-Match Tater Topper ideas:

Low-fat cottage cheese
Sapsago cheese
Farmer cheese
Neufchatel cheese
Imitation bacon bits (made from soy)
Chunks of lean meat or poultry
Boiled shrimp, lobster, crabmeat, or imitation crabmeat
Steamed vegetables (mushrooms, broccoli, carrots, spinach,
   zucchini, tomatoes, or onions)
Meatless tomato sauce
Meatless chili
Beans and legumes
Tofu
Chives
Herbs and spices

Mexican Tater Topper

PREPARATION TIME: 5 MINUTES.
   COOKING TIME (USING JUST-BAKED POTATOES): 10 TO 15 MINUTES.

Here's another "meal-in-one" that's high in protein and has no meat. The protein is provided by the beans, cheese, and potato.

2 cups cooked kidney beans   ½ teaspoon cayenne pepper
¼ cup minced onion   1 teaspoon chili powder

1 teaspoon garlic powder
2 tablespoons water
4 medium baked potatoes, hot

Shredded lettuce
½ cup diced tomato
½ cup grated cheese

1. In a hot skillet, combine the beans, onion, seasonings, and water. Mash with a fork as the mixture heats, for a chunky-smooth texture.
2. Spoon the "refried beans" into the hot, split potatoes. Top with as much shredded lettuce as you like, and 2 tablespoons each of tomatoes and cheese for each potato.

4 servings. Serving size is about ½ cup sauce, 1 potato, plus condiments.

Per Serving: 330 calories, 15 mg. cholesterol, 15 g. dietary fiber, 6 g. fat, 108 mg. sodium.

Italian Tater Topper

PREPARATION TIME: 5 MINUTES.   COOKING TIME
                        (USING JUST-BAKED POTATOES): 5 MINUTES.

1 cup Real Italian Tomato
  Sauce (pp. 290–91) OR your
  favorite tomato sauce

4 medium baked potatoes, hot
½ cup part-skim mozzarella
  cheese, grated

1. Heat the sauce in a small saucepan.
2. Top each hot, split potato with ¼ cup of sauce and 2 tablespoons of cheese.

4 servings. Serving size is ¼ cup sauce, 1 potato, 2 tablespoons cheese.

Per Serving: 204 calories, 8 mg. cholesterol, 5 g. dietary fiber, 3 g. fat, 453 mg. sodium.

Broccoli-and-Chicken (or Lean-Beef) Tater Topper

PREPARATION TIME: 5 MINUTES.   COOKING TIME
(USING JUST-BAKED POTATOES): 15 MINUTES.

¼ cup chopped onion
1 cup sliced mushrooms
1 tablespoon vegetable oil
2 tablespoons water
¼ cup whole-wheat flour
1½ cup skim OR low-fat milk
Herb blend and/or
  fresh-ground black pepper to
  taste

2 cups cooked chicken
  OR lean beef, cubed
1 large bunch broccoli, steamed
  and chopped (about 2 cups)
4 medium baked potatoes, hot
  (medium potato = 5–6
  ounces or 3 per pound)

1. Sauté the onion and mushrooms in the oil in a large skillet.
   Stir in the water and flour.
2. Gradually add the milk, stirring until slightly thickened.
3. Add the seasonings, chicken or beef, and the broccoli.
   Cook uncovered, stirring occasionally, for 2 to 3 minutes.
4. Slice open the baked potatoes, and pour the broccoli mixture on top.

4 servings. Serving size is about 1½ cups over 1 potato.

Per Serving: 462 calories, 98 mg. cholesterol, 10 g. dietary fiber, 8
g. fat, 153 mg. sodium.

Twice-Baked Stuffed Potatoes

PREPARATION TIME: 12 MINUTES.   COOKING TIME
(USING JUST-BAKED POTATOES): 10 MINUTES.

4 medium baked potatoes
1 cup low-fat cottage cheese OR
  ½ cup low-fat shredded
  cheese, such as mozzarella,
  Monterey jack, OR Swiss
1 egg white
¼ teaspoon salt

2 teaspoons prepared mustard
1 tablespoon minced onion
Dash fresh-ground black
  pepper
Dried parsley OR paprika
  (optional)

1. Cut the potatoes in half, lengthwise. Scoop out the insides into a mixing bowl, leaving the skins intact.
2. Add the remaining ingredients to the bowl, and beat with a wire whisk or electric mixer until smooth and fluffy.
3. Arrange the potato skins on an ungreased baking sheet. Spoon the potato mixture into the skins. Sprinkle with dried parsley or paprika if desired.
4. Bake at 375 degrees for about 10 minutes, or until lightly browned.

4 servings.

Per Serving: 203 calories, 5 mg. cholesterol, 4 g. dietary fiber, 1 g. fat, 416 mg. sodium.

Zucchini Soufflé

PREPARATION TIME: 20 MINUTES.   COOKING TIME: 45 MINUTES.

¾ cups shredded zucchini
3 tablespoons onion, minced
4 ounces fresh mushrooms, sliced
2 teaspoons cornstarch
¾ cup skim milk
2 eggs

½ teaspoon salt
¼ teaspoon fresh-ground black pepper
¼ teaspoon nutmeg
⅓ cup mozzarella cheese, diced

1. In a large bowl, combine the zucchini, onion, and mushrooms.
2. In a medium bowl, mix together the cornstarch and 1 tablespoon of milk, then stir in the remaining milk. Beat in the eggs and seasonings.
3. Stir the egg mixture into the vegetables, then stir in the cheese.
4. Pour into a 9-inch pie plate, and bake at 350 degrees for 45 minutes.

4 servings. Serving size is about ¾ cup.

Per Serving: 151 calories, 151 mg. cholesterol, 4 g. dietary fiber, 9 g. fat, 423 mg. sodium.

Three-Way Beans and Rice

PREPARATION TIME: 5 MINUTES.   COOKING TIME: 4 HOURS AND
                                                                15 MINUTES.

You may substitute chicken or beef stock for the water if you
are not concerned about whether this meal is totally meatless.

1 cup black beans
1 cup white beans
¼ cup lentils
6 cups water
  OR vegetable stock
2 medium onions

½ bulb (about 4 to 5 cloves)
  garlic, minced
2 teaspoons salt
1 tablespoon olive oil
1 cup brown rice

1. Wash and drain the beans and lentils, picking over to be
   sure there are no stones. Reserve the lentils.
2. Place the black and white beans in a large soup pot with
   the water or stock, and bring to a boil.
3. Turn the heat down to simmer. Add the onions, garlic, salt,
   and oil. Let simmer for about 3½ hours, stirring occasionally.
4. Add the lentils and the rice. Bring to a boil again, then
   reduce heat and let simmer for 40 minutes, until rice and
   lentils are tender, and the broth is like a thick gravy.

12 servings of about 1 cup each.

Per Serving: 152 calories, no cholesterol, 7 g. dietary fiber, 2 g.
fat, 373 mg. sodium.

Stir-Fry Vegetables

PREPARATION TIME: 5 MINUTES.   COOKING TIME: 15 TO 20 MINUTES.

2 cups finely chopped fresh
  vegetables
1 tablespoon peanut oil
1 clove garlic, minced
¼ teaspoon ginger

2 tablespoons grated hard
  cheese
Tamari sauce
  OR soy sauce to taste

1. Have your vegetables ready; use any combination you like. In a large skillet or wok, heat the oil. Add the garlic and ginger, then add the vegetables requiring the most cooking, such as carrots, broccoli, green pepper, and so on.
2. Stir constantly, adding the vegetables that require less cooking as you go along. If necessary, add a tablespoon or two of water to prevent sticking. Cook until tender-crisp.
3. Spoon over cooked grain, sprinkle with cheese and tamari sauce if desired, and serve.

Serves 1 as a main course, 4 as a side dish.

Per Complete Recipe (with ½ cup each carrots, onions, celery, and broccoli): 257 calories, 8 mg. cholesterol, 7 g. dietary fiber, 17 g. fat, 314 mg. sodium.

Per Serving (as a side dish, ½ cup mixed stir-fry vegetables recipe, with ½ cup brown rice): 180 calories, 2 mg. cholesterol, 4 g. dietary fiber, 5 g. fat, 78 mg. sodium.
    Note: ½ cup brown rice (cooked) contains 118 calories, no cholesterol, 2 g. dietary fiber, 1 g. fat, no sodium.

Spinach Pizza

PREPARATION TIME: 50 MINUTES.   COOKING TIME: 30 MINUTES.

If you like spinach and pizza, you will love this combination! You can use the same crust as in the Summer Squash Pizza (pp. 252–53), or you can use this rapid-rise version. The water needs to be a little warmer than usual (but never hot!) for the rapid-rise version, since you are combining the yeast with so many ingredients at once.

Serve with a salad on the side.

The crust:

½ cup whole-wheat flour
⅛ cup all-purpose flour
¼ cup soy flour
½ teaspoon salt
1 tablespoon rapid-rise yeast

½ cup lukewarm water (120° to 130° F.)
Nonstick vegetable cooking spray

The filling:

½ medium onion, minced
4 ounces fresh mushrooms, sliced
1 package (10 ounces) frozen chopped spinach, thawed
1¼ cups shredded low-fat mozzarella cheese

¾ cup skim-milk ricotta
OR dry-curd nonfat cottage cheese
1 egg OR 2 egg whites
1 clove garlic, crushed
1 tablespoon Traditional Italian Herb Blend (p. 335)

1. To prepare the crust, combine the flours, salt, and yeast in a large bowl with the water. Mix well. If necessary, add a little more all-purpose flour to make the dough the right consistency. Knead the dough for 5 minutes on a floured board or other flat surface.
2. Replace the dough in the bowl, and cover with a damp dish towel to let rise in a draft-free place. Let double (about 30 minutes), then punch down. Let the dough rest for 5 minutes, then roll out to fit a 9 × 13-inch baking pan.
3. Spray the pan with nonstick cooking spray, and place the crust in the pan.
4. Steam the onions and mushrooms over a small amount of

water until tender. Meanwhile, drain the thawed spinach in a colander, pressing out as much liquid as possible. (You can save the liquid for stock, if you wish.)

5. Combine cooked onions and mushrooms with the spinach and all remaining ingredients in a large bowl, mixing well. Pour into the crust, and bake at 375 degrees for 30 minutes.

4 servings. Serving size is ¼ pizza.

Per Serving: 307 calories, 102 mg. cholesterol, 6 g. dietary fiber, 12 g. fat, 594 mg. sodium.

White-Bean Casserole

PREPARATION TIME: 10 MINUTES.　　　COOKING TIME: 1 HOUR.

2 cups dried white beans
1 teaspoon butter
　OR margarine
2 tablespoons olive oil
1 can (10 ounces) tomato purée
1 cup shredded cheddar cheese

1 cup shredded mozzarella
　cheese
3 tablespoons whole-wheat
　flour
2 tablespoons dried oregano

1. Cook the beans according to the Basic Bean recipe (p. 241), cooking off as much liquid as possible.
2. Lightly butter an 8½ × 11-inch casserole dish. Mix the cooked beans with the olive oil and tomato purée, and pour into the dish.
3. Combine the cheeses, flour, and oregano, and spread on top of the beans.
4. Bake uncovered at 275 degrees for 1 hour.

8 servings. Serving size is about 1 cup.

Per Serving: 267 calories, 27 mg. cholesterol, 8 g. dietary fiber, 12 g. fat, 159 mg. sodium.

Summer Squash Pizza

PREPARATION TIME: 1 HOUR AND 10 MINUTES.   COOKING TIME: 30 MINUTES.

This is *marvelous!* Tastes like a "real" pizza, even though it has no meat or tomato sauce. Serve it hot or cold as a main dish with a salad on the side, or cut it up in small pieces and serve as an hors d'oeuvre.

The crust:
- 1 tablespoon active dry yeast
- ½ cup lukewarm water (105° to 115° F.)
- ⅛ teaspoon sugar
- ½ cup whole-wheat flour
- ¼ cup all-purpose flour
- ¼ cup soy flour
- ½ teaspoon salt
- 2 additional tablespoons all-purpose flour

The filling:
- 1 tablespoon olive oil
- 1 medium onion, chopped
- 1 clove garlic, minced or crushed
- 2 cups yellow crookneck squash, sliced thin
- 2 cups zucchini, sliced thin
- 2 eggs
- 2 cups grated part-skim mozzarella cheese
- 2 tablespoons fresh parsley, chopped
- 1½ teaspoons Traditional Italian Herb Blend (p. 335)
- ½ teaspoon fresh-ground black pepper

1. Dissolve the yeast in ¼ cup of the warm water, along with the sugar. In another bowl, combine the whole-wheat flour, ¼ cup of the all-purpose flour, the soy flour, and the salt.
2. Stir the other ¼ cup warm water into the yeast mixture, then stir the mixture into the dry ingredients. Turn out on a lightly floured board or flat surface and knead for about 5 minutes, or until smooth and elastic, adding a little more all-purpose flour as needed. Return the dough to the bowl, cover with a damp dish towel, and set in a warm, draft-free place to rise for 45 minutes.
3. Meanwhile, heat the oil in a large skillet over medium heat, and add the onion and garlic. Cover, and sauté/ steam until onions are translucent.

4. Add the yellow squash and zucchini, cover, and reduce heat to low. Cook for 10 minutes, or until squash is tender.
5. Preheat the oven to 375 degrees.
6. Combine the eggs, the cheese, and the seasonings in a large bowl. When the vegetables are cooked, drain them thoroughly, and stir them into the egg mixture.
7. Punch down the dough after it doubles, and let it rest for 5 minutes on the board. Then roll it out to fit a 9 × 13-inch baking dish. Place the dough into the ungreased dish, and press into the sides. (If it cracks in places, pat it with lightly floured fingers to smooth it out.) Pour the vegetable mixture on top and spread evenly.
8. Bake for about 30 minutes, or until a knife or toothpick inserted in the center comes out clean. Let cool for 10 minutes before slicing.

4 servings. Serving size is ¼ pizza.

Per Serving: 377 calories, 169 mg. cholesterol, 7 g. dietary fiber, 17 g. fat, 572 mg. sodium.

Peas and Rice

PREPARATION TIME: 10 MINUTES.   COOKING TIME: 45 TO 50 MINUTES.

Here's a special-tasting vegetable-and-grain dish that cooks in one pan.

1 tablespoon vegetable oil
1 small onion, chopped
1 clove garlic, crushed
1 teaspoon dried basil
1 cup brown rice
1½ cups vegetable
  OR chicken stock

1 bay leaf
Salt and fresh-ground black
  pepper to taste
1 cup fresh or frozen peas

1. Heat the oil in a large saucepan over medium heat. Add the onion, garlic, and basil. Cover and sauté, stirring occasionally, until onions are translucent. Add the rice, and stir.
2. Add the stock, the bay leaf, salt and pepper, and bring to a boil.
3. Cover, and reduce heat to simmer. Let cook about 20 to 25 minutes.
4. Pour the peas on top. Do not stir.
5. Cover and let cook until the peas are just tender and the liquid has boiled away.

4 servings. Serving size is about ¾ cup.

Per Serving: 258 calories, no cholesterol, 5 g. dietary fiber, 5 g. fat, 427 mg. sodium.

Italian Squash Casserole

PREPARATION TIME: 10 MINUTES.   COOKING TIME: 1 HOUR.

2½ pounds zucchini squash
1 teaspoon butter
  OR margarine
1 cup shredded cheddar cheese
1 cup shredded mozzarella
  cheese

1 can (10 ounces) tomato purée
4 tablespoons whole-wheat
  flour
1 tablespoon olive oil

1 teaspoon basil   ½ teaspoon garlic powder
½ teaspoon salt

1. Wash the squash and chop into chunks.
2. Lightly butter an 8 × 11½-inch casserole dish or similar-sized baking dish. Put in the squash. Spread the cheeses over the squash, then the tomato purée. Sprinkle the flour over the top, then the oil, and then the spices, spreading all the ingredients as evenly as possible.
3. Cover and bake at 350 degrees for 1 hour.

6 servings. Serving size is about 1 cup.

Per Serving: 221 calories, 38 mg. cholesterol, 4 g. dietary fiber, 4 g. fat, 392 mg. sodium.

Welsh Rarebit

PREPARATION TIME: 7 MINUTES.   COOKING TIME: 12 MINUTES.

1 cup Swiss cheese, diced   ¼ teaspoon salt
1 egg   ¼ teaspoon fresh-ground black
½ cup skim milk   pepper
1 teaspoon dry mustard   1 teaspoon cornstarch
¼ teaspoon Tabasco sauce   4 slices whole-grain toast

1. Melt the cheese in a double boiler. While the cheese is melting, beat together the remaining ingredients except for the cornstarch and toast.
2. When cheese is melted, add the cornstarch, stirring constantly until it is absorbed.
3. Add the egg mixture and stir constantly (a wire whisk is best for this) until the sauce thickens. Serve immediately over whole-grain toast.

4 servings. Serving size is about ⅓ cup each, plus toast.

Per Serving: 221 calories, 95 mg. cholesterol, 4 g. dietary fiber, 11 g. fat, 449 mg. sodium.

Tofu

Tofu, soybean curd, soy cheese—these terms all refer to the same thing. At best, they may sound unusual to most of us. At worst, they sound downright unappetizing!

Yet this light, mild-tasting, and versatile meat substitute is extremely high in protein and extremely low in calories, saturated fat, and salt. It has no cholesterol to speak of, and is a staple in many Oriental countries where meat is not as readily available as it is in the Western world. Plus, it's high in calcium, iron, and other valuable minerals and vitamins.

Due to its delicate flavor, tofu blends well with practically everything. It can be grilled, sautéed, stir-fried, added to soups, or mashed or blended to resemble cottage cheese and then used as a base for desserts, dips, salads, sandwiches, and main courses.

Tofu is available in an array of textures—regular, firm, silken, wine-fermented, and so on—but the recipes in this book use the kind you are likely to find in a small plastic tub in the produce section of your local supermarket. Or, better still for the tofu, it may be refrigerated in the dairy section.

Drain and rinse the tofu in fresh water before using. You can keep it in the plastic tub while you do this. Be sure to follow any directions in the recipes for draining or pressing the tofu before using it in order to get the right consistency.

Although we had used tofu occasionally before writing this cookbook, we learned a great deal more about this versatile and healthful food as we tested the following recipes, many of

which were created especially for us by Margaret Nofziger
Dotzler.

Shrimp and Tofu

PREPARATION TIME: 7 MINUTES.   COOKING TIME: 10 MINUTES.

Another of Chef Wang Chai Hsin's creations from the Peking
Garden restaurant. If you're not already a fan of tofu, this will
do the trick.

2 teaspoons vegetable oil	Dash of salt
½ inch piece of gingerroot, peeled and chopped	Fresh-ground black pepper to taste
1 scallion, chopped	Dash of sugar
8 ounces shrimp, shelled	½ cup chicken stock
6 ounces tofu, cut into 1-inch pieces	¼ teaspoon cornstarch, dissolved in a bit of water

1. In a wok or skillet, heat the oil, add the gingerroot and
   scallions and stir for 10 seconds, then add the shrimp and
   tofu and cook until the shrimp are almost done (about 3
   minutes).
2. Add the salt, pepper, sugar, chicken stock, and dissolved
   corn starch. Bring to a boil, stirring frequently. Reduce
   heat, and simmer for about 1 minute more, or until sauce
   is at desired consistency.

2 servings. Serving size is about 1 cup.

Per Serving: 245 calories, 168 mg. cholesterol, 2 g. dietary fiber,
10 g. fat, 534 mg. sodium.

Tofu Manicotti

PREPARATION TIME: 30 MINUTES.   COOKING TIME: 1 HOUR AND 5 MINUTES.

You can make regular, supermarket variety tofu into "firm" tofu by placing the rinsed tofu on a dish towel or several paper towels. Set a foil pan with some water in it, or another light weight such as a plate or two, on top of the cake of tofu, and let stand for about 10 to 20 minutes. Then crumble it as directed below, and proceed with the recipe.

In some areas of the country, you may be able to purchase firm tofu in a health-food store or international market.

1 pound firm tofu
½ teaspoon salt
1 cup grated part-skim
    mozzarella cheese
¼ cup fresh parsley, finely
    chopped
1 can (28 ounces) whole
    tomatoes

1 can (6 ounces) tomato paste
1 tablespoon leaf oregano
2 teaspoons basil leaf
¼ teaspoon garlic powder
2 cups water
1 package (8 ounces) manicotti
    noodles

1. Rinse the tofu, and crumble finely into a mixing bowl. Add the salt, mozzarella, and parsley. Mix well, and set aside.
2. Place the tomatoes with their juice, the tomato paste, oregano, basil, garlic powder, and water in a blender. Blend briefly, for a chunky consistency.
3. Place 2 cups of the tomato sauce in the bottom of a 9 × 12-inch glass or stainless steel baking pan (*not* aluminum).

4. Fill the uncooked manicotti noodles with the tofu mixture. Using your hands, pack the noodles firmly. You should have exactly enough filling for all of the noodles in the package.

5. Place the noodles side by side in the baking pan. Pour the remaining sauce over the top. Make sure the noodles are completely covered. Cover the pan with foil.

6. Bake at 400 degrees for 45 minutes. Then remove the foil, being careful not to let the hot steam burn your hands. Turn the manicotti with tongs. Cover again, and bake another 20 minutes. Remove from the oven and let stand for 10 minutes before serving.

6 servings. Serving size is 1 filled noodle each, plus sauce.

Per Serving: 217 calories, 10 mg. cholesterol, 4 g. dietary fiber, 7 g. fat, 518 mg. sodium.

"Tonight I plan to have something for dinner you never had before but it is *very* good for you." DRAWING BY MODELL; © 1985 THE NEW YORKER MAGAZINE, INC.

Oriental Tofu Soup

PREPARATION TIME: 15 MINUTES.   COOKING TIME: 30 MINUTES.

5 cups vegetable
  OR chicken stock (see Onion
  Stock, pp. 66–67)
1 medium carrot, sliced thinly
  on the diagonal
1 cup chopped Chinese
  cabbage
1 small stalk celery, with leaves,
  sliced thinly (about ¼ cup)
½ can (5-ounce can) sliced
  bamboo shoots, drained

1 tablespoon tamari sauce
  OR soy sauce
4 large mushrooms, sliced
1 tablespoon cornstarch
¼ cup water
½ pound tofu
¼ teaspoon crushed red
  pepper
3 slices fresh gingerroot,
  dime-size
1 whole black peppercorn

1. Bring the stock to a boil in a large pot. Add the carrot, cabbage, and celery, and bring back to a boil. Then reduce the heat to medium or medium low, and simmer, covered, for 10 minutes.
2. Add the bamboo shoots, tamari sauce or soy sauce, and the mushrooms.
3. Put the cornstarch in a small bowl, and stir in the water to make a smooth paste. Add this to the soup.
4. Bring the soup back to a gentle boil. Meanwhile, handling the tofu carefully, cut it into julienne strips, and add to the soup. The tofu will become firmer after it simmers for a short time.
5. Put the red pepper, gingerroot, and black pepper into a stainless steel teaball or a cheesecloth bag. Add to the soup, and let simmer for 10 minutes.
6. Remove the teaball or bag, and serve the soup at once, ladling the tofu carefully.

6 servings. Serving size is about 1½ cups.

Per Serving: 84 calories, 1 mg. cholesterol, 2 g. dietary fiber, 3 g. fat, 835 mg. sodium.

Potato-Tofu Salad

PREPARATION TIME: 20 MINUTES

As a complete lunch, this recipe will serve four. Use the sugar if you like a sweeter tasting salad. It is also good served on a bed of your favorite lettuce and garnished with sliced hard-boiled eggs.

(*Note:* No cooking time if potatoes have been previously cooked.)

6 medium red potatoes
¼ cup water
¼ cup vegetable oil
1 tablespoon lemon juice
2 tablespoons vinegar
2 teaspoons prepared mustard
2 teaspoons sugar (optional)

½ to 1 teaspoon salt
⅛ teaspoon garlic powder
1 pound tofu, crumbled
½ cup celery, sliced thinly
4 radishes, sliced thinly
¼ cup minced onion

1. Steam, microwave, or boil the potatoes until tender. Drain (if boiled) and let cool. (You can set the pan of potatoes over ice cubes to hurry this process, or put the potatoes in the refrigerator or freezer. Don't let them freeze though!) Trim any blemishes.
2. Meanwhile, place the water, oil, lemon juice, vinegar, mustard, sugar if desired, salt, and garlic powder in a blender or food processor and blend briefly to mix. Add the crumbled tofu, and blend until smooth.
3. When the potatoes are cool, dice them. Add the celery, radishes, and onions, tossing gently. Add the tofu mixture, and mix gently. Adjust the salt if necessary.

4 servings. Serving size is about 2 cups.

Per Serving: 309 calories, no cholesterol, 5 g. dietary fiber, 19 g. fat, 327 mg. sodium.

Tofu Stir-Fry

PREPARATION TIME: 6 MINUTES.   COOKING TIME: 20 MINUTES.

Serve this over cooked grain, along with a dark green or yellow vegetable on the side. See the introduction to the preceding recipe for Tofu Manicotti for directions on how to make your tofu firmer, if desired.

½ pound tofu, regular or firm
1 tablespoon peanut oil
 OR vegetable oil
1½ teaspoons tamari sauce
 OR soy sauce
½ cup celery, sliced thinly
1 cup coarsely shredded white
 cabbage

3 cups fresh bean sprouts
1 can (2½ ounces) water
 chestnuts, drained
1 tablespoon cornstarch
2 tablespoons water
1½ tablespoons tamari
 OR sauce soy sauce

1. Cut the tofu into pieces about ½-inch wide by ¼-inch thick by 1-inch long.
2. Heat the oil in a large frying pan or wok. Carefully place the pieces of tofu in the pan, side by side. Sprinkle with the 1½ teaspoons of tamari sauce. Fry over medium heat until the bottom of the tofu starts to brown. Carefully turn over, and cook the other side until it starts to brown. Remove the tofu, and set aside.
3. Add the celery and cabbage, and stir-fry for 3 minutes. Add the bean sprouts and water chestnuts, and stir-fry for 3 more minutes.
4. Mix the cornstarch with the water and the 1½ tablespoons of tamari sauce. Pour the mixture over the vegetables, and stir well. Add the tofu, mix gently, and cover. Steam for a few minutes, until the liquid has thickened and the tofu is hot. Serve immediately.

4 servings. Serving size is about 1½ cups.

Per Serving: 117 calories, no cholesterol, 3 g. dietary fiber, 6 g. fat, 26 mg. sodium.

Crêpes with Tofu Filling

PREPARATION TIME: 20 MINUTES.   COOKING TIME: 10 MINUTES.

1½ quarts water
1 pound tofu
Dash or two of lemon juice
Dash of salt
½ cup whole-wheat flour
½ cup all-purpose flour
1 teaspoon baking powder
1 tablespoon sugar
1 large egg

1¼ cups low—fat milk
½ teaspoon vanilla extract
1 to 2 tablespoons vegetable oil
1 package (10 ounces) frozen
  berries, thawed
½ cup plain low-fat yogurt
  (optional)
½ cup sour cream (optional)

1. In a 2-quart saucepan, bring the water to a boil. Gently crumble the tofu, and add to the boiling water. Reduce heat and let simmer for 1 minute. Drain in a mesh strainer until fairly dry, and stir in the lemon juice and salt. Set aside.
2. Combine the flours, baking powder, and sugar in a medium bowl.
3. In another bowl, beat the egg. Beat in the milk and vanilla, and add to the flour mixture. Stir until smooth.
4. Heat a small (5-inch) nonstick pan on medium heat. Place the oil in a small bowl, and brush the pan with a small amount of oil. Pour in a scant ¼ cup of the batter, tipping the pan around to spread the batter thinly and evenly. Cook over medium-high heat until the top is dry and the bottom is browned. Turn over using a pancake turner and cook for about 10 seconds.
5. Fill the crêpe with 2 tablespoons of tofu, roll up, and set in a warm oven as the others are cooked. When the crêpes are all cooked and assembled, top with about 2 tablespoons of berries. If you are using the yogurt and sour cream, blend them together in a small bowl, and top each serving with 2 tablespoons of the mixture.

8 crêpes. Serving size is 1 crêpe.

Per Serving: 211 calories, 42 mg. cholesterol, 5 g. dietary fiber, 10 g. fat, 96 mg. sodium.

Tofu "Cheesecake"

PREPARATION TIME: 20 MINUTES. COOKING TIME: 40 MINUTES.

¾ cup graham cracker crumbs
   (about 9 squares)
1 teaspoon brown sugar
1½ tablespoons melted butter
   OR margarine
1 pound tofu
2 eggs
1 tablespoon vegetable oil

½ cup sugar
¼ teaspoon salt
1 teaspoon vanilla
2 tablespoons all-purpose flour
8 ounces frozen strawberries
   OR other berries, thawed, OR
1 cup of unsweetened
applesauce

1. Preheat the oven to 350 degrees. Combine the crumbs, the brown sugar, and the melted butter or margarine in a small bowl. Press firmly into the bottom of an 8-inch pie pan. Bake for 10 minutes, then set aside and let cool.
2. Crumble the tofu into a blender or food processor. Add all the other ingredients except the fruit, and blend for about 3 minutes or until very smooth.
3. Pour the mixture into the cooled crust, and bake at 350 degrees for 40 minutes.
4. Turn off the oven, open the oven door, and let the pie stand in the open oven for 20 minutes. Then chill in the refrigerator overnight or at least 4 hours. Keep chilled until serving time. Just before serving, top with the fruit.

8 servings.

Per Serving: 196 calories, 74 mg. cholesterol, 2 g. dietary fiber, 8 g. fat, 159 mg. sodium.

Vegetable Side Dishes

Almost any cooked vegetable tastes fantastic simply steamed over hot water. You can eat them plain, or add a touch of salt and pepper if you wish. The naturally sweet flavor of fresh vegetables needs no other enhancement.

Here's how to steam vegetables: Put about an inch of water in a pot. Place a stainless steel, bamboo, or ceramic steamer in the water. (The stainless steel steamers are cheap, conduct heat quickly, and are available in almost any supermarket or cookware store.) Put the vegetables that need the longest cooking time in the steamer. Cover, and bring to a boil. Then reduce the heat to medium low, allowing the steam to cook the vegetables. After about 3 to 5 minutes, add the vegetables that need less cooking time.

Hard vegetables, such as carrots, broccoli, cauliflower, bell peppers, and so on, need about 10 to 20 minutes of cooking time, depending on how thinly you've sliced them, and how tender you like your vegetables to be. The less cooked they are, the more vitamins and minerals are retained, so getting them just barely tender is best. Onions, summer squashes, mushrooms, and similarly textured vegetables take less time, while spinach and other greens take only a minute or two.

Of course, it's also fun to doctor up the taste of fresh vegetables with seasonings and spices. We hope you enjoy the "fancier" recipes we have here. Most of them are really quite simple—fast yet festive. But if you're ever in such a rush that you don't want to bother with a recipe, plain steamed vegetables are the answer.

You can also use a microwave oven to good advantage with vegetables. If you have a microwave, check the instruction manual that came with it. Vegetables cooked in a microwave retain their nutrients better perhaps than through any other way of cooking.

To prepare vegetables for *any* cooking method, leave edible skins on most vegetables and fruits (such as potatoes, carrots, apples, tomatoes); the skins contain healthful fiber and nutrients. If your produce has been waxed for longer shelf-life, as is often the case these days with apples, try scraping the wax off with a paring knife, or washing the produce under hot, soapy water with a scrub brush. The wax is *supposed* to be harmless and quite edible (there is some controversy about that), but regardless, it seems to give an off-flavor to the peel.

Frozen vegetables are good to have on hand in case you run out of fresh ones. In terms of time, however, it really doesn't take longer to rinse a couple of squashes, slice them, and toss them in the steamer, than it does to unwrap a freezer package, take the vegetables out of the box, and put them in a pot with water.

Canned vegetables are usually overcooked, over-salted, or preserved with other ingredients you may wish to avoid, so check labels carefully.

Nutritionists formerly suggested that we have green or yellow vegetables every other day for their vitamin A content, but many are now changing and increasing that recommendation to a leafy green every day because of the additional calcium contained in greens. Collards, for example, are about as good a source of calcium as milk products—and they contain no fat! For the record, a recent survey of research in the journal *Contemporary Nutrition* suggests that oxalic acid in spinach does not prevent the absorption of calcium from that green to any appreciable extent. So, go to it, spinach lovers!

"Why, yes . . . we do have two children who won't eat their vegetables." *THE FAR SIDE.*
COURTESY CHRONICLE FEATURES, SAN FRANCISCO.

Spaghetti Squash Parmesan

PREPARATION TIME: 5 MINUTES.   COOKING TIME: 1 TO 1¼ HOURS.

1 whole spaghetti squash, about 8 inches long

2 tablespoons butter OR margarine

4 tablespoons grated Parmesan cheese

1 teaspoon garlic powder

1. Boil the whole squash in a large pot of water for about 1 hour to 1¼ hours or until tender, turning it every 15 minutes.
2. Cut the squash in half and remove the seeds. Scoop out the squash and toss with the remaining ingredients.

8 servings. Serving size is about ½ cup.

Per Serving: 90 calories, 10 mg. cholesterol, 4 g. dietary fiber, 4 g. fat, 81 mg. sodium.

Shades of Green

PREPARATION TIME: 8 MINUTES.   COOKING TIME: 15 TO 20 MINUTES.

2 stalks celery, sliced
½ green pepper, diced
3 scallions, chopped (separate
  white part from green)
1 tablespoon water

3 ounces green beans, cut into
  1-inch pieces
1 stalk broccoli, chopped into
  flowerets
1 large zucchini, sliced

1. In a covered pan, sauté/steam the celery, green pepper, and the white part of the scallions in the water until tender.
2. Add the green beans and steam until the beans are tender. Then add the broccoli, zucchini, and the green parts of the scallions. Steam until just tender, and serve.

4 servings. Serving size is about 1 ¼ cup.

Per Serving: 33 calories, no cholesterol, 3 g. dietary fiber, no fat, 16 mg. sodium.

Cherry Tomato Bake

PREPARATION TIME: 7 MINUTES.   COOKING TIME: 6 MINUTES.

Serve hot or cold, as a side dish, an appetizer, or a salad.

1 pint ripe cherry tomatoes
3 tablespoons scallion, diced
¼ cup fresh parsley, minced
1 medium clove garlic, crushed
¼ teaspoon thyme

½ teaspoon salt
⅛ teaspoon black pepper
2 tablespoons grated Parmesan
  cheese

1. Remove any stems from the tomatoes, and place the tomatoes in a baking dish. Sprinkle the scallions on top.
2. In a small bowl, combine the remaining ingredients. Sprinkle this mixture over the tomatoes.

3. Bake at 375 degrees for 3 minutes. Stir, turning the tomatoes, and bake an additional 3 minutes. Mix, and serve.

4 servings. Serving size is about ½ cup.

Per Serving: 31 calories, 2 mg. cholesterol, 2 g. dietary fiber, 1 g. fat, 322 mg. sodium.

Cheese-Baked Cauliflower

PREPARATION TIME: 15 MINUTES.   COOKING TIME: 10 MINUTES.

1 large head cauliflower   1 teaspoon dried dillweed
2 eggs   2 tablespoons grated Swiss
2 tablespoons skim milk   OR cheddar cheese

1. Trim the leaves and stem off the cauliflower, and steam
   · the whole head for about 10 to 15 minutes, until just tender. (If you don't have a steamer big enough, cut the cauliflower into chunks.)
2. Meanwhile, beat together the eggs, milk, dillweed, and cheese.
3. Place the cooked cauliflower in a casserole dish, and pour the egg mixture on top. Cover and bake at 375 degrees for about 10 minutes, until the egg has begun to set and the cheese has melted.

8 servings. Serving size is about ½ cup.

Per Serving: 56 calories, 70 mg. cholesterol, 3 g. dietary fiber, 2 g. fat, 38 mg. sodium.

Broccoli with Water Chestnuts

PREPARATION TIME: 5 MINUTES.   COOKING TIME: 10 TO 15 MINUTES.

1 onion, chopped
1 can (2½ ounces) water
  chestnuts, drained and
  chopped
1 tablespoon butter

1 small head fresh broccoli
OR 1 package (10 ounces)
  frozen chopped broccoli
Salt and fresh-ground black
  pepper to taste

1. Sauté onion and water chestnuts in butter until onion is translucent.
2. Add the broccoli. Cover and cook on low heat until the broccoli is tender. Add a small amount of water during cooking if necessary, to keep the vegetables from sticking to the pan.
3. Add salt and pepper to taste, or leave unseasoned so everyone can add their own at the table.

4 servings. Serving size is about ½ cup.

Per Serving: 61 calories, 8 mg. cholesterol, 3 g. dietary fiber, 3 g. fat, 183 mg. sodium.

Yellow Squash with Dill

PREPARATION TIME: 5 MINUTES.   COOKING TIME: 15 MINUTES.

This attractive and easy dish, created by my wife, Enid, is also delightful with zucchini; or try mixing the two types of squash.

4 to 6 yellow squash
1 medium onion, diced
1 tablespoon butter
  OR margarine

¼ teaspoon salt
Fresh-ground black pepper to
  taste
Dried or fresh dillweed to taste

1. Cut the larger summer squashes in halves or quarters; leave the small ones whole. Place the squash in a steamer over hot water, and let cook until tender.

2. Meanwhile, sauté the onion in the butter or margarine until translucent. Add the seasonings.
3. When the squash is done, place it in a serving bowl, top with the seasoned onions, and serve.

4 servings. Serving size is about 1 cup.

Per Serving: 79 calories, 8 mg. cholesterol, 5 g. dietary fiber, 4 g. fat, 167 mg. sodium.

Ginger Carrots

PREPARATION TIME: 10 MINUTES.   COOKING TIME: 30 MINUTES.

This is a mild recipe that goes well with just about any main course. However, if you like your carrots spicier, add more ginger to taste.

8 medium carrots (4 cups, sliced)
1 tablespoon butter
  OR margarine

2 teaspoons lemon juice
1 teaspoon fresh gingerroot, minced

1. Scrub the carrots well and slice into julienne strips. Heat a skillet on medium heat, and add the butter. When the butter is melted, reduce the heat to low, and add the remaining ingredients.
2. Cover the skillet, and sauté/steam about 25 minutes, stirring occasionally, until the carrots are tender. Add a little bit of water if necessary to prevent sticking.

8 servings. Serving size is about ½ cup.

Per Serving: 31 calories, 4 mg. cholesterol, 1 g. dietary fiber, 2 g. fat, 41 mg. sodium.

Sautéed Zucchini (Villa Romano)

PREPARATION TIME: 5 MINUTES.   COOKING TIME: 8 TO 10 MINUTES.

This recipe from the Villa Romano illustrates how a small amount of butter, when mixed with an oil and seasoning (in this case, olive oil and basil), can add flavor.

2 teaspoons butter
2 tablespoons minced shallots
2 teaspoons minced garlic
1 large OR 2 small zucchini, sliced into rounds (about 4 cups raw slices)
1 teaspoon dried basil

OR 2 tablespoons fresh, chopped
Coarse fresh-ground black pepper to taste
Pinch of salt
1 teaspoon olive oil (extra-virgin if available)

1. Melt the butter in a skillet over medium heat. Add the shallots, garlic, and zucchini. Sauté for 3 to 4 minutes.
2. Season with the basil, pepper, and salt, and cook 3 to 4 additional minutes, until zucchini is cooked but still firm.
3. Sprinkle the olive oil over all, stir well, and serve.

4 servings. Serving size is about ½ cup.

Per Serving: 47 calories, 5 mg. cholesterol, 1 g. dietary fiber, 3 g. fat, 75 mg. sodium.

Sunshine Vegetable Medley

PREPARATION TIME: 8 MINUTES.   COOKING TIME: 30 TO 35 MINUTES.

1 tablespoon olive oil
1 medium yellow onion, sliced
1 large tomato, chopped
1 pound yellow squash, sliced (about 3 cups raw)
½ pound carrots, sliced (about 1½ cups raw)

2 medium red or yellow bell peppers, cut into chunks
1 teaspoon Traditional Italian Herb Blend (p. 335)

1. Heat the oil in a large skillet over medium heat. Add the onions, and sauté until onions are translucent.
2. Add the tomatoes, and reduce the heat to low. Cover, and sauté/steam for 3 minutes.
3. Add the remaining ingredients, and continue cooking until vegetables are just tender, about 20 to 25 minutes. Add a little water if necessary to prevent sticking.

6 servings. Serving size is about 1 cup.

Per Serving: 73 calories, no cholesterol, 4 g. dietary fiber, 3 g. fat, 32 mg. sodium.

Honey-Nut Glazed Carrots

PREPARATION TIME: 5 MINUTES.   COOKING TIME: 20 MINUTES.

2 cups carrots, sliced into rounds ¼-inch thick
Water
2 teaspoons sliced almonds

1 teaspoon butter
2 teaspoons honey
Dash nutmeg

1. Steam the carrots over a small amount of water until just tender.
2. Heat a small skillet over medium heat. Measure the almonds into the skillet and toast, stirring constantly, until golden brown. Remove the pan from the heat and remove the almonds, setting aside.
3. When the carrots are done, melt the butter in the same skillet you used for the almonds. Add 2 to 3 teaspoons of liquid from the steaming carrots, and add the carrots.
4. Stir in the honey and toasted almonds until the carrots are well coated. Sprinkle with nutmeg, and serve.

4 servings. Serving size is ½ cup.

Per Serving: 63 calories, 3 mg. cholesterol, 3 g. dietary fiber, 2 g. fat, 62 mg. sodium.

Eggplant Stove-Top Casserole

PREPARATION TIME: 5 MINUTES.　　　　COOKING TIME: 20 MINUTES.

1 medium eggplant (about 1
　pound)
1 tablespoon vegetable oil
1 teaspoon instant beef bouillon
　granules
¼ cup water

2 stalks celery, chopped
1 small onion, diced
½ teaspoon salt
⅛ teaspoon cardamom
1 tablespoon unsalted,
　dry-roasted peanuts, chopped

1. Cut eggplant into ¾-inch cubes.
2. Heat the oil in a large skillet, add the eggplant, and toss to coat.
3. Mix the bouillon and water, and add to the pan. Cover and let cook over medium-low heat for 15 minutes, stirring every 5 minutes or so.
4. Stir in the remaining ingredients, cover, and cook an additional 5 minutes.

6 servings. Serving size is about ½ cup.

Per Serving: 48 calories, no cholesterol, 3 g. dietary fiber, 3 g. fat, 193 mg. sodium.

Beans with Tomato Sauce

PREPARATION TIME: 10 MINUTES.　　　　COOKING TIME: 1 TO 4 HOURS,
　　　　　　　　　　　　　　　　　DEPENDING ON VARIETY OF BEANS.

½ pound dried beans (red, or
　your choice)
Water OR stock
1 medium onion
6 whole cloves
2 cloves garlic, pressed
1 can (10½ ounces) tomato
　sauce OR 1⅜ cup Real

Italian Tomato Sauce (pp.
　290–91)
½ teaspoon basil
2 tablespoons red wine
Meat scraps (optional)
Fresh-ground black pepper to
　taste

1. Soak the beans overnight, covered with water or stock, together with the onion, in which you have stuck the cloves. Remove the cloves from the onion and discard them before cooking the beans.
2. Bring the beans together with the onion to a boil, covered, then reduce heat and simmer until fork-tender (this can take from one to several hours, depending on the variety of beans you have chosen). Add water as needed to keep the beans covered during cooking.
3. Pour off any remaining liquid from the cooked beans, and save it to be used as stock for other dishes. Then add the garlic, tomato sauce, basil, and remaining ingredients. Blend, and simmer for about 30 minutes. Depending upon the sauce you use, you may wish to add a dash of salt, and if you like your beans hot, a dash of cayenne pepper.

8 servings. Serving size is about ¹/₂ cup.

Per Serving: 82 calories, no mg. cholesterol, 7 g. dietary fiber, no fat, 63 mg. sodium.

Spinach Bake

PREPARATION TIME: 15 MINUTES.   COOKING TIME: 30 MINUTES.

This recipe is easy to prepare.

2 pounds fresh
  OR 1 package (10 ounces)
  frozen spinach, cooked and
  drained
1 cup fresh mushrooms, sliced

¹/₂ cup mozzarella cheese,
  diced
¹/₂ teaspoon salt
¹/₄ teaspoon fresh pepper
1 teaspoon basil

1. Mix all ingredients thoroughly and bake at 350 degrees for 30 minutes.

6 servings. Serving size is about ¹/₃ cup.

Per Serving: 47 calories, 8 mg. cholesterol, 2 g. dietary fiber, 3 g. fat, 258 mg. sodium.

Fresh Beets

Many of us are used to canned beets, and have never bothered to cook fresh beets ourselves. Yet it's as easy as baking a potato. You can also boil beets, a slightly messier but quicker method. Try them either way, plain or with a dollop of plain low-fat yogurt and a dash of salt and pepper. Or use them in another beet recipe. Beware the beet juice, as it is a powerful staining agent!

To bake:

PREPARATION TIME: 5 MINUTES.   COOKING TIME: 1½ HOURS.

1 pound fresh beets   **Aluminum foil**

1. Preheat the oven to 350 degrees. Wash the fresh beets, trim off the stems, and tightly wrap each beet in aluminum foil. Place them in the oven for about 1½ hours.
2. Remove the beets from the oven and unwrap the foil. Peel the beets with a knife or paring knife as soon as they're cool enough to handle, and enjoy!

To boil:

PREPARATION TIME: 5 MINUTES.   COOKING TIME: 35 MINUTES.

1. Place the washed, trimmed beets in a kettle and cover with cold water. Bring to a boil and simmer, uncovered, about 35 minutes, or until the beets are tender.
2. Pour the beets in a colander and run cold water over them to stop the cooking process, drain, and peel.

4 servings. Serving size is about ½ cup.

Per Serving: 35 calories, no cholesterol, 3 g. dietary fiber, no fat, 56 mg. sodium.

Sweet Spiced Beets

PREPARATION TIME: (USING FRESH BEETS) 30 MINUTES.   COOKING TIME:
10 MINUTES.

Here's a recipe that calls for boiling fresh beets. You can use canned if you're in a hurry; just skip the first two steps, add the raisins and cloves with the ginger, and the beets later. Delicious hot or cold.

1 pound small fresh beets,
  washed and trimmed
Water to cover
3 whole cloves
¼ cup raisins
Dash allspice
2 teaspoons butter
  OR margarine

1 slice fresh gingerroot, ¼-inch
  thick, minced
1 teaspoon grated orange
  OR lemon rind
1 teaspoon red wine vinegar
2 teaspoons honey

1. Place the beets in water to cover in a saucepan. Bring to a boil, add the cloves, and reduce the heat to simmer. Let cook, uncovered, for 20 minutes. Add the raisins and allspice and cook 5 minutes more.
2. Drain, and rinse with cold water until the beets are cool enough to handle. Peel, and cut them into bite-size chunks.
3. Heat a large saucepan over medium heat. Add the butter. When the butter is melted, add the ginger, orange or lemon rind, and vinegar, and cook, covered, about 5 minutes.
4. Add the beets and raisins, and the honey. Stir, and cook until heated through.

4 servings. Serving size is about ½ cup.

Per Serving: 95 calories, 5 mg. cholesterol, 3 g. dietary fiber, 2 g. fat, 77 mg. sodium.

Poached Vegetables with Shallots (Arthur's)

PREPARATION TIME: 3 MINUTES.   COOKING TIME: 5 MINUTES.

The chef at Arthur's restaurant suggests trying this with carrots, yellow squash, or zucchini.

¼ cup water
¼ cup white wine
1 teaspoon chopped shallots

½ cup vegetable of choice
Dash salt, pepper
Herbs to taste

1. Put the water, wine, and shallots in a hot frying pan and simmer for 1 minute on medium heat.
2. Add the ½ cup vegetables, cover, and simmer for 2 minutes. Add the seasonings, and serve at once.

1 serving.

Per Serving (with yellow squash): 14 calories, no cholesterol, 1 g. dietary fiber, no fat, 100 mg. sodium (with dash of salt). If you use carrots, the calories will be about 25 per ½ cup.

Kohlrabi

PREPARATION TIME: 8 MINUTES.   COOKING TIME: 20 MINUTES.

Some say kohlrabi tastes like a cross between an artichoke and a mild turnip. Others compare it to cabbages, radishes, and cucumbers (singly or combined). We have decided that kohlrabi tastes like kohlrabi; try expanding your vegetable repertoire to include it. For variety, you might occasionally substitute it in recipes that call for some of the other vegetables listed above. Buy the small knobs of kohlrabi, which are more tender than the larger ones. Here is the basic recipe for cooking them.

16 small kohlrabi   Boiling water

1. Wash the kohlrabi, cut off and reserve the tops, and pare the knobs.

2. Slice and drop the knobs into a small amount of boiling water. Cook, uncovered, about 20 minutes. Drain.
3. Meanwhile, in another pot, boil the tops of the kohlrabi, and drain when tender.
4. Finely chop the tops and add to the cooked knobs.

4 servings. Serving size is 4 kohlrabi.

Per Serving: 66 calories, no cholesterol, 3 g. dietary fiber, no fat, 47 mg. sodium.

Brussels Sprouts with Wine Sauce

PREPARATION TIME: 7 MINUTES. COOKING TIME: 20 MINUTES.

2 cups fresh Brussels sprouts
  OR 1 package frozen (10 ounces), thawed
¼ cup white wine
1 teaspoon lemon juice

8 fresh mushrooms, sliced
¼ teaspoon salt
Fresh-ground black pepper to taste
Dash oregano

1. Place the trimmed sprouts, wine, and lemon juice in a saucepan, cover, and heat over medium-low heat for 10 minutes.
2. Add the mushrooms and seasonings. Cover and let simmer for another 10 minutes, or until sprouts and mushrooms are tender.

4 servings. Serving size is ½ cup sprouts, plus sauce.

Per Serving: 35 calories, no cholesterol, 3 g. dietary fiber, no fat, 142 mg. sodium.

Chinese Cabbage Stir-Fry

PREPARATION TIME: 12 MINUTES.   COOKING TIME: 10 MINUTES.

This vegetable combination is especially good with Oriental Pork Chops (p. 148).

1 small head fresh
   OR 1 package (10 ounces)
   frozen cauliflower
¼ cup water
2 teaspoons peanut oil
1 cup Chinese cabbage (or
   other cabbage), chopped

¼ bell pepper, diced
¼ cup chopped mushrooms
½ teaspoon salt
1 teaspoon tamari sauce
   OR soy sauce
1 tablespoon dry-roasted,
   unsalted peanuts, chopped

1. Partially cook the cauliflower in the water, about 7 minutes.
2. Brush a wok or skillet with the oil, and heat over medium to medium-high heat. Add the cauliflower and cabbage, and stir. Add the remaining ingredients and cook, stirring often, until tender.

4 servings. Serving size is about ½ cup.

Per Serving: 52 calories, no cholesterol, 2 g. dietary fiber, 4 g. fat, 375 mg. sodium.

Carrot Crunch

PREPARATION TIME: 15 MINUTES.   COOKING TIME: 20 MINUTES.

The carrots in this recipe stay slightly crunchy—very satisfying for those who are cutting back on food intake and feel the urge to do a lot of chewing!

2 teaspoons olive oil
1½ tablespoons onion, diced
1 egg
¼ cup skim milk
½ teaspoon salt
½ teaspoon fresh-ground black
   pepper

1 teaspoon oregano
1 small clove garlic, crushed
1 teaspoon Traditional Italian
   Herb Blend (p. 335)
2 cups grated carrots

¾ cup frozen peas (you may use a 10-ounce package and reserve the leftover peas for another recipe)

1. Brush a skillet with oil, heat over medium heat, and add onions. Sauté, stirring constantly, until onions are translucent.
2. Beat together the egg and milk. Add the seasonings. Blend in the cooked onions and grated carrots. Pour the mixture into a casserole dish, and bake at 350 degrees for 20 minutes.
3. While the casserole is baking, cook the peas according to package directions, but without added salt.
4. Stir the cooked peas into the carrots, mixing well.

6 servings. Serving size is about ½ cup.

Per Serving: 72 calories, 46 mg. cholesterol, 4 g. dietary fiber, 3 g. fat, 247 mg. sodium.

Zucchini with Olives

PREPARATION TIME: 5 MINUTES.   COOKING TIME: 10 MINUTES.

This is another recipe that can be served hot or cold.

2 medium zucchinis
1 tablespoon olive oil
1 large clove garlic, crushed
6 black olives, diced

1 teaspoon dried parsley
¼ teaspoon salt
¼ teaspoon black pepper
½ teaspoon marjoram

1. Wash and dice the zucchini.
2. Heat the oil in a saucepan. Stir in all ingredients, and reduce the heat to low. Cook, covered, for about 10 minutes.

4 servings. Serving size is about ⅔ cup.

Per Serving: 70 calories, no cholesterol, 3 g. dietary fiber, 5 g. fat, 188 mg. sodium.

Brussels Sprouts in Light Béchamel Sauce

PREPARATION TIME: 5 MINUTES.   COOKING TIME: 10 MINUTES.

Small, baby Brussels sprouts have a tender, more delicate flavor than the full-grown ones, although you may use full-grown instead if they are all you can find.

4 cups fresh Brussels sprouts
¼ cup water
1 teaspoon basil
1 tablespoon butter
   OR margarine

1 tablespoon all-purpose flour
1 cup low-fat milk
2 to 4 cloves garlic, minced or
   crushed
Pinch of chervil (optional)

1. Wash the Brussels sprouts, and pull off any yellowing leaves, then trim the ends, and make a small gash in the bottom of each one to help them cook to tenderness. Place them in a saucepan with the water and the basil, and bring to a boil. Then reduce heat and simmer for about 10 minutes.
2. Melt the butter or margarine in a large skillet over medium-low heat. Add the flour and brown, stirring constantly, to form a roux. Stir in the milk and garlic, and cook until the sauce has thickened slightly. Serve over the cooked Brussels sprouts. (This makes about 1 cup sauce.)

8 servings. Serving size is ½ cup sprouts, with 2 tablespoons of sauce.

Per Serving: 64 calories, 7 mg. cholesterol, 3 g. dietary fiber, 2 g. fat, 37 mg. sodium.

Oven-Fried Potato Sticks

PREPARATION TIME: 8 MINUTES.   COOKING TIME: 35 MINUTES.

Potatoes are a powerhouse when it comes to nutritional value: they are good-to-excellent sources of protein, phosphorus, thiamine, niacin, vitamin C, potassium, and a broad array of other vitamins and minerals. You could survive for months, possibly years, on potatoes alone, plus some green vegetables, and a small amount of dairy products! We eat a lot of potatoes, usually just baked, but here is a recipe for people (like ourselves) who just can't do without something that resembles a french fry occasionally.

4 medium potatoes
1 tablespoon oil
⅛ teaspoon garlic powder
⅛ teaspoon onion powder

1½ teaspoons paprika
¼ teaspoon salt
¼ teaspoon black pepper

1. Wash the potatoes well, and slice them lengthwise into strips, leaving the skins on.
2. Line a shallow baking pan with foil, and put all the ingredients into the pan, tossing well to coat the potatoes with the oil and seasonings.
3. Bake at 425 degrees for about 35 minutes, stirring often, until the potatoes are tender. Adjust the seasoning if necessary.

4 servings of about 1 cup each.

Per Serving: 178 calories, no cholesterol, 4 g. dietary fiber, 4 g. fat, 142 mg. sodium.

Creamy Potatoes with Herbs

PREPARATION TIME: 25 MINUTES.   COOKING TIME: 35 MINUTES.

4 medium potatoes, unpeeled,
  boiled or baked until tender
6 ounces Neufchatel cheese,
  softened
¼ cup skim or low-fat milk
1 egg
½ teaspoon basil

½ teaspoon thyme
½ teaspoon salt
½ teaspoon fresh-ground black
  pepper
1 medium bell pepper, diced
Nonstick vegetable cooking
  spray

1. Mash potatoes in a large bowl. Using an electric mixer, blend potatoes with Neufchatel, milk, egg, and seasonings.
2. Stir in diced bell pepper.
3. Place mixture in 8-inch square baking dish that has been sprayed with cooking spray. Bake uncovered at 350 degrees for 35 minutes.

10 servings. Serving size is about ½ cup.

Per Serving: 114 calories, 41 mg. cholesterol, 2 g. dietary fiber, 5 g. fat (with low-fat milk), 188 mg. sodium.

Sweet Potato Strudel

PREPARATION TIME: 15 MINUTES.   COOKING TIME: 50 MINUTES.

3 medium sweet potatoes
  OR yams
1 tablespoon vegetable oil
4 tablespoons grated Parmesan
  cheese

1 tablespoon toasted sesame
  seeds
1 teaspoon dried parsley
¼ teaspoon black pepper
¼ teaspoon salt

1. Peel and slice the raw sweet potatoes as thinly as possible.
2. Measure oil into a small bowl.
3. Combine the dry ingredients in another small bowl.
4. Layer one-quarter of the potatoes in a casserole dish, brushing the tops of the potatoes lightly with oil as you go, using a pastry brush. Then sprinkle about a tablespoon of the Parmesan cheese mixture on top.

5. Repeat step 4 until potatoes and cheese are used up.
6. Bake, covered, at 425 degrees for 30 minutes. Uncover, and bake about 20 minutes more, until browned on top.

6 servings. Serving size is about ½ cup.

Per Serving: 125 calories, 3 mg. cholesterol, 2 g. dietary fiber, 5 g. fat, 164 mg. sodium.

Dill Potatoes

PREPARATION TIME: 5 MINUTES.　　　COOKING TIME: 20 MINUTES.

This recipe is simple, tasty, and filling.

4 medium potatoes, cut into chunks
¾ cup vegetable OR meat stock

1 teaspoon dried dillweed
¼ teaspoon salt (optional)
Fresh-ground black pepper to taste

1. Place all ingredients except salt and pepper in a saucepan and bring to a boil. Then lower the heat to simmer and cook until the potatoes are tender and the broth has reduced somewhat.
2. Mash potatoes just a little with a fork, add the salt (if desired) and the pepper, and serve.

4 servings. Serving size is about 1 cup, plus broth.

Per Serving: 123 calories, no cholesterol, 3 g. dietary fiber, no fat, 281 mg. sodium.

Orange-Glazed Sweet Potatoes

PREPARATION TIME: 5 MINUTES.   COOKING TIME: 35 TO 45 MINUTES.

Potatoes, sweet potatoes, and winter squashes are considered to be "grains" rather than "vegetables" in the famous Four-Food-Group plan because of their starch content, which makes them somewhat higher in calories. But, in contrast with grains, sweet potatoes (and winter squash) are high in vitamins A and C, and potassium. A boiled sweet potato has 30 percent less calories than a baked sweet potato because some of the sugars are dissolved in the water.

4 medium sweet potatoes	¼ teaspoon cinnamon
Boiling water to cover	⅛ teaspoon salt
¼ cup orange juice	

1. Wash the sweet potatoes, and drop them in enough boiling water to cover them. Cover the pan. When the water comes to a boil again, reduce the heat to low, and cook until tender.
2. Drain the potatoes, let cool for a few minutes, and peel. (Rinsing in tepid water will help make them cool enough to hold.)
3. In a medium saucepan, combine the orange juice, cinnamon, salt, and cooked sweet potatoes. Cook over low heat, stirring occasionally, until most of the juice is gone, about 6 to 7 minutes.

4 servings of 1 potato each.

Per Serving: 167 calories, no cholesterol, 4 g. dietary fiber, no fat, 84 mg. sodium.

Spanish Rice

PREPARATION TIME: 10 MINUTES.   COOKING TIME: 1 HOUR.

1 tablespoon olive oil
½ cup brown rice, uncooked
½ cup chopped onions
1¼ cups canned tomatoes
1 medium green bell pepper,
  chopped fine

1 clove garlic, minced or
  crushed
¼ teaspoon salt
1 teaspoon paprika

1. Heat the oil in a large skillet on medium heat. Add the rice and cook until browned, stirring constantly. Add the onions, and cook until golden, still stirring constantly. Add a little water if necessary to prevent sticking.
2. Place the rice and onions in the top part of a double boiler, and set it over boiling water. Add the remaining ingredients to the rice, cover, and steam for about 1 hour.

4 servings. Serving size is about ¾ cup.

Per Serving: 141 calories, no cholesterol, 2 g. dietary fiber, 4 g. fat, 260 mg. sodium.

Yellow Rice

PREPARATION TIME: 5 MINUTES.   COOKING TIME: 15 MINUTES.

1 medium onion, diced
1 clove garlic, crushed
4 large mushrooms, diced
¼ teaspoon salt
¼ teaspoon pepper
¼ teaspoon turmeric
1 tablespoon fresh parsley,
  minced

1 tablespoon oil
2 cups cooked brown rice
⅓ cup golden raisins
¼ cup chopped unsalted,
  dry-roasted nuts

1. Sauté the onions, garlic, mushrooms, and seasonings in the oil in a large skillet until onions are translucent.
2. Stir in the rice, raisins, and nuts. Heat through, and serve.

6 servings. Serving size is about 1 cup.

Per Serving: 164 calories, no cholesterol, 3 g. dietary fiber, 5 g. fat, 93 mg. sodium.

Zucchini–Brown Rice Pilaf

PREPARATION TIME: 15 MINUTES.   COOKING TIME: 20 MINUTES.

This dish has a remarkable taste, similar to a clam sauce. Try making it without the rice sometime. You can pour the sauce over linguine. You may need to thicken it with a tablespoon or more of cornstarch, however.

2 medium zucchinis
1 tablespoon olive oil
2 cloves garlic, minced or
   crushed
1 cup brown rice, uncooked

1½ cups stock
½ cup dry white wine
1 bay leaf
1 teaspoon dried basil

1. Wash and dice the zucchini. Sauté it in the oil and garlic, then remove it from the pan.
2. Add the rice to the pan, stirring to coat the grains with whatever oil is remaining. Add the stock, wine, and bay leaf, and bring to a boil. Add the basil, and return the zucchini to the pan. Cover, and let simmer until rice is tender, about 20 minutes.

6 servings. Serving size is about ½ cup.

Per Serving: 173 calories, no cholesterol, 5 g. dietary fiber, 4 g. fat, 373 mg. sodium.

Sauces

Looking through the sauce recipes in the average cookbook is almost like watching a contest to see how much butterfat a chef can squeeze into a sauce using, well, nothing but butter. In fact, usually there are recipes for herb butters, garlic butters, and a host of cream sauces with a base of heavy cream and, you guessed it, butter.

We like butter as well as anyone, but find that small amounts mixed with a bit of olive oil, and with herbs and spices, do perfectly well for flavor, and are much easier on the arteries!

You will see that our sauces rely more on seasonings or wine than on butter and cream. As always, we substitute skim or low-fat milk for cream, sometimes in combination with yogurt. We also use yogurt alone, or in a mixture of part sour cream, part yogurt, which is higher in fat, but milder in taste than plain yogurt (see especially Mushroom Sauce, pp. 294–95).

We also include a low-fat béchamel sauce in our vegetable side dishes section (see Brussels Sprouts in Light Béchamel Sauce, p. 282), which can be used with other vegetables or on fish.

Barbecue Sauce

PREPARATION TIME: 15 MINUTES.   COOKING TIME: 30 MINUTES.

This sauce will keep for about a week and a half in the refrigerator. Liquid smoke is usually available in the condiments section of supermarkets.

1 can (12 ounces) tomato paste	2 tablespoons brown sugar
⅓ cup dry red wine (OR substitute water)	1 tablespoon honey
	2 teaspoons liquid smoke
1½ cups water OR stock	1 teaspoon garlic powder
	1 tablespoon chili powder
2 tablespoons red wine vinegar	1 tablespoon dry mustard
2 teaspoons lemon juice	Crushed red pepper to taste
½ medium onion, chopped fine	Dash of Tabasco
½ medium bell pepper, chopped fine	2 tablespoons fresh parsley, minced
1 tablespoon Worcestershire sauce	¼ teaspoon celery seed
	½ teaspoon salt (optional)

1. Combine all ingredients except parsley and celery seed (and salt, if you're using any) in a large kettle or saucepan. Bring to a low boil, then reduce heat and simmer about 20 minutes.
2. Add the parsley, celery seed, and salt if desired, and simmer for another 5 minutes or so.

Makes about 1 quart. Serving size is 1 tablespoon.

Per Serving (without added salt, and using water): 8 calories, no cholesterol, no dietary fiber, no fat, 5 mg. sodium.

Real Italian Tomato Sauce

PREPARATION TIME: 10 MINUTES.   COOKING TIME: 1 HOUR.

The Italians we have met tell us that the only *real* Italian tomato sauce uses basil, garlic, a bit of salt and pepper, and maybe a bay leaf for seasonings. That's all. No oregano!

Here is our favorite basic sauce. This sauce can be used for any recipe calling for tomato sauce, from pasta to eggplant to fish. It's wonderful with our Sage Sausage or Meatballs (p. 192). You can leave out the mushrooms if you prefer; we just happen to like mushrooms.

If you don't care if your tomato sauce is authentically Italian, try adding about a teaspoon of crushed, dried red pepper. This gives the sauce a little bite.

Also, look for the no-salt-added variety of canned tomato products if you're trying to cut down on salt.

You can store this in a tightly sealed container in the refrigerator for up to a week, or freeze it indefinitely in freezer containers for later use.

1 tablespoon olive oil
1 medium onion, cut in chunks
8 ounces fresh mushrooms, sliced or quartered
1 to 3 *tablespoons* dried basil (even more if you use fresh!)
2 large cloves garlic, crushed or minced
1 large bay leaf
1 can (28 ounces) whole tomatoes
1 can (10¾ ounces) tomato purée
1 can (6 ounces) tomato paste
Salt and fresh-ground black pepper to taste

1. Heat a large kettle on medium heat. Put in the oil, onion, mushrooms, basil, and garlic. Cover, and reduce the heat to medium low. Stir frequently—you may need to add a tablespoon or two of water to keep it from sticking.
2. When the onions are translucent, add the remaining ingredients, except the salt and pepper. Bring to a boil on high heat, then reduce to simmer and let cook for an hour or so, stirring occasionally.
3. Add salt and pepper to taste.

Makes about 6 cups. Serving size is 1 cup.

Per Serving: 110 calories, no cholesterol, 4 g. dietary fiber, 3 g. fat, 326 mg. sodium.

"He's on a diet. Tell him he looks thin." DRAWING
BY MODELL; © 1984 THE NEW YORKER
MAGAZINE, INC.

Roux

PREPARATION TIME: 1 MINUTE.   COOKING TIME: 5 TO 10 MINUTES.

This roux can be used to thicken soups, sauces, or just about
any cooked item that needs thickening. It is also the basis for
gravies.

1 tablespoon vegetable oil   or whole wheat or
  OR other butter   combination)
2 tablespoons flour (all-purpose

1. Heat the oil in a skillet over medium heat. Slowly add the
   flour, stirring constantly. Cook until golden brown, stirring constantly. Stir into the main recipe.

Gravy

PREPARATION TIME: 1 MINUTE.   COOKING TIME: 20 TO 30 MINUTES.

Add to the above roux 1 cup of stock, and stir over medium-low
to medium heat until thickened. Season your gravy with a dash

of salt and fresh-ground black pepper if desired; we like to add a few pinches of rosemary, sage, marjoram, and/or thyme to our yearly Thanksgiving turkey gravy. Sodium content will vary with the stock you use and the amount of salt. We use ¼ teaspoon salt and a low-sodium, homemade stock.

Makes about 1 cup. Serving size is ⅛ cup.

Per Serving: 22 calories, no cholesterol, no dietary fiber, 2 g. fat, 63 mg. sodium.

Nutty Pesto

PREPARATION TIME: 10 MINUTES.

Many pesto recipes combine basil, huge amounts of oil, and sometimes pine nuts. The resulting mixture is then tossed with cooked pasta. The recipe below is a lot lighter on the oil, and goes well with cooked vermicelli, baked potatoes, and other cooked vegetables or grains. (If you were to use butter or oil alone on a potato for flavoring instead of this sauce, it would have over twice the calories of this mixture, per tablespoon.)

½ cup unsalted, raw nuts (almonds, pecans, whatever you like)
¼ cup fresh parsley
½ cup fresh basil leaves
  OR ¼ cup dried basil

2 cloves garlic, chopped
2 tablespoons olive oil
¼ teaspoon salt (optional)

1. Blend all ingredients in a food processor or blender.

Makes about ¾ cup. Serving size is 1 tablespoon.

Per Serving: 58 calories, no cholesterol, 1 g. dietary fiber, 6 g. fat, 1 mg sodium.

Savory Spoon-Topping

PREPARATION TIME: 5 MINUTES.   COOKING TIME: 12 TO 15 MINUTES.

Try sprinkling this on baked potatoes, hot cooked vegetables, salads, or cottage cheese. Or mix it into dips or meat loaves for added flavor and fiber.

2 tablespoons Worcestershire sauce
1 tablespoon lemon juice

½ teaspoon hot pepper sauce
2 cups All-Bran cereal

1. Mix together the Worcestershire sauce, lemon juice, and hot pepper sauce, blending thoroughly. Pour the cereal into a large bowl, and pour the sauce over it. Immediately toss to moisten evenly.
2. Spread evenly on a lightly greased baking sheet.
3. Bake at 325 degrees until dry and crisp, about 12 to 15 minutes. Cool completely, and store in an airtight container.

Makes about 2 cups. Serving size is 1 tablespoon.

Per Serving: 15 calories, no cholesterol, 2 g. dietary fiber, no fat, 60 mg. sodium.

Mushroom Sauce

PREPARATION TIME: 10 MINUTES.   COOKING TIME: 15 TO 20 MINUTES.

Though you may prepare this sauce with yogurt alone, the tartness of the yogurt is mellowed by the addition of a small amount of sour cream. If you are being especially careful about fat in your diet, replace the ½ cup sour cream with ¼ cup more yogurt and ¼ cup skim milk. The milk also helps reduce the tart taste.

Serve the sauce over baked or boiled potatoes, cooked grain, or pasta.

1 tablespoon olive oil
12 ounces fresh mushrooms, sliced
2 medium onions, sliced or diced
2 cloves garlic, minced or crushed
2 cups plain low-fat yogurt
1 tablespoon cornstarch

½ cup sour cream
1 tablespoon tamari sauce
   OR soy sauce
2 teaspoons dried basil
1 teaspoon dried thyme
Fresh-ground black pepper to taste
6 pimientos, chopped (optional)

1. Heat a skillet over medium heat. Add the oil, mushrooms, onion, and garlic, and turn the heat to medium low. Cover, and let cook until onions are translucent, stirring occasionally.
2. Meanwhile, mix 1 tablespoon of the yogurt with the cornstarch, then mix in the rest of the yogurt. Stir in the sour cream, and set aside.
3. When the onions are done, remove from heat, and turn heat to low. Add tamari sauce and seasonings to the pan, stir, and add the yogurt-sour cream mixture.
4. Place the skillet back on the burner, and heat through. Do not boil.

Makes about 4 cups, or 4 main course servings over 1 cup of cooked grain or pasta, or 1 medium potato per serving. Makes 16 servings as a sauce for a side dish.

Per Serving (4): 215 calories, 20 mg. cholesterol, 3 g. dietary fiber, 12 g. fat, 359 mg. sodium.

Red Clam Sauce

PREPARATION TIME: 5 MINUTES.   COOKING TIME: 10 MINUTES.

For a quick, easy dinner, try this sauce over chicken. Simply place 4 skinned chicken breasts, or 8 thighs, in a casserole dish. Spread 1 cup of Red Clam Sauce on top of the chicken, cover, and bake at 350 degrees for about an hour. Delicious!

3 cups Real Italian Tomato
   Sauce (pp. 290–91)
¼ cup dry red wine (optional)
1 can (6½ ounces) minced
   clams, drained (reserve juice)

⅓ cup clam juice
2 teaspoons dried parsley

1. Heat the tomato sauce in a large saucepan. Stir in the remaining ingredients, and heat through. Serve over pasta or in any Italian recipe.

Makes 4 cups. Serving size is 1 cup.

Per Serving: 132 calories, 29 mg. cholesterol, 3 g. dietary fiber, 4 g. fat, 304 mg. sodium.

Basil-Tomato Sauce

PREPARATION TIME: 5 MINUTES.   COOKING TIME: 10 TO 15 MINUTES.

Here is a basic, traditional Italian tomato sauce in the manner of Chef Ramovich, at Nashville's Villa Romano. We've reduced the fat content and use it with our version of two of Chef Ramovich's specialties, *Capellini di angelo al filetto di pomodoro* (pp. 230–31) and the incredibly good *Linguine al frutti di mare* (pp. 224–25). If you can't get to the Villa Romano, well, the next best thing is to make it yourself.

1 tablespoon olive oil
   (extra-virgin if available)
4 to 5 cloves garlic,
   minced

1 large shallot, minced
1 medium can (28 ounces)
   Italian plum tomatoes,
   quartered,

OR 3 large ripe tomatoes,   Salt and coarse fresh-ground
skinned, seeded, and   black pepper to taste
chopped   ¼ cup fresh basil, chopped

1. Heat the oil over medium heat. Add the garlic and shallot, and sauté until wilted and golden. Add the tomatoes. Season with salt, pepper, and basil.

Makes about 2 to 3 cups, depending on the size of your tomatoes.

Per Recipe: 270 calories, no cholesterol, 11 g. dietary fiber, 15 g. fat, 578 mg. sodium (assuming ¼ teaspoon of added salt and fresh tomatoes. The recipe will contain about 25 mg. sodium if you add no salt, and about 1200 mg. sodium if you use canned tomatoes; ¼ teaspoon of salt contains about 550 mg. sodium.)

Seafood Sauce

PREPARATION TIME: 5 MINUTES.

This versatile sauce needs no cooking, and can be used as a dipping sauce for seafood, vegetables, even meat. Usually served unheated, it can be served hot. Add it to an Oriental-style dish in the final stages of cooking, and heat through.

1 cup catsup   ¼ cup water
2 tablespoons prepared mustard   ⅛ teaspoon Tabasco sauce
2 tablespoons tamari sauce
   OR soy sauce

1. Combine all ingredients, blending well. Store in the refrigerator.

Makes about 1½ cups. Serving size is 1 tablespoon.

Per Serving: 14 calories, no cholesterol, no dietary fiber, no fat, 221 mg. sodium.

Dijon Dressing

PREPARATION TIME: 5 MINUTES.

For meats, especially lamb, this pungent sauce is fantastic. Try it with Sesame-Ginger Lamb Chops (p. 160). The sauce is at its best when prepared a day ahead of time.

¼ cup Dijon mustard
¼ cup lemon juice
2 teaspoons tamari sauce
  OR soy sauce

1 teaspoon salt
1 teaspoon pepper
2 large cloves garlic, crushed

1. Combine all ingredients, and chill. Serve cold.

Makes about ½ cup. Serving size is 1 tablespoon.

Per Serving: 11 calories, no cholesterol, no dietary fiber, no fat, 450 mg. sodium.

Fresh Tomato Sauce with White Wine

PREPARATION TIME: 7 MINUTES.   COOKING TIME: 15 MINUTES.

This sauce is a good way to dress up leftovers of all kinds, as an accompaniment to simple baked chicken, fish, or other entrées and vegetables. With only 1 teaspoon of oil in the entire recipe, it is very low in fat. The fresh tomatoes add enough liquid to the sauté to keep the ingredients from sticking to the pan.

1 teaspoon vegetable oil
  OR olive oil
1 medium onion, diced
2 large tomatoes, diced
¼ green pepper, diced

4 ounces fresh mushrooms,
  sliced (about 1¼ cups)
¼ teaspoon salt
½ teaspoon pepper
1 tablespoon white wine

1. Brush a skillet with the oil, and heat over medium heat. Add the onions, stir, and cover. Sauté, stirring often, until onions are translucent.

2. Stir in the remaining ingredients, and let cook, covered, stirring occasionally, until vegetables are tender. Drain if you want a more solid sauce, or leave as is.

Makes about 2 1/2 cups. Serving size is about 1/2 cup.

Per Serving: 51 calories, no cholesterol, 3 g. dietary fiber, 3 g. fat, 98 mg. sodium.

Horseradish Sauce

PREPARATION TIME: 5 MINUTES.

Use this versatile low-fat sauce for topping baked potatoes, beets, or other cooked vegetables, as a sauce for meats, a dip for raw vegetables, or as a spread for sandwiches in place of or mixed with a little mayonnaise.

2 tablespoons pure horseradish　　**1/2 teaspoon dried dillweed**
1 cup plain low-fat yogurt　　**Salt and fresh-ground black**
2 tablespoons skim milk　　　　**pepper to taste**

1. Combine all ingredients, chill, and serve.

VARIATION: Omit dill and horseradish; use 2 tablespoons of chives instead.

Makes about 1 1/4 cups. Serving size is 1 tablespoon.

Per Serving: 8 calories, 1 mg. cholesterol, no dietary fiber, no fat, 37 mg. sodium.

Orange-Cranberry Sauce

PREPARATION TIME: 15 MINUTES.   COOKING TIME: 25 TO 30 MINUTES.

Fruit juice and rind replace much of the sugar that is normally called for in cranberry sauce recipes.

1 package (12 ounces) fresh cranberries
1 cup orange juice

½ cup sugar
Grated rind of 1 small orange

1. Rinse and drain the cranberries. Combine the orange juice, sugar, and orange rind in a saucepan and bring to a boil.
2. Add the cranberries. Bring to a boil again. Reduce the heat and let cook for 10 minutes, stirring occasionally. Remove from the heat, cover, and let cool. Refrigerate after the sauce reaches room temperature.

Makes about 2 cups. Serving size is ¼ cup.

Per Serving: 83 calories, no cholesterol, 4 g. dietary fiber, no fat, 1 mg. sodium.

Pineapple-Cranberry Sauce

PREPARATION TIME: 5 MINUTES.   COOKING TIME: 25 TO 30 MINUTES.

We like this sauce even better than the tasty orange version. Perhaps we have gone overboard by including two cranberry sauce recipes in this book, but since this is a "lifetime" cookbook, we wanted recipes that would be appropriate all year long. Most people tend to put on a few pounds over the Thanksgiving-Christmas-Chanukah holiday season, because goodies are so prevalent, but you can avoid gaining weight every year at holiday time by staying active and by preparing lower-calorie treats, such as this one. Once you taste this, you may want to serve cranberry sauce on all sorts of occasions.

1 package (12 ounces) fresh   Water
  cranberries   ½ cup sugar
1 can (16 ounces) crushed
  unsweetened pineapple

1. Rinse and drain the cranberries. Press the juice from the pineapple into a measuring cup, and add enough water to make 1 cup.
2. In a saucepan, combine the sugar and pineapple-juice mixture. Bring to a boil. Add the cranberries and bring to a boil again, then reduce the heat and boil for 10 minutes. Remove from the heat and let cool. Store refrigerated.

Makes about 4½ cups. Serving size is ¼ cup.

Per Serving: 48 calories, no cholesterol, 2 g. dietary fiber, no fat, 1 mg. sodium.

Apricot Sauce

PREPARATION TIME: 4 MINUTES.   COOKING TIME: 20 MINUTES.

This pungent, sweet sauce is good with lean pork. A small amount is enough; this is more like a relish than a sauce. You may substitute other nuts for the peanuts.

6 whole dried apricots, diced   ¼ teaspoon salt
Water   ¼ teaspoon pepper
1 tablespoon honey   1 tablespoon chopped, unsalted,
5 tablespoons white wine   dry-roasted peanuts
1 clove garlic, crushed

1. Cook the apricots in a small amount of water until tender.
2. In a small saucepan, heat the honey until warm. Add the wine, stirring well to blend. Add the remaining ingredients, along with the cooked apricots, and heat through.

Makes about ½ cup. Serving size is 1 tablespoon.

Per Serving: 28 calories, no cholesterol, 1 g. dietary fiber, no fat, 72 mg. sodium.

Breads and Muffins

BREADS

There is good reason to call bread the staff of life: when made with whole wheat it contains a very broad spectrum of vitamins and minerals. In fact, except for vitamin B_{12}, whole-wheat bread has much the same vitamin and mineral content as beef. When you eat bread with certain foods, such as legumes, nuts, seeds, or a small amount of a dairy product, the combination makes the protein in bread more available to the human body. Thus, peanut butter sandwiches on whole wheat bread not only taste good to those of us who enjoy them (as we do), they are nourishing, especially when you use natural peanut butter without added sugar. (See our discussion of complementary protein on p 234.)

Calorie for calorie, whole-grain foods are far less expensive to produce and yield far more nutritional value than animal foods. An acre of land devoted to grain production for human consumption can feed many more people than an acre devoted to grain production for livestock, especially cattle. In the future, this may prove to be very important as the world's population increases.

Bread in its earliest forms some eight thousand years ago, before the discovery of leavening, was not very appetizing. Produced in rock-hard slabs, it wore down the teeth of the ancient peoples who gnawed on it for nourishment. Perhaps by accident, as the story goes, an Egyptian baker let his flour-

and-water mixture lie for a time in the sun, and it began to ferment. The bread rose as it baked and this was the beginning of bread in the form that we know it.

If you've never baked bread, you've missed out on one of the most satisfying creations of the kitchen. Many people are afraid to bake bread, thinking it's too difficult. However, many persons who have become wonderful home bread-bakers will tell you that their first loaves were disappointing: hard, flat, and unappetizing, if not inedible.

Please don't be put off by the long directions included in some of our bread recipes. The steps are simple, and we want to take you through each one of them so you will have a perfect loaf when you're through.

It usually takes a couple of "practice loaves" to get the hang of it. One essential step is to make sure your yeast is mixed with a liquid at the correct temperature. Mix it with lukewarm liquid, usually water, as listed in the recipes, and go on from there. The suggested temperature of the liquid is between 105 and 115 degrees Fahrenheit—i.e., lukewarm. (We call it "baby-bottle warm.") You may use a thermometer if you wish; you will probably soon learn to do it by "feel."

Yeast is actually made up of microorganisms that feed on sugar and liquid, and that release carbon dioxide, which is one part of what makes your dough rise. So remember, yeast is alive—or should be. Proof it (make sure it's alive) by combining it with a small amount of water, sugar, and maybe a pinch of ground ginger. Within 15 minutes, it should be bubbly. If not, throw it out and start a new batch. (If the water is the correct temperature, check the "use-by" date on your yeast package for its expiration date.) Some of our recipes call for the new rapid-rise yeast, which works very well and requires far less rising time. It can also be mixed directly with dry ingredients, eliminating the proofing step, although you may proof it if you so desire. You can always substitute regular active dry yeast for rapid-rise. Remember, however, that rapid-rise yeast can withstand slightly higher temperatures in liquids than can regular yeast.

As yeast feeds on sugars in the bread dough, it gives off alcohol and carbon dioxide, which are what make the bread rise. When you put the dough in the oven, the high heat kills the yeast, the dough stops rising, the crust forms, and you have your bread.

HOW MUCH FLOUR?

You may need slightly more or less flour, depending on the humidity and temperature of the kitchen and other factors. This is why a bread recipe often calls for extra flour. Always add your flour slowly. You can add more as you go along, but you can't take any out! If you do find you've added too much, you can wet your hands a little while kneading, and add moisture that way, but it's best to avoid this.

THE NEED TO KNEAD

Kneading is fun, burns a few calories, doesn't take long, and gets you used to how the dough is supposed to feel. You can use kneading attachments on food processors and the like, but Terri and our bread-baking friends prefer getting in there with their hands.

Kneading, which develops the gluten in the dough, works with the yeast to help the dough to rise. Different flours have different protein contents, and since the gluten is formed when liquids are mixed with the protein in flour, flours with high protein levels produce the best breads. Bread flour and all-purpose flour (a blend of hard and soft wheat flours), have high protein levels (over 10 percent). They absorb more water and, when kneaded, give larger volume and lighter texture than soft flours (less than 10 percent protein). An enriched flour has been fortified with thiamin, riboflavin, niacin, and iron, which were removed in the milling process. Bleaching does what it says it does, and doesn't help the flour (white flour is still often a bit brownish). Some enriched, all-purpose flours contain a small amount of other flours, such as malted barley flour. There are quick yeast breads that require no kneading and are still healthful and delicious, but it seems the best-textured breads are kneaded. The following sequence will familiarize you with the basics of the bread-making process.

Rising: Some doughs need no rising time, including non-yeast and some batter breads. Others require several risings.

DRAWING BY LEVIN; © 1983 THE NEW YORKER MAGAZINE, INC.

Usually, you will place the dough in a bowl, cover it with a damp dish towel, and set it in a warm, draft-free place. We just put it in the oven so it's out of the way. In winter, if the house is cold, warm the oven on its lowest setting for a few minutes, turn it off, and put the dough in. Or use a cupboard next to the oven if the oven is in use—the warmth from the oven will permeate the cupboard and keep the dough happy.

Punch down: This is just what it says. Punch the dough with your fist, and it will collapse so you can allow the dough to rise again.

The floured board: When you knead or roll out dough, do so on a large surface lightly dusted with flour. You can add more flour as you go along, if necessary. If you don't have a board, wipe an area of your kitchen counter or table with a damp cloth, cover it with a large piece of wax paper, and dust the wax paper with flour. The damp underneath keeps the paper from sliding.

How to knead: Press the heels of your hands into the dough, fold the dough over, turn it about one-quarter of the way around, and repeat the process. Dough is ready to rise when it appears smooth, elastic, and bounces back from a poke with a finger.

Greasing and dusting: Usually, baked bread will fall out of the pan easily if you follow this procedure: spray pans lightly with nonstick cooking spray, or lightly grease with some oil, margarine, or butter smeared on a paper towel. To dust the pans, add about 2 teaspoons whole-wheat flour or cornmeal to each pan, and tap it while holding it at different angles until flour coats all sides. Then tap out the excess flour. Your completed raw loaf will meet the corners of the pan and will usually fill a loaf pan about two-thirds full.

To test for doneness, tap on the top and *bottom* of the loaf with your knuckles. If it sounds hollow, and if the crust is nicely browned, it's done. If your knock *isn't* hollow, return the loaf to the pan and the oven, but be cautious about how long it stays in the oven.

It's easy to overeat fresh, hot, homemade bread that's just out of the oven. There really is no better food we can imagine. BUT—restrain yourself. Allow yourself one slice, if you must. Tell yourself it doesn't slice as well when it's warm (it doesn't: it tears.) Let bread cool completely before serving, preferably on a wire rack, or your crust may get damp from the steam in the loaf. Joyce Weingartner, who created a number of the breads in this cookbook, never slices hers until it has cooled for 2 hours. How she can resist, we will never know, but we admire her for it.

After the bread cools, slice it with a long serrated knife. You can store the bread in airtight plastic bags and freeze a loaf for later use.

You can vary the type of crust on your breads in the following ways. Brushing the crust with 1 beaten egg mixed with 1 tablespoon of water results in a shiny crust. A soft, glazed crust is obtained by brushing with 1 egg white beaten with 1 tablespoon water. For a soft crust, brush a smidgen of melted butter or vegetable oil on top just before the last rising of the dough, or while baking. For a crisp crust, brush with cold water, a noncaloric alternative to a soft crust! Sweeteners and/or milk in the dough will make a darker crust.

Whole-Wheat Bread Crumbs

Take any whole—wheat or non—sweet whole—grain bread, and whir in a blender or food processor. (Yes, in a pinch, you may use white bread.)

One average slice of fresh bread makes about ½ cup, while 1 average slice of dry (stale) bread makes about ⅓ cup. Use for casserole toppings, breading meats, etc. Commercial breads vary greatly in their nutritional value, so read the labels to determine calories, cholesterol, dietary fiber, fat, and sodium.

Italian Whole-Wheat Bread

PREPARATION TIME: 3 HOURS.   BAKING TIME: 40 MINUTES.

2 packages active dry yeast
¼ cup lukewarm water (105° to
   115° F.)
¼ teaspoon sugar
¼ teaspoon ground ginger
1½ cups lukewarm water
1 tablespoon sugar
¼ cup melted butter
2 teaspoons salt

2 cups whole-wheat flour
3 cups all-purpose flour
   (approximately)
Nonstick vegetable cooking
   spray
2½ tablespoons cornmeal
1 egg white
1 tablespoon water

1. Proof the yeast by pouring it into a small bowl with the ¼ cup water, ¼ teaspoon sugar, and the ginger. Wait about 5 to 15 minutes, or until bubbly.
2. In a large bowl, combine the remaining lukewarm water, the sugar, the butter, and the salt. Add the proofed yeast.
3. Add 1 cup of whole-wheat flour and 1 cup of all-purpose flour. Mix 100 strokes. Add another 1 cup each of the flours, mixing well. Then slowly add the remaining cup of all-purpose flour, a little at a time, to make sure the dough is the correct consistency.
4. Knead for 8 to 10 minutes, adding up to ¼ cup more all-purpose flour if necessary. Place in a lightly greased bowl, cover with a damp towel, and set in a draft-free place until doubled in bulk.
5. Punch down the dough with your fist. Knead on a lightly floured surface for about 2 minutes until smooth and elastic. Divide the dough into 2 equal balls. Cover with the damp towel and let stand for 10 minutes.
6. Spray a baking sheet with cooking spray, and dust with cornmeal, pouring off excess cornmeal.
7. Shape each ball of dough into a long loaf—like a French loaf—about 14 inches in length, by holding each end and gently stretching the dough, shaking it gently at the same time. Pat into shape if necessary. Place loaves—not touching—on the baking sheet, cover with wax paper, and let

rise in a warm, draft-free place until doubled in bulk, about 1 hour.

8. Beat the egg white with the 1 tablespoon of water, and brush the tops of the loaves with it. Make five shallow diagonal slashes in the tops of each loaf to let steam escape while baking.

9. Bake at 425 degrees for 40 minutes, or until the loaves are a rich golden color. If they begin getting too dark, you may cover them with a piece of foil; however, don't open the oven during the first 20 minutes, or your bread may collapse. To test for doneness, tap the bread top and bottom; if it does not sound hollow, return it to the oven until it taps hollow. Cool on a wire rack.

Makes 2 loaves of 16 slices each. Serving size is 1 slice.

Per Serving: 86.5 calories, 4 mg. cholesterol, 1.5 g. dietary fiber, 1.5 g. fat, 150 mg. sodium.

Homemade Croutons

PREPARATION TIME: 5 MINUTES.   COOKING TIME: 8 TO 10 MINUTES.

4 slices whole-grain bread
1 tablespoon margarine
   OR butter
1 teaspoon basil
¼ teaspoon oregano

¼ teaspoon onion powder
⅛ teaspoon thyme
½ teaspoon garlic powder
Other herbs and spices of your
   choice (optional)

1. Cut the bread into ½-inch cubes. In a skillet, melt the margarine, then add the seasonings.
2. Stir in the bread cubes and sauté until crisp.

Makes about 2 cups. Serving size is ¼ cup.

Per Serving: 56 calories, 4 mg. cholesterol, 2 g. dietary fiber, 2 g. fat, 133 mg. sodium.

Whole-Wheat French Bread

PREPARATION TIME: 3 HOURS.   BAKING TIME: 25 TO 30 MINUTES.

If you enjoy French bread, which goes with just about any meal, you may want to invest in a French-bread pan, which is a heavy pan made especially for its long shape. You can find one in most cookware shops. This bread freezes well wrapped in foil and placed in a sealed plastic bag.

2 packages yeast
1/4 cup warm water
1/4 teaspoon sugar
1/4 teaspoon ground ginger
3/4 cup plus 2 tablespoons lukewarm water
1 tablespoon sugar
2 tablespoons unsalted melted butter
OR margarine

2 teaspoons salt
1 1/2 cups all-purpose flour
3/4 cup whole-wheat flour
1 to 2 teaspoons vegetable oil
2 1/2 tablespoons cornmeal
1 egg white
1 tablespoon water

1. Proof the yeast by putting it in a small bowl with the 1/4 cup warm water, the sugar, and the ginger. In about 5 to 15 minutes, it should be bubbly. If not, throw it out and start over with two more packages of yeast.
2. Meanwhile, in another bowl, combine the 3/4 cup plus 2 tablespoons warm water, the tablespoon of sugar, the butter, and the salt.
3. Add the proofed yeast to the water mixture. Mix in 1 cup of all-purpose flour, and the whole-wheat flour. Stir 100 strokes.
4. Mix in another 1/4 cup all-purpose flour, then slowly add up to an additional 1/4 cup. Knead the dough for 10 minutes.
5. Rub a small amount of vegetable oil over the surface of a bowl, place the dough in it, and cover with a damp towel until doubled, about 1 hour. Punch down the dough, knead 2 minutes more, then let rest with the towel over it for 10 minutes.
6. Divide the dough into 2 pieces. Shape into loaves by holding each end of a piece and gently stretching and shaking

the bread into the shape of a long French loaf. Pat into shape if necessary.

7. Brush a baking sheet lightly with vegetable oil, and evenly spread cornmeal over it. Place the loaves on the baking sheet, and cover with a damp cloth. Let double, about 30 to 45 minutes.

8. Brush each loaf with the egg white mixed with the 1 table-spoon of water. Put several diagonal slashes, ¼ inch deep, in the bread to let steam escape while it bakes. Bake the bread at 425 degrees for 25 to 30 minutes, until golden brown. Remove from the oven immediately and let cool on a rack.

9. If you serve the bread the same day you bake it, simply crisp it in the oven for 5 minutes before serving. This is the secret to getting traditional "crusty" French bread. To thaw frozen bread and serve, warm in foil for 15 minutes at 350 degrees. Then remove the foil, and leave in the oven for another 5 minutes.

VARIATION: For a pungent, East Indian-style loaf, add to the above recipe ½ teaspoon Indian Spice Blend (p. 334) or other curry powder, and 3 tablespoons scallion, minced, green part only. Reduce salt to 1½ teaspoons.

Makes 2 loaves of 8 slices each. Serving size is 1 slice.

Per Serving: 91 calories, 4 mg. cholesterol, 1 g. dietary fiber, 2 g. fat, 271 mg. sodium.

Buttermilk Corn Bread

PREPARATION TIME: 30 MINUTES.　　　BAKING TIME: ¾ TO 1 HOUR.

For several weeks, Enid tested revision after revision of this recipe until she triumphed with a light, tasty corn bread that rivals any other we have tasted. You can make this recipe into a loaf or muffins. If you decide to make muffins, lightly coat the muffin tins with a small amount of the butter, and bake for 25 to 30 minutes.

¼ cup butter
　OR margarine
1½ cups yellow cornmeal,
　sifted
½ cup whole-wheat flour,
　sifted

1½ cups buttermilk
½ teaspoon baking soda
¼ teaspoon salt

1. Use a small amount of the butter to coat a loaf pan. Melt the remaining amount in a small saucepan.
2. Combine all ingredients in a mixing bowl. Let stand for 20 minutes. Pour into the loaf pan, and bake at 350 degrees for 45 minutes to 1 hour, until beginning to lightly brown on top.

Makes 1 loaf of 16 slices, or a dozen muffins. Serving size is 1 slice or 1 muffin.

Per Serving (16 slices): 94 calories, 9 mg. cholesterol, 1 g. dietary fiber, 3 g. fat, 113 mg. sodium. (Each muffin will contain one-third more of each nutrient.)

Good Bread

PREPARATION TIME: ¾ TO 1 HOUR.　　　BAKING TIME: 1 TO 1¼ HOURS.

Our longtime friend Denni Llovet says of her bread creation: "Only 1½ hours from bowl to mouth!"

We think she's more efficient than we are, because it usually takes us 2 hours to make this bread. Regardless of how long it takes to make, it is truly plain-old, down-home *good* bread.

1 teaspoon or less butter
Whole-wheat flour—a little
½ cup lukewarm water (105° to 115° F.)
3 packages yeast (may use rapid-rise)
⅔ cup vegetable oil
⅔ cup honey
1 teaspoon salt
5 cups hot water
About 10 cups whole-wheat flour

1. Lightly grease 3 loaf pans with the butter, and dust with a little bit of flour.
2. Place the ½ cup of lukewarm water in a small bowl, and sprinkle the yeast on top. Do not stir.
3. Measure the oil into a measuring cup, then pour into a small bowl. Measure the honey into the same measuring cup you used for the oil; this will keep the honey from sticking in the cup. Pour the honey into the bowl with the oil, and add the salt.
4. Mix the 5 cups of hot water with 7 cups of the flour in the largest mixing bowl you have—use a soup pot if you want! Keep the flour handy. Add the yeast-and-water mixture, then add the oil-honey-salt mixture, and blend. Keep mixing in flour, a little at a time, to make a pliant dough, firm but not stiff. Turn the dough out onto a floured board and knead for 10 minutes with a folding-over, punching-down motion.
5. Divide the dough into three loaves and place in loaf pans. Cover with a damp cloth and let rise until half again as big.
6. Bake at 350 degrees until dark brown on top (about 1 hour to 1 hour and fifteen minutes). Let cool on a wire rack 5 to 10 minutes before slicing if you want it to slice cleanly.

3 loaves of 16 slices each. Serving size is 1 slice.

Per Serving: 126 calories, no cholesterol, 3 g. dietary fiber, 4 g. fat, 47 mg. sodium.

Four-Grain Wheatless Bread

PREPARATION TIME: 35 MINUTES.   BAKING TIME: 1¼ HOURS.

We asked Joyce Weingartner, who helped us test many recipes, to create a wheatless bread for us. She delighted us with this, a batter bread that has a rich, nutty flavor, great in sandwiches or all by itself. For those who are allergic to wheat, this bread is a suitable substitute, as buckwheat is actually not in the wheat family. This loaf will not rise as high as most kneaded wheat breads, because there is far less gluten in these flours. Store the loaf in the refrigerator, and slice thin to serve.

2 packages yeast
¼ cup lukewarm water (105° to 115° F.)
¼ teaspoon sugar
⅛ teaspoon ground ginger
1 cup lukewarm water
¼ cup molasses
2 tablespoons melted butter

2 teaspoons salt
2 cups rye flour
¼ cup buckwheat
¼ cup soy flour
½ cup oat flour
Nonstick vegetable cooking spray

1. Proof the yeast in the ¼ cup water, sugar, and ginger (the mixture should be bubbly after about 5 to 15 minutes).
2. In a large bowl, combine the 1 cup water, molasses, butter, and salt. Add the proofed yeast, and mix well.
3. In another bowl, combine 1½ cups of the rye flour, and the remaining flours. Add the flours to the yeast mixture, and mix 100 strokes. Be sure to get all the flour at the bottom of the bowl mixed in with the dough.
4. Gradually add the remaining ½ cup rye flour, stirring well.
5. Preheat the oven to 350 degrees.
6. Spray a loaf pan with nonstick cooking spray, and place the dough in the pan, spreading with a knife to meet the corners and smooth out the top of the loaf. Place the loaf pan in a larger pan that has about 1 inch of hot water in it. Cover the loaf pan with foil, and place both pans in the center of your oven.

7. Bake for 30 minutes, then remove the foil *and* the pan of water. Bake the loaf an additional 45 minutes. This loaf will not sound hollow when you tap it, but will have a rich, dark brown crust. Remove it from the pan and place on a rack to cool.

Makes 1 loaf of 20 thin slices. Serving size is 1 slice.

Per Serving: 78 calories, 3 mg. cholesterol, 1 g. dietary fiber, 1 g. fat, 226 mg. sodium.

Sesame Poppy-Seed Loaf

PREPARATION TIME: 10 MINUTES.   BAKING TIME: 40 MINUTES.

¾ cup whole-wheat flour
¾ cup all-purpose flour
1 tablespoon baking powder
½ teaspoon salt
2 tablespoons sesame seeds
2 teaspoons poppy seeds

¾ cup orange juice
2 tablespoons honey
1 egg
2 tablespoons vegetable oil
½ cup All-Bran cereal

1. In a medium bowl, stir together the whole-wheat flour, all-purpose flour, baking powder, salt, and seeds. Set aside.
2. In a large mixing bowl, beat together the orange juice, honey, egg, oil, and cereal until well-combined. Let stand 2 minutes.
3. Add the flour mixture, stirring only until combined. Spread the batter evenly into a lightly greased 9 × 5 × 3-inch loaf pan.
4. Bake at 350 degrees about 40 minutes, or until a toothpick inserted near the center comes out clean. Let cool 10 minutes before removing from the pan. Cool completely before slicing.

Makes 1 loaf of 16 slices. Serving size is 1 slice.

Per Serving: 100 calories, 20 mg. cholesterol, 2 g. dietary fiber, 3 g. fat, 380 mg. sodium.

Whole-Wheat Tortillas

PREPARATION TIME: 1½ HOURS.   COOKING TIME: 1 HOUR.

Tortillas are the bread of Mexico. You can use them as you would bread, although we still think the traditional Mexican recipes are the best. You can also find whole-wheat tortillas at a health-food store.

As for the use of vegetable *shortening,* which is often processed into a solid form that is similar to saturated fat, there is so little per serving in this recipe that we felt it was acceptable. You can substitute oil if you wish, although the resulting texture is not quite as good. There are some commercial health-food brands, however, that use sesame oil to good effect.

When cooking these, a little bit of cooking spray goes a long way. You can probably cook several tortillas before needing more fat.

These are great with Fajitas (pp. 114–15); or make your own burritos or soft tacos. They can substitute for bread in Cheese Toast (pp. 340–41); you can sprinkle them with grated cheese, chopped tomato, and/or onion, broil them, and top with chopped lettuce, and maybe some Mexican-Style Hot Sauce (p. 58).

You can also freeze these for later use.

2 cups whole-wheat flour
2 cups all-purpose flour
2 teaspoons salt
⅓ cup vegetable shortening

1 cup warm water (or slightly more if needed)
Whole-wheat flour as needed
Nonstick cooking spray

1. Combine all ingredients in a large bowl to make a light-textured dough. Form into 16 egg-sized balls, and place the balls in the bowl. Let stand for about 20 minutes.
2. Roll each ball of dough out on a lightly floured board to form a very thin circle, about ⅛-inch thick.
3. Spray a griddle or large skillet with cooking spray, and fry each tortilla over medium-low heat for a minute on one side, and a minute on the other. NOTE: When one side is done, the tortilla will begin puffing up. Turn it over, and

fry the other side. They will be slightly browned in spots, not all over. Serve warm.

Makes 16 tortillas. Serving size is 1 tortilla.

Per Serving: 140 calories, no cholesterol, 4 g. dietary fiber, 5 g. fat, 267 mg. sodium.

Caraway-Onion-Bran Loaf

PREPARATION TIME: 20 MINUTES.   BAKING TIME: 30 TO 35 MINUTES.

¼ cup margarine (regular, not light)
½ cup finely chopped onion
1 cup minus 1 tablespoon skim milk
1 tablespoon lemon juice
1 cup All-Bran cereal

1 egg, slightly beaten
1½ cups all-purpose flour
1 teaspoon baking powder
1 teaspoon baking soda
1 teaspoon salt
2 teaspoons caraway seeds

1. In a medium saucepan, melt the margarine. Add the onion, and cook over low heat until tender. Remove from the heat.
2. Combine the milk and the lemon juice to make sour milk. Stir the cereal and the milk into the onions. Let stand for 2 minutes, or until most of the liquid is absorbed. Add the egg and blend well.
3. In a large mixing bowl, mix the flour, baking powder, soda, salt, and caraway seeds. Add the cereal mixture to the flour. Stir just until moistened.
4. Spread in a lightly greased 9 × 5 × 3-inch loaf pan. Bake at 350 degrees for 30 to 35 minutes, or until a knife inserted in the center comes out clean. Let cool for 10 minutes. Remove from the pan, and let cool completely before slicing.

Makes 1 loaf of 16 slices. Serving size is 1 slice.

Per Serving: 90 calories, 20 mg. cholesterol, 2 g. dietary fiber, 4 g. fat, 400 mg. sodium.

Swedish Limpa Rye

PREPARATION TIME: 3 HOURS.   BAKING TIME: 40 MINUTES.

2 packages yeast
¼ cup lukewarm water (105° to 115° F.)
¼ teaspoon sugar
⅛ teaspoon ground ginger
1¼ cup lukewarm water
½ cup unsweetened orange juice
2 tablespoons melted butter

⅓ cup molasses
2½ teaspoons salt
2 tablespoons orange peel
1¾ cups whole-wheat flour
1¾ to 2 cups all-purpose flour
1 cup rye flour
1 egg white
1 tablespoon water

1. In a small bowl, proof the yeast by combining it with the ¼ cup water, sugar, and ginger.
2. In a large bowl, combine the 1¼ cups water with the orange juice, butter, molasses, salt, and orange peel.
3. After the yeast has proofed (about 5 to 15 minutes), add to the orange-juice mixture. Stir in 1 cup of each of the flours, and mix 100 strokes. Add another ½ cup of whole-wheat, then ½ cup of all-purpose, stirring well after each addition. Slowly add about ¼ cup more of both whole-wheat and all-purpose flours. The dough will be sticky.
4. Dust your hands, the kneading board, and the dough with flour, and knead for 8 to 10 minutes, adding more all-purpose flour a little at a time, if necessary.
5. Place the dough in a lightly greased mixing bowl and cover with a damp towel. Place in a warm, draft-free area, and let rise until it doubles, about 1 hour.
6. Punch down, and let rest for 10 minutes with the towel over it.
7. Form the dough into 2 round loaves, or use 2 loaf pans, 8 × 4 inches each. Let rise again until doubled, about 45 minutes.
8. Mix the egg white with the tablespoon of water, and brush each loaf with the mixture. Put several diagonal slashes on the bread to let out steam while baking.
9. Bake at 350 degrees for 40 minutes, or until the loaves

sound hollow when tapped on the top and bottom. Cool on a wire rack for 2 hours before slicing.

2 loaves of 16 slices each. Serving size is 1 slice.

Per Serving: 76 calories, 2 mg. cholesterol, 1 g. dietary fiber, 1 g. fat, 175 mg. sodium.

Breadsticks

PREPARATION TIME: 40 MINUTES.   BAKING TIME: 15 MINUTES.

2 packages active dry yeast
2 teaspoons sugar
Pinch ground ginger
1 cup lukewarm water
2 tablespoons vegetable oil

1 teaspoon salt
3 cups all-purpose flour
    OR half all-purpose, half
    whole-wheat flour

1. Combine the yeast, sugar, ginger, and water in a large bowl. Let stand for 10 minutes.
2. Mix in the oil and salt, then slowly mix in the flour, adding just enough to get past the sticky stage and allow you to knead the dough.
3. Knead for 5 minutes. Roll into long sticks, about ½-inch thick × 8 inches long. Place the sticks on a lightly oiled baking sheet.
4. Bake at 375 degrees on the high rack of the oven for 15 minutes, or until golden brown. Serve hot.

Makes about 2 dozen sticks. Serving size is 1 stick.

Per Serving: (with half all-purpose and half whole-wheat flour), 63 calories, no cholesterol, 1 g. dietary fiber, 1 g. fat, 90 mg. sodium.

Quick Whole-Wheat Buttermilk Bread

PREPARATION TIME: 1¼ HOURS.   BAKING TIME: 25 MINUTES.

This bread has a lovely, even texture.

2 cups whole-wheat flour
2½ cups all-purpose flour
2 packages rapid-rise yeast
½ cup wheat germ
2 teaspoons baking powder
2 teaspoons salt
1¼ cups buttermilk

¾ cup water
¼ cup melted butter
   OR margarine
2 tablespoons molasses
Nonstick vegetable cooking
   spray

1. In a large bowl, mix together 1½ cups of the whole-wheat flour, 1½ cups of all-purpose flour, the yeast, wheat germ, baking powder, and salt.
2. In a saucepan, heat the buttermilk and water on medium-low heat until lukewarm, not hot (105 to 115 degrees Fahrenheit). Stir into the flour mixture.
3. Melt the butter or margarine, and blend into the flour mixture. Blend in the molasses, and stir 100 strokes.
4. Slowly stir in the other ½ cup of whole-wheat flour, and ½ cup all-purpose flour. When the flour is mixed into the batter, add another ¼ cup all-purpose flour, mix well, and add another ¼ cup all-purpose flour if necessary. Your dough will be a bit sticky, so dust your kneading board, your hands, and the dough with flour.
5. Knead the dough for 8 to 10 minutes. Place in a lightly greased bowl, and cover with a damp dish towel.
6. Spray 2 loaf pans, 8 × 4 inches, with nonstick cooking spray, and preheat your oven to 425 degrees.
7. Divide the dough into 2 pieces. Pat each piece into a square about 7 × 8 inches, and about 1-inch thick. Fold the square in thirds. Seal the seam, and place each loaf, seam down, in a loaf pan.
8. Cover the loaves with a damp towel and let rise again until doubled in bulk, about 30 minutes.

9. Place the loaves in the center of the oven, evenly distanced and not touching each other. Bake for 25 minutes, or until the loaves sound hollow when tapped on the top and bottom. They should be nicely browned. Let them cool on a wire rack.

2 loaves of 16 slices each. Serving size is 1 slice.

Per Serving: 86 calories, 4 mg. cholesterol, 1 g. dietary fiber, 2 g. fat, 182 mg. sodium.

Bran Cheese Twists

PREPARATION TIME: 35 MINUTES.   BAKING TIME: 15 MINUTES.

This "snack" bread is good with salads, for example, instead of whole-grain crackers, for a change of pace.

1 cup All-Bran cereal
1⅓ cups skim milk
1 tablespoon lemon juice
2 cups all-purpose flour
1 tablespoon baking powder

1 teaspoon baking soda
1 teaspoon salt
2 tablespoons margarine,
   softened
½ cup grated cheddar cheese

1. In a small bowl, combine the cereal and the milk, which has been soured with the lemon juice. Set aside.
2. In a large mixing bowl, combine the flour, baking powder, soda, and salt. Cut in the margarine to make a coarse meal. Add the cereal mixture and blend well. Stir in the cheese.
3. Shape the dough into 20 ropes, 3½ × 3 inches each, by rolling the dough between your hands. Fold each rope in half and twist each end. Place on a lightly greased baking sheet.
4. Bake at 425 degrees for 15 minutes or until golden brown.

Makes 20 twists. Serving size is 1 twist.

Per Serving: 80 calories, 3 mg. cholesterol, 2 g. dietary fiber, 2 g. fat, 270 mg. sodium.

Applesauce Bran Bread

PREPARATION TIME: 1¼ TO 1½ HOURS.   BAKING TIME: 30 MINUTES.

¾ cup All-Bran cereal
2 to 2½ cups all-purpose flour
2 tablespoons firmly packed
 brown sugar
½ teaspoon salt
1 package active dry yeast

¾ cup unsweetened
 applesauce
¼ cup skim milk
3 tablespoons margarine
 OR butter
1 egg, at room temperature

1. Stir together the cereal, ½ cup of the flour, the sugar, salt, and yeast in a large mixing bowl. Set aside.
2. In a small saucepan, heat the applesauce, milk, and margarine until very warm (120 to 130 degrees Fahrenheit; the margarine does not need to melt). Gradually add to the cereal mixture, and beat 2 minutes at a medium speed with the electric mixer, occasionally scraping the bowl.
3. Add the egg and ½ cup of flour. Beat 2 minutes at high speed, scraping the bowl. By hand, stir in enough remaining flour to make a stiff, sticky dough. Cover loosely with a damp towel. Let rise in a warm place until double in volume.
4. Punch down the dough and shape into a loaf. Place in a lightly greased 9 × 5 × 3-inch loaf pan. Cover and let rise in a warm place until double in volume.
5. Bake at 375 degrees about 30 minutes or until done. To prevent over-browning, cover loosely with foil during the last few minutes of baking time. Remove the loaf from the pan, and cool on a wire rack.

Makes 1 loaf of 17 slices. Serving size is 1 slice.

Per Serving: 110 calories, 20 mg. cholesterol, 2 g. dietary fiber, 3 g. fat, 130 mg. sodium.

Bran-Batter Rolls

PREPARATION TIME: 45 MINUTES.   BAKING TIME: 18 TO 20 MINUTES.

1 cup All-Bran cereal
2½ to 3 cups all-purpose flour
2 tablespoons sugar
1½ teaspoons salt
1 package rapid-rise yeast

1 cup skim milk
½ cup water
2 tablespoons margarine
1 egg, slightly beaten
Poppy seeds (optional)

1. In a large mixing bowl, stir together the cereal, 1 cup of the flour, the sugar, salt, and yeast. Set aside.
2. In a small saucepan, heat the milk, water, and margarine until warm (115 to 120 degrees Fahrenheit). Add to the cereal mixture. Reserve 1 tablespoon of the egg. Add the remaining egg to the cereal mixture. Beat for 30 seconds at low speed on the electric mixer, then beat for 3 minutes at high speed.
3. By hand, stir in enough of the remaining flour to make a stiff batter. Cover loosely with a damp towel. Let rise in a warm place until double in volume. Stir down the batter. Portion the batter evenly into 16 lightly greased 2½-inch muffin-pan cups. Brush the tops of the rolls with the reserved egg. Sprinkle with poppy seeds if desired.
4. Bake at 400 degrees for 18 to 20 minutes, or until golden brown. Serve warm.

Makes 16 rolls. Serving size is 1 roll.

Per Serving: 120 calories, 20 mg. cholesterol, 2 g. dietary fiber, 2 g. fat, 290 mg. sodium.

MUFFINS

We are inveterate muffin-makers; nothing seems to give as much pleasure in the making and the eating for so little effort. A muffin is really a "quick bread" made, basically, from a batter that is baked in a muffin pan.

Our muffins blend a high-fiber source, such as a cereal product, with a flour. The batter is produced with the addition of low-fat milk, oil, an egg or two, and the sweetener, which can be sugar, honey, molasses, or a combination of the three. To this you can add an almost limitless combination of various dried fruits and nuts. Because it is so easy to be creative when you make muffins, we usually make two or three different kinds at a time. One might contain raisins, while another has dates and nuts; one might be a blend of oat- or wheat-bran cereal with whole-wheat flour, while another might have small quantities of barley or soy flour blended with the wheat flour.

When it comes to satisfying a desire for something sweet or for something cake-like to go with a good cup of fresh-ground coffee, a muffin is a far healthier alternative than baked goods like pastry, pie, or cake. Also, it is *far* cheaper to bake your own than to buy them in the bakery, and, because you select the ingredients, you know how fresh *and* healthy these muffins are.

Some of the recipes in this section were developed and tested for us in the Kellogg kitchens, so you will note that the recipes in question call for Kellogg products. You can, of course, try these recipes using your own favorite equivalent cereals, e.g., any 100% bran for All-Bran (but not 40% bran-content flakes for All-Bran).

Mixed Raisin-Bran Muffins

PREPARATION TIME: 10 MINUTES. BAKING TIME: 15 MINUTES.

Whole-wheat pastry flour is available in most health food stores, and gives a slightly finer texture than regular whole-wheat flour. However, you may use regular whole-wheat flour instead.

Nonstick vegetable cooking spray	2 teaspoons baking powder
1¼ cups oat bran	¼ teaspoon salt
1 cup whole-wheat pastry flour	1 cup low-fat milk
¼ cup brown sugar	1 large egg, beaten
½ cup raisins	¼ cup molasses
	2 tablespoons vegetable oil

1. Heat oven to 425 degrees. Spray bottoms of 12 2½″ muffin pan cups with nonstick cooking spray, or line with paper cups.
2. Combine dry ingredients in a large mixing bowl.
3. In separate bowl, mix milk, egg, molasses, and oil.
4. Add the liquid mixture to the dry, and mix only until the dry ingredients are moistened (the mixture should be lumpy).
5. Fill muffin cups until ¾ full, and bake at 425 degrees for 15 minutes, or until tops are golden brown.

Makes 12 muffins. Serving size is 1 muffin.

Per Serving: 152 calories, 25 mg. cholesterol, 2 g. dietary fiber, 5 g. fat, 238 mg. sodium.

Honey Bran Muffins

PREPARATION TIME: 10 MINUTES.   BAKING TIME: 25 MINUTES.

2 cups All-Bran cereal
⅓ cup honey
1¼ cups skim milk
1 egg

1 cup all-purpose flour
1 teaspoon baking soda
½ teaspoon salt

1. Combine the cereal, honey, and milk, and let stand for 2 minutes. Add the egg, beating well.
2. Stir together the flour, soda, and salt; add to the cereal mixture, stirring *only until combined.* Portion the batter evenly into lightly greased 2½-inch muffin-pan cups.
3. Bake at 400 degrees for 25 minutes or until a toothpick inserted in the center of a muffin comes out clean. Let stand about 5 minutes before removing from the pans. Serve immediately.

Makes 12 muffins. Serving size is 1 muffin.

Per Serving: 115 calories, 25 mg. cholesterol, 5 g. dietary fiber, 1 g. fat, 340 mg. sodium.

Apricot Bran Muffins

PREPARATION TIME: 20 MINUTES.   BAKING TIME: 25 MINUTES.

1½ cups all-purpose flour
2 tablespoons sugar
1 tablespoon baking powder
½ teaspoon salt
1½ cups All-Bran cereal

1½ cups skim milk
1 egg
2 tablespoons vegetable oil
½ cup chopped dried apricots

1. In a small bowl, stir together the flour, sugar, baking powder, and salt. Set aside.
2. In a large bowl, combine the cereal and the milk; let stand 2 minutes. Add the egg and oil, blending well. Add the flour mixture, stirring only until combined. Stir in the apricots.

3. Portion the batter evenly into lightly greased 2½-inch muffin-pan cups. Bake at 400 degrees for 25 minutes, or until a toothpick inserted in the center of a muffin comes out clean. Serve warm.

Makes 12 muffins. Serving size is 1 muffin.

Per Serving: 135 calories, 25 mg. cholesterol, 4 g. dietary fiber, 3 g. fat, 580 mg. sodium.

Bran Muffins

PREPARATION TIME: 20 MINUTES.   BAKING TIME: 18 TO 20 MINUTES.

1¼ cups all-purpose flour	1½ cups All-Bran cereal
1 tablespoon baking powder	1¼ cups skim milk
¼ teaspoon salt	2 egg whites
2 tablespoons sugar	2 tablespoons vegetable oil

1. Stir together the flour, baking powder, salt, and sugar, and set aside.
2. Measure the cereal and milk into a large mixing bowl. Stir to combine. Let stand 1 to 2 minutes or until cereal is softened.
3. Place the egg whites in a small mixing bowl. Beat until foamy. Add the egg whites and the oil to the cereal mixture, and beat well. Add the flour mixture, stirring only until combined. Portion the batter evenly into 12 lightly greased 2½-inch muffin-pan cups.
4. Bake at 400 degrees for 18 to 20 minutes, or until a toothpick inserted in the center of a muffin comes out clean.

Makes 12 muffins. Serving size is 1 muffin.

Per Serving: 110 calories, 1 mg. cholesterol, 4 g. dietary fiber 3 g. fat, 265 mg. sodium.

Herb Bran Muffins

PREPARATION TIME: 12 TO 15 MINUTES.   BAKING TIME: 18 TO 20
MINUTES.

1¼ cups all-purpose flour
1 tablespoon baking powder
¼ teaspoon salt
2 tablespoons sugar
2 tablespoons toasted sesame
  seeds
¼ teaspoon dry mustard
½ teaspoon herb of your
  choice (suggestions: sage,

dillweed, oregano, sweet
basil, chives, parsley,
marjoram, summer savory,
rosemary, coriander, or
cardamom)
1 cup All-Bran cereal
1 cup skim milk
1 egg
2 tablespoons melted margarine

1. Stir together the flour, baking powder, salt, sugar, sesame
   seeds, dry mustard, and herb of choice. Set aside.
2. In a large mixing bowl, combine the cereal and the milk.
   Let stand 2 minutes. Add the egg and margarine, blending
   well. Add the flour mixture, stirring only until combined.
3. Portion the batter evenly into lightly greased 2½-inch
   muffin-pan cups. Bake at 400 degrees for 18 to 20 minutes,
   or until a toothpick inserted in the center of a muffin
   comes out clean.

Makes 12 muffins. Serving size is 1 muffin.

Per Serving: 110 calories, 25 mg. cholesterol, 3 g. dietary fiber,
3 g. fat, 520 mg. sodium.

Whole-Wheat Honey Tea Muffins

PREPARATION TIME: 15 MINUTES.   BAKING TIME: 18 TO 20 MINUTES.

¾ cup whole-wheat flour
1½ teaspoons baking powder
1 cup All-Bran cereal
¾ cup skim milk

1 egg
¼ cup honey
3 tablespoons vegetable oil

1. Stir together the flour and the baking powder. Set aside.

2. Combine the cereal and the milk in a large mixing bowl. Let stand for 2 minutes, or until the cereal is softened. Add the egg, honey, and oil. Beat well.
3. Add the flour mixture, stirring only until combined.
4. Portion the batter evenly into lightly greased 2½-inch muffin-pan cups. Bake at 400 degrees for 18 to 20 minutes, or until a toothpick inserted in the center of a muffin comes out clean.

Makes 12 muffins. Serving size is 1 muffin.

Per Serving: 115 calories, 20 mg. cholesterol, 4 g. dietary fiber, 2 g. fat, 170 mg. sodium.

Seasonings

Human sensitivity to taste has certain peculiarities. It adapts to the use of salt and sugar, so that the more we use, the less sensitive to the flavor we become. This adaptation does not occur in our perception of bitter and sour.

Some people are "salt-sensitive": their blood pressure rises when they consume salt. The effect is due, in actuality, to the sodium in salt. Table salt is 40 percent sodium and 60 percent chloride.

Although sodium is an essential nutrient, we Americans consume 8 to 10 times more than our bodies need to stay alive and healthy. About 25 to 35 percent of us are "salt sensitive" and can develop high blood pressure if we consume too much salt. For this reason, most health professionals encourage us to cut back on salt. We can do this by cutting back on added salt in our own cooking, and by reducing the consumption of certain processed foods, such as processed meats, soups, and snack foods.

We agree with the suggestion to cut back on salt and have done it ourselves over the past few years. But we don't think you need to cut it out entirely from your cooking unless you are on a severely salt-restricted diet. The reason we include salt or other seasonings that contain some sodium in many of our recipes is that salt seems to bring out the flavors in other ingredients, especially herbs and spices. Try it yourself: mix up a batch of herbs, taste them, and then add about one part salt to a mixture of six or seven parts other herbs. You will agree, we're quite sure, that the flavor of the other herbs fairly explodes to the taste with a bit of salt.

For this reason, our Herb Salt (pp. 334–35) is usually made with one part salt to six or seven parts other herbs, yielding a mixture that has perhaps 285 milligrams of sodium per teaspoon, compared with 2200 milligrams in a teaspoon of salt.

We keep a wide assortment of herbs and spices on our shelves, including just about everything we itemized on pages 34 to 36. We also keep a variety of our own blends, such as the recipes included here. In addition, we keep some commercial preparations on hand for the times we are in a hurry, or seek other variety. These include Mrs. Dash, which is strong on garlic and rather hot; Old Bay, which, although quite high in sodium, is good when lightly sprinkled on fish and poultry; and Perc, which is a salt-free herb blend, somewhat strong on onion, but acceptable in most recipes to which you might ordinarily sprinkle blended dried herbs. Both Mrs. Dash and Perc, for example, will add interest to cottage cheese or cheese toast, and can be sprinkled lightly on just about any meat or vegetable when you are not feeling particularly creative.

We also occasionally use the original Worcestershire in small quantities, over steaks or in a meat loaf. Recently we discovered White Wine Worcestershire, which is an excellent seasoning for fish and chicken and gets our highest recommendation. We almost always use soy sauce in place of salt whenever possible, since a teaspoon of soy sauce, in the usual commercial preparation, has about 1/7 the sodium content of salt.

And here's a hint for seasoning meat, chicken, and turkey before roasting: place your selection of seasonings (a total of 4 to 6 teaspoons of crushed herbs and spices) in a small bowl, add 1 tablespoon of oil and 1 tablespoon of soy sauce. Mix it until it forms a paste, and then, before roasting, rub it well into the meat or poultry with your fingers. In 1986, we used Indian Spice Blend in this way before smoking our Christmas turkey Tandoori style and it got rave reviews from our dinner guests. (We think that smoked foods should be used with extreme moderation, since smoking may increase the activity of certain carcinogenic substances. We will smoke a turkey or roast two or three times each year; we avoid smoked foods at other times.)

After they are emptied, save several of the spice jars you obtain when you purchase commercial spices. Wash and dry them well and use them to store your own blends. You can also use them to store any herbs and spices that you buy in bulk. The flavor of herbs and spices is preserved best when they are stored in air-tight containers.

When you cannot use the fresh form of an herb, substitute a powder. Garlic and onion powders (and celery seed) are far lower in sodium content than their salt equivalents. The sodium content of the blend is far higher than necessary. If you find that your recipe needs additional salt, add it yourself. You will end up using far less.

Finally, whenever we say "dash" of salt, we mean about 1/16th of a teaspoon, which is what some cooks refer to as a "pinch." When we say "salt to taste," go lightly and let people add a bit more at the table if they wish. We discovered that the instruction was the source of tremendous variation among the "army" of chefs who helped design and taste our recipes. Until we made ourselves understood, this misunderstanding sometimes resulted in food that was so salty we could not believe they had ever tasted it before emptying the salt shaker!

Since nutrients in herbs and spices are so minimal in the quantities sold, we haven't provided nutritional analyses for our herb blends.

Garam Masala

PREPARATION TIME: 3 MINUTES.

A traditional Indian "masala" is simply a mixture of spices. A "garam masala" is typically added to a dish just before serving. The preferences of the cook often determine which spices are included in the mixture, and in what quantities. This one is a little sweeter than our Indian Spice Blend (p. 334). If you like it, you may want to double or triple this recipe in order to have plenty on hand.

1 tablespoon ground cardamom
1 teaspoon cinnamon
1 teaspoon cumin
½ teaspoon ground cloves
½ teaspoon fresh-ground black
  pepper
¼ teaspoon nutmeg

1. Combine all ingredients and store in an airtight jar.

Makes a little over 2 tablespoons.

"Is that all it says about eye of newt—add to taste?" DRAWING
BY MODELL; © 1983 THE NEW YORKER MAGAZINE, INC.

Indian Spice Blend

PREPARATION TIME: 3 MINUTES.

Curry powder is actually a combination of several of various spices, including ginger, coriander, cardamom, cayenne pepper, cinnamon, chilis, mustard seed, turmeric, cumin, black pepper, poppy seeds, fenugreek, fennel, mace, and cloves. There are many different versions of the blend, depending on the type of dish and the cook. You can create your own special curry using some of these spices. Or mix the blend below to have on hand "in a pinch," and use it any time curry powder is called for.

8 teaspoons cumin
4 teaspoons ground ginger
2 teaspoons ground coriander
2 teaspoons cayenne pepper

4 teaspoons turmeric
2 teaspoons fresh-ground black pepper

1. Combine all ingredients and store in an airtight spice jar.

Makes about 7 tablespoons.

Herb Salt

PREPARATION TIME: 3 MINUTES.

Though the following combination of herbs is one of our favorites, you can experiment with your own combination of herbs. You will soon find that an Herb Salt is an excellent substitute for plain salt, and instead of about 2200 milligrams of sodium per teaspoon, it has only 285 milligrams. Thus a sprinkle (about ⅛ teaspoon) of Herb Salt will give you perhaps 30 or 40 milligrams of sodium, instead of the almost seven times that amount (200 to 300 milligrams) plain salt would provide.

½ teaspoon basil
¼ teaspoon thyme

¼ teaspoon dillweed
¼ teaspoon celery seed

¼ teaspoon salt   ¼ teaspoon dried parsley

1. Combine all ingredients and grind with a mortar and pestle. Store in a small herb jar.

Makes about 1¾ teaspoons.

Traditional Italian Herb Blend

PREPARATION TIME: 3 MINUTES.

Use this blend whenever Italian seasoning is called for but you don't want to take the time to mince or crush garlic, and so on. Add a bay leaf to your recipe along with this blend for the perfect Italian flavor. This mixture will contain 96 milligrams of sodium per teaspoon (less than ¹⁄₂₀ the sodium content of a teaspoon of salt itself, which contains 2200 milligrams sodium, so it can be considered a low-sodium seasoning).

6 tablespoons dried basil   2 teaspoons fresh-ground black
   leaves   pepper
1 tablespoon garlic powder   1 teaspoon salt

1. Combine all ingredients and store in a tightly sealed jar in a cool, dry place.

Makes 8 tablespoons.

Sandwiches, Sandwich Spreads, and the Working World Lunch

My typical quick lunch consists of two slices of whole-grain bread topped with one ounce or two of cheese and a dash of seasoning, then broiled or microwaved for a minute (see Cheese Toast, pp. 340–41). Unlike the English Lord Sandwich, who wouldn't leave his card games long enough to eat a "proper" lunch, and requested two slices of bread with meat between them, thus inventing the "sandwich," Terri and I are more likely to be glued to our word processors, with our sandwiches on the side. Lord Sandwich probably had no idea he was starting a trend that would still be the last word in lunches right up through the twentieth century.

For starters, you don't have to limit yourself to whole-grain bread as your sandwich foundation. Try whole-grain English muffins, bagels, or pita (Middle Eastern pocket) bread. Even a whole-wheat or corn tortilla can function as sandwich bread.

We prefer cooked chicken, turkey, or cheese, and low-calorie tuna salads and spreads such as we show in our recipes, to processed meats such as bologna or salami, which contain salt, sugar, and other additives. In addition, processed meats are usually higher in fat than in any other nutrient. Because a high consumption of the saturated fats found in meat appears to be related to a high blood cholesterol level, which in turn is a risk factor for cardiovascular disease, many food processors have taken to producing reduced-fat processed meats. But be sure to read the labels: many of the so-called reduced-fat processed meats from one food packager can be higher than the regular meats of another.

Read about the Combination Sandwich (p. 340) for basic preparation tips for sandwiches.

And now, a brief word about lunch in general. What do you do if you're an office worker whose usual lunch consists of either a fast-food burger, fries, and a soft drink, or a quick candy bar and a soft drink from a vending machine? Many of us are hampered by lack of time for lunch and less than adequate kitchen facilities in our workplaces.

Of course, more and more restaurants are becoming health-

"Sandwiches!" *THE FAR SIDE.*
COURTESY CHRONICLE FEATURES,
SAN FRANCISCO.

conscious, and offer low-calorie selections that go way beyond the boring old "dieter's special" of a bland hamburger patty, cottage cheese, and a limp lettuce leaf. If you are lucky enough to have a good restaurant near you that caters to health, you're ahead of the game. And remember that many restaurants will be happy to prepare a special low-calorie meal for you, even if they may not list it on the menu. All you have to do is ask.

Bringing your own lunch is one of the best alternatives.

Then you really have control of what you're eating. Sandwiches, fruit, and salads in plastic containers last until lunchtime without refrigeration, and don't require heating up.

In some workplaces, workers band together to fund a "kitchen," with everyone contributing money to buy appliances like a hot plate, a toaster oven, a small camper-sized refrigerator, or even a small microwave. Having these kinds of appliances expands the lunch possibilities tremendously. Soups, stir-fries, leftovers—indeed, whole meals, can be stored in the refrigerator and prepared later for a quick, low-cost lunch.

A refrigerator is especially handy for those who like to bring yogurt for lunch or for a snack. And do bring a snack! Mid-afternoon "blahs" are conducive to raids on the candy machines. Fruit and homemade muffins are tops on our list for snacks, or high-fiber cereal and milk.

So, although we present sandwiches in the following section, many of our recipes, especially soups, stews, stir-fries, or leftovers, can do double-duty as all or part of a nutritious lunch.

Meat Spread

PREPARATION TIME: 8 TO 10 MINUTES.

½ pound cooked meat
  OR poultry
1 small onion, diced
¼ cup wheat germ
  OR cooked red beans

2 tablespoons soy flour
Herb Salt (pp. 334–35)
  OR other herb blend to taste
Freshly ground black pepper to
  taste

1. Blend all ingredients in a food processor. Moisten as needed with catsup, mustard, or salad dressing.

Makes about 1¼ cups. Serving size is about 2 ounces, or ¼ cup.

Per Serving: 99 calories, 38 mg. cholesterol, no dietary fiber, 2 g. fat, 85 mg. sodium. (With ¼ cup cooked red beans: 97 calories, 39 mg. cholesterol, 1 g. dietary fiber, 2 g. fat, 85 mg. sodium.)

Turkey Melt

PREPARATION TIME: 10 MINUTES.   COOKING TIME: 20 MINUTES.

The original recipe called for ham. You can, of course, use lean ham, but try it with turkey, as suggested below, or chicken, for less sodium and fat content. Serve over whole-grain toast or English muffins.

1 teaspoon vegetable oil
4 ounces fresh mushrooms,
 sliced
1 tablespoon butter
 OR margarine
1 tablespoon all-purpose flour
1 cup skim
 OR low-fat milk

¼ cup white wine
¼ teaspoon nutmeg
¼ teaspoon tarragon
⅓ cup grated Gruyère cheese
2 cups diced cooked turkey

1. Brush a skillet with the oil, and heat over medium heat. Add the mushrooms, cover, and reduce heat slightly. Let cook for several minutes, until mushrooms are tender, stirring occasionally.
2. Meanwhile, melt the butter or margarine in a large skillet. Stir in the flour and let cook, stirring constantly, until golden brown. Stir in the milk, wine, nutmeg, and tarragon.
3. Combine the cheese and turkey, and stir into the milk mixture. Add the mushrooms, and heat the mixture through without boiling.

4 servings. Serving size is about 1 cup.

Per Serving: 235 calories, 74 mg. cholesterol, 1 g. dietary fiber, 11 g. fat, 147 mg. sodium.

Combination Sandwich

This is another frequent suggestion on the original *Rotation Diet* menus. The label "combination sandwich" refers to any combination of ingredients between 2 slices of whole-grain bread, such as any slice of meat, and cheese, or spreads with vegetables or cheese.

The way to prepare sandwiches with limited calories is to use lean cuts of meat or poultry, and only limited amounts of mayonnaise or catsup. You may use as much mustard as you like since it is very low in calories. Then you add lettuce, tomato, or other *free vegetables* as desired.

Two slices of whole-grain bread, with one ounce each of meat and cheese, will contain approximately 295 calories. Mayonnaise is about 33 calories a teaspoonful, catsup 16 calories a tablespoon, and mustard is negligible. Along with the *free vegetables,* or a piece of fresh fruit, a Combination Sandwich gives you a satisfying lunch for about 350 to 380 calories. (Compare the calorie content of this lunch with the 650 or so calories you obtain in the typical fast-food hamburger sandwich. The fast-food hamburger, *all by itself,* will have about twice the fat content of your lean slice of meat, and 3 to 6 times more mayonnaise or salad dressing will be used to enhance the flavor.)

For variety, try one of the following spreads. They make especially attractive open-faced sandwiches. Serve with sprouts, or a slice of tomato or cheese; broil in the oven for a hot sandwich.

Cheese Toast

PREPARATION TIME: 3 MINUTES.   COOKING TIME: 3 TO 5 MINUTES.

2 slices whole-grain bread   2 slices tomato (optional)
1 ounce cheese, sliced thin, to
  cover 2 slices of bread

1. Place the bread on a foil-lined baking sheet. Arrange the cheese, and tomato slices if desired, on top of the bread, and place under the broiler for a few minutes, until the cheese is melted.

VARIATIONS: Before broiling, sprinkle the cheese toast with basil, chili powder, cumin, or other herbs and spices.

Serves 1.

Per Serving: 248 calories, 26 mg. cholesterol, 3 g. dietary fiber, 11 g. fat, 452 mg. sodium. (Nutrient values computed for Monterey Jack cheese, one of our favorites.)

Shrimp Spread

PREPARATION TIME: 15 MINUTES.

1 pound cooked, peeled shrimp	1 teaspoon dried tarragon
1 cup low-fat cottage cheese	Dash of Worcestershire sauce
2 ounces Neufchatel cheese	(optional)
½ cup plain low-fat yogurt	Salt and fresh-ground black
1 clove garlic, crushed	pepper to taste

1. Mince the shrimp (or use baby shrimp).
2. Put the cottage cheese and the Neufchatel in a blender or food processor, and blend until smooth. Pour into mixing bowl.
3. Add the remaining ingredients, mixing well. Chill and serve.

Makes about 4 cups. Serving size is ¼ cup.

Per Serving: 60 calories, 48 mg. cholesterol, no dietary fiber, no fat, 160 mg. sodium.

Tuna Salad

PREPARATION TIME: 8 TO 10 MINUTES.

This is our basic tuna salad. As a halfway measure for reducing mayonnaise in our diet, we mix a little mayonnaise (for flavor) with yogurt and mustard. This same dressing goes equally well with cooked chicken, turkey, salmon, crab, lobster, or shrimp. You can vary it by adding a dash of tarragon, dillweed, or other herbs and spices. Use about a pound of cooked seafood, or 2 medium cans, 9¼ ounces each.

On a day when you feel like splurging, add a tablespoon or two of chopped nuts or olives.

2 medium cans (9¼ ounces each) water-packed tuna
½ cup plain low-fat yogurt
2 tablespoons mayonnaise
2 teaspoons Dijon mustard
1 hard-boiled egg, chopped

1½ stalks celery, chopped
1 tablespoon fresh parsley, chopped
Fresh-ground black pepper to taste

1. Combine all ingredients in large bowl. Serve chilled on lettuce leaves or in half a melon or tomato.

4 servings. Serving size is about 1 cup.

Per Serving: 253 calories, 134 mg. cholesterol, 1 g. dietary fiber, 8 g. fat, 331 mg. sodium.

Tuna Salad with Fruit Vinaigrette Dressing

PREPARATION TIME: 5 MINUTES.

We suggest a raspberry vinegar for this salad, although you may use any fruit vinegar; substitute regular wine vinegar if that's all you have on hand or if you don't like fruit vinegars.

1 medium can (9¼ ounces) water-packed tuna, drained

¼ cup chopped apples, unpeeled

¼ cup raisins
¼ cup fruit vinegar
  OR red wine vinegar

½ teaspoon Dijon mustard
½ teaspoon dillweed
½ teaspoon celery seed

1. Combine all ingredients. Serve on lettuce leaves or mixed greens, if desired.

2 servings. Serving size is about 1 cup.

Per Serving: 283 calories, 74 mg. cholesterol, 2 g. dietary fiber, 2 g. fat, 741 g. sodium. (Two leaves of lettuce, about 1 ounce, will add 4 calories, no cholesterol, no dietary fiber, and 2 mg. sodium.)

Mexican Bean Spread

PREPARATION TIME: 8 TO 10 MINUTES.

This can substitute for a Mexican bean dip, and it's great broiled in the oven covered with a slice of cheese or tomato, and sprinkled with oregano.

2 cups cooked OR 1 can (16 ounces) dark-red kidney beans, drained
1 small onion

3 tablespoons catsup
⅛ teaspoon cayenne pepper
Herb Salt (pp. 334–35)
Freshly ground black pepper

1. Blend the above ingredients in a food processor or blender, adding more catsup if needed for desired consistency.

Makes about 1½ cups. Serving size is about 2 ounces, or ¼ cup.

Per Serving: 78 calories, no cholesterol, 6 g. dietary fiber, no fat, 456 mg. sodium.

Curried Turkey Salad

PREPARATION TIME: 10 TO 15 MINUTES.

2 cups cooked turkey, diced
½ cup plain low-fat yogurt
2 tablespoons mayonnaise
¼ cup raisins
¼ cup finely chopped nuts
  OR seeds (walnuts, peanuts,
  sunflower seeds, etc.)

1½ stalks celery, chopped
½ teaspoon Indian Spice Blend
  (p. 334) OR other curry
  powder
Fresh-ground black pepper to
  taste

1. Combine all ingredients in large bowl. Serve chilled on
   lettuce leaves, in half a melon or tomato, or surrounded by
   other fresh fruit in season.

4 servings. Serving size is about 1 cup.

Per Serving: 261 calories, 54 mg. cholesterol, 2 g. dietary fiber,
13 g. fat, 125 mg. sodium.

Crabmeat Spread

PREPARATION TIME: 8 TO 10 MINUTES.

1 cup crabmeat
½ cup celery, diced
1 small onion, diced
Herb Salt (pp. 334–35) to taste

½ green pepper, diced
1 cup sprouts (your choice)
1 cup low-fat cottage cheese

1. Blend all the ingredients with enough salad dressing to
   moisten. (We use about 2 tablespoons of mayonnaise.)

Makes about 3 cups. Serving size is about 2 ounces, or ¼ cup.

Per Serving: 32 calories, 13 mg. cholesterol, no dietary fiber, no
fat, 215 mg. sodium. (With 2 tablespoons mayonnaise: 49 calories,
14 mg. cholesterol, no dietary fiber, 2 g. fat, 228 mg. sodium.)

Beverages

We must start by talking about plain, fresh WATER!

Although it may not have occurred to you, water is our most essential nutrient. No beverage (including those in this chapter) should replace plain, fresh water as the primary beverage in your diet. Aim for eight 8-ounce glasses per day.

For many people this is very hard advice to follow. Water doesn't taste very good anymore when it comes out of the tap in many parts of the country. In fact, the consumption of soda pop is greater than that of water in the United States.

Won't diet drinks do? In my opinion, no. Perhaps in moderation they don't do any harm, but using intensely sweetened drinks of any kind seems to dull our sensitivity to sweetness and to keep alive a sweet tooth in those who may find it hard to manage their weight.

But plain water won't do for all occasions and we are constantly asked, "What am I supposed to drink?" Well, coffee or tea may do no harm provided you limit yourself to 2 or 3 cups per day, and many nutritionists believe it's okay to count them among the recommended daily total of 64 fluid ounces of fluids. But what about treats and special occasions? Isn't there anything you can drink that's really tasty and not bad for you?

This chapter contains some suggestions for making flavored teas and coffees and for other beverages that are satisfying and good for you, such as some tasty blended fruit drinks. Notice the use of vanilla flavoring: it makes beverages taste sweeter without adding any calories and it reduces the need for sugar.

346 | THE ROTATION DIET COOKBOOK

Other extracts can do the same. If you live in a part of the country where you can enjoy a real winter, you will find that Herb Rum Tea is even more satisfying on snowy nights than it is on rainy nights. It's a favorite of mine after a long walk or run in chilly weather. All of our recommendations are good for entertaining.

An important consideration for making beverages is the taste of the water you're using. If your tap water doesn't taste particularly good, it may be adding an off-flavor to other beverages that you make with it. That may be why you prefer sweetened bottled drinks over water or the drinks that you blend yourself using tap water. Try some bottled spring water for tea, coffee, and the other beverage suggestions in this chapter. If you notice a pleasant improvement, you might consider using bottled water for drinking and cooking. Or you might want to purchase an activated-charcoal filter for your kitchen faucet to remove chlorine and other objectionable organic matter. Be sure to get one that's bacteriostatic, to prevent bacteria from multiplying in water from which chlorine has been removed. You will find it easier to replace sweet-flavored beverages in your diet if your water tastes fresh and clean. You can also try seltzer water.

Two warnings: I do not recommend that you use distilled water as your primary source of fluids. Tap water and spring water contain a number of essential minerals that are removed in the distillation process, and appliances that soften water may add a considerable amount of sodium. Be sure that your water requires softening before you buy this type of water conditioner. The activated charcoal filters that I advise for making tap water more palatable do not remove essential minerals, nor do they add unnecessary sodium.

Fruit and vegetable juices are good, and for variety, there are many blended juices available in supermarkets and health-food stores if you don't want to combine your own. Fruit juice blended with herb tea also makes a satisfying punch, and the possibilities for combining are practically endless. If you are interested in limiting your calorie intake, however, we recommend you turn to whole fresh fruit rather than juice. Most people end up consuming fewer calories when they eat fresh fruit, which contains considerable fiber, than they do when they drink juice, which is almost devoid of fiber.

Banana-Strawberry Frozen Delight

PREPARATION TIME: 7 TO 8 MINUTES.   FREEZING TIME: 2 HOURS.

2 medium bananas, peeled
½ cup evaporated skim milk
½ teaspoon vanilla extract
Strawberry, banana,
  OR almond extract (optional)

1 package (10 ounces) frozen
  whole unsweetened
  strawberries

1. Wrap the peeled bananas in plastic wrap and place in the freezer for at least 2 hours, until frozen.
2. Cut the frozen bananas into chunks. Place the chunks in a blender or food processor.
3. Combine the milk and the extract(s) and pour over the bananas. Blend until smooth.
4. Reserve a couple of strawberries to slice for a garnish, if desired. Gradually add the remaining strawberries to the blender or food processor, blending briefly after each addition. Serve immediately.

4 servings. Serving size is about ¾ cup.

Per Serving: 102 calories, 1 mg. cholesterol, 3 g. dietary fiber, no fat, 39 mg. sodium.

Herb Rum Tea

PREPARATION TIME: 8 TO 10 MINUTES.

Also known as "Chilly, Rainy Night Tea." We combine a favorite black tea, such as Earl Grey or Darjeeling, with a favorite herb tea (usually mint, lemon, or almond). Then we put a teaspoon of rum in a mug, and pour in the hot, brewed tea. Try adding a whole clove, a piece of cinnamon stick, or an orange or lemon slice. A great warmer-upper.

Coffee Suggestions

For those who are used to drinking coffee with sugar and/or cream, here are a few hints that may help you reduce or completely omit those high-calorie additions. When brewing coffee, add to the grounds one or more of the following:

A dash or two of ground cinnamon, cardamom, or other sweet spices
A piece of vanilla bean (about ⅛-inch per cup)
A bit of orange peel
Ground almonds (about ¼ teaspoon per cup)

We also suggest that you use dairy products rather than the non-dairy substitutes if you don't take coffee black. The substitutes may contain even more saturated fat than the dairy product; for example, half-and-half has about the same calories as non-dairy creamers, and, in our opinion, the substitute can't compare in flavor. (Both half-and-half and non-dairy liquids contain 20 calories per tablespoon. The powders contain about 10 per teaspoon. Whole milk is only 10 calories per tablespoon.)

Cool Coffee Special

PREPARATION TIME: 15 TO 20 MINUTES.

For a refreshing dessert drink, try this with either regular or decaffeinated coffee, or a blend of the two, which is how we drink it. You can substitute instant coffee if you prefer.

2 cups hot brewed coffee
2 cups cold skim milk
2 cups cold water

2 eggs, separated
4 teaspoons sugar
1 teaspoon vanilla extract

1. Put the hot coffee in a large saucepan.
2. Add the cold milk and cold water and stir. Beat the egg yolks and add to the coffee mixture. Stir in the sugar and vanilla.
3. Beat the egg whites until stiff. Gently fold them into the coffee mixture. Serve over ice.

6 servings. Serving size is about 1 cup.

Per Serving: 67 calories, 93 mg. cholesterol, no dietary fiber, 2 g. fat, 66 mg. sodium.

Great Shakes

PREPARATION TIME: 8 TO 10 MINUTES.

Here is the basic recipe for a satisfying, sweet substitute for the common, sugar-loaded milkshake. Vary this recipe by using any combination of fruit. Our favorites are orange-banana, as shown below, strawberry-banana, and strawberry-peach. Try different flavorings as well, such as almond extract, cinnamon, cloves, or cardamom. This makes a complete breakfast or lunch for one person, or a dessert drink for one or two people.

2 1 cup plain low-fat yogurt ½ teaspoon vanilla
1 small banana Dash nutmeg
1 medium orange

1. Place yogurt in blender or food processor. Cut the fruit into chunks and add to the yogurt. Blend for 30 seconds. Add vanilla and nutmeg, and blend until smooth. Serve immediately.

1 serving. Serving size is 2 cups.

Per Recipe: 310 calories, 14 mg. cholesterol, 6 g. dietary fiber, 4 g. fat, 160 mg. sodium.

Fruit 'n' Juice Shake

PREPARATION TIME: 5 TO 10 MINUTES.

This recipe combines whole fruit with fruit juice for a refreshing, low-calorie "shake." You can use your imagination with this one; for starters, try banana, orange, apple, and/or berries; mix and match your favorite fruit flavors.

10 ounces fruit juice 1 medium piece of fruit, sliced

1. Combine the ingredients in a blender, and blend for about 30 seconds.

2 servings. Serving size is about 1 cup.

Per Serving (using orange juice and pineapple): 82 calories, no cholesterol, 1 g. dietary fiber, no fat, 2 mg. sodium.

Spiced Tea

PREPARATION TIME: 10 MINUTES.

Many spiced teas call for premixed instant teas and lemonades, which are often high in sugar, as well as other additives. Here is our refreshing alternative that lets you control the amount of sugar. Serve hot or cold.

4 cups brewed black tea
2 cinnamon sticks
1 cup unsweetened orange
  juice

1 to 2 teaspoons sugar
1 teaspoon ground cloves
1 to 2 teaspoons lemon juice
  OR 4 slices of fresh lemon

1. When brewing the tea, place the cinnamon sticks in the same pan or teapot. When the tea is ready, discard the cinnamon sticks.
2. Add the remaining ingredients and serve, or chill first and serve over ice cubes if you want iced tea.

4 servings. Serving size is about 1 1/4 cups.

Per Serving: 38 calories, no cholesterol, no dietary fiber, no fat, 9 mg. sodium.

"That settles it Carl! . . . From now on, you're getting only decaffeinated coffee!" *THE FAR SIDE.* COURTESY CHRONICLE FEATURES, SAN FRANCISCO.

Irish Spiced Coffee

PREPARATION TIME: 10 MINUTES.   COOKING TIME: 10 MINUTES.

This is a dessert drink, which is satisfying served alone, or with a barely-sweet dessert such as Sweet Pineapple Squares (p. 374) or Carrot-Nut Tea Bread (p. 367). You may use "store-bought" bottled lemon and orange peel in this recipe. Though they tend to have small amounts of sugar added, the total sugar in this recipe is minimal for a dessert.

2 cups strong black coffee (regular or decaffeinated)
2 teaspoons sugar
2 whole cloves
1 stick cinnamon

1 teaspoon finely grated lemon peel
1 teaspoon finely grated orange peel
¼ cup Irish whiskey

1. Bring the coffee, sugar, cloves, cinnamon, and lemon and

orange rind to a boil in a saucepan. Let boil for a couple of minutes, then remove from heat. Remove the cloves and cinnamon stick and discard.
2. Add the whiskey, and serve. Or chill—it is delicious cold, for a summer dessert drink.

VARIATION: For an exotic chilled dessert, add to the recipe 1 envelope of unflavored gelatin, as follows:

1. Follow step one.
2. Soften the gelatin in the Irish whiskey. Then add the hot coffee mixture, and stir until the gelatin dissolves.
3. Pour into 2 small serving dishes or parfait glasses, and chill overnight. Garnish with a curl of lemon or orange peel, if desired.

The taste and texture will surprise you!

2 servings. Serving size is about 1 cup.

Per Serving: 90 calories, no cholesterol, no dietary fiber, no fat, 3 mg. sodium.

Desserts

WARNING! It is dangerous to read this chapter without also reading the next chapter!

If you put the recipes of this chapter "into practice," and if you are a sedentary person, you must "go all the way": you must develop the active life-style that will permit you to enjoy them without gaining weight!

We have made a special effort to include desserts that are relatively low in fat and sugar, and high in more valuable nutrients, so that you will see that a treat need not necessarily be a "cheat." Our goal is to reduce fat, sugar, and salt in basic dessert recipes by significant amounts, often by as much as 50 percent in comparison with other recipes of a similar nature.

Sometimes we combine more healthful ingredients with the less healthful processed ingredients that have worked their way into our style of food preparation because they are easier to use, "fluffier," or in other ways more satisfying to the human preference for fat and sugar. We blend whole-grain flour with all-purpose flour, or use only whole-grain flour when appropriate, and we use honey and molasses when they enhance flavor, rather than relying on just granulated white sugar. (If you find that 100 percent whole-wheat flour makes a cookie or cake too heavy for you, try using whole-wheat pastry flour or blending it with unbleached white flour. Whole-wheat pastry flour has had a small part of the fibrous portion removed to make it lighter than 100 percent whole-wheat and we frequently use it. We also suggest skim and low-fat milk in place of whole milk, and low-fat yogurt, half-and-half, or sour cream, in place of heavy cream, whenever these will do the job both satisfactorily and tastily.

Some of our recipes, such as the Oatmeal Pecan Cookies (p. 368), use vegetable oil instead of solid shortenings such as butter or margarine. You can often make this kind of substitution with perfectly acceptable results. Although the calorie content in all fats is about the same, the amounts and types of fats you use, especially in desserts, which tend to be relatively high in fat, can make a difference in your health.

Fats are present in foods in three forms: saturated, monounsaturated, and polyunsaturated. *Saturated fats* have a chemical structure that tends to make them harden at room temperature; lard, butter, some margarines, and some vegetable oils are saturated fats.

Research has shown that there is a link between high intake of fat in the diet, and the risk of certain forms of cancer. *Saturated fats* raise the blood level of cholesterol, which is a primary risk factor for heart disease. On the other hand, monounsaturated and polyunsaturated fats either reduce or have no effect on blood cholesterol.

The typical American diet contains 40 to 50 percent calories from fat, yet health authorities recommend 30 percent or less. Saturated fats should equal no more than 10 percent of total calories for the day, or, in other words, one-third of the 30 percent total of all fat calories per day. The average American diet contains 17 percent.

Various foods contain various combinations of the different types of fats, but in any given food, there is usually more of one type. Animal fats, for instance, are primarily saturated. Even some vegetable fats are highly saturated, such as coconut oil, palm oil, and cocoa butter.

Polyunsaturated fats, which tend to lower blood cholesterol, are usually liquid at room temperature. They are: corn oil, safflower oil, sunflower oil, soybean oil, or margarines made from these oils. However, hydrogenation, the process which "saturates" or hardens vegetable fats, gives these fats some of

the same characteristics as animal fats. Check labels for hy-
drogenated margarines that have been chemically saturated.
The softer the margarine, the better. You can buy margarines
in a tub, for example, that are more polyunsaturated than stick
margarine.

Monounsaturated fats, which also tend to have a choles-
terol-lowering effect, are olive oil and peanut oil. Avocados,
too, mainly have monounsaturated fat, but they are high in
total fat and calories compared with other fruits and vegetables, so eat them in moderation.

When vegetable oil is called for in a dessert recipe, I usually
use corn oil. I normally use olive oil or peanut oil for sautéeing,
and I sometimes use a little butter with these oils, since nothing can quite equal the flavor that butter imparts to many
foods. If you like popcorn, try avocado oil for popping. It adds
a faint, but delicious nutty flavor. We don't care much for
air-blown popcorn, and corn popped with avocado oil will
contain only about 54 calories per cup, popped. (Our recipe is
2 tablespoons oil with ½ cup popcorn, or enough to make 6
cups popped.) We add no additional fat to the popcorn after
popping, and use one of various seasonings, such as nutritional
yeast, garlic or onion powder, or chili powder. I like just a light
sprinkle of salt on mine.

Although our desserts are relatively low in fat, sugar, and
salt, we make no effort to have every recipe come in at, say,
just 30 percent of total calories from fat. THAT IS THE AVER-
AGE, TOTAL TARGET FOR A DAY, NOT EVERY SINGLE
MEAL OR DISH. If you eat a well-balanced diet throughout
the day, with plenty of fresh fruit and vegetables, low-fat meats
and milk products, and if you avoid fried foods, your basic diet,
before dessert, may contain as little as 20 to 25 percent fat.
Thus, there is no need to fear an occasional dessert of 300
calories, in which 50 percent of the calories come from fat:
your total fat for the day will still fall within the guidelines of
a nutritious diet.

However, we must issue one more warning. In spite of the
lowered fat and sugar, the desserts in this chapter are really

good! Don't have too many, or too much, around at one time!

During the period in which we were developing and testing recipes in great numbers, we had to sample eight of these desserts in one evening. (That was our "cookie-testing" week.) To resist overeating at least a little under these circumstances would have required the willpower of a saint. Neither of us qualified!

Finally, a word of advice when you decide to "go all the way" at your favorite restaurant and indulge in the super-rich

"Let's just go in and see what happens."
DRAWING BY BOOTH; © 1986 THE NEW YORKER MAGAZINE, INC.

New York-style cheesecake or the seven-layer cake in which the layers of frosting are thicker than the layers of cake. If you are an active person in good health, we don't think an occasional indulgence of this sort is harmful. We sometimes do it ourselves, and, having relatively low cholesterol levels and no hypertension, we don't feel guilty about it. You don't need to kick yourself, either. But we *don't* go overboard on a regular basis, and you won't want to either, especially in your own cooking, once you see how you can reduce the fat in your own recipes.

Take a look at Kahlua Chocolate Cheesecake (pp. 362–63), for example. There is simply no need to use cream cheese and heavy cream in your own baking once you learn how to use lower-fat ingredients for desserts in the appropriate proportions. I challenge anyone to make a better cheesecake, no matter how much fat you use! And do write to me if you can devise a better cheesecake! I love cheesecake and promise to find a way to share your expertise with others who share your (and my) predilections.

Apricot-Banana Bread

PREPARATION TIME: 15 MINUTES.   BAKING TIME: 35 TO 40 MINUTES.

This makes a lightly sweet, wholesome dessert bread.

2 medium bananas, mashed
4 whole dried apricots,
    chopped (8 halves)
1½ cups whole-wheat flour
2 teaspoons baking powder

½ teaspoon salt
Dash nutmeg
⅓ cup vegetable oil
⅓ cup honey
1 egg

1. Combine the bananas and apricots in a small bowl.
2. In another bowl, combine the dry ingredients. Add the oil and the honey, then beat in the egg. Add the banana-apricot mixture, blending well.
3. Spray a 9×5-inch loaf pan with nonstick vegetable cooking spray, or oil very lightly by rubbing a bit of oil on the pan with a paper towel. Pour the batter into the pan, which will be about ⅓ full.
4. Bake at 350 degrees for 35 to 40 minutes or until slightly browned, and a toothpick inserted in the middle comes out clean.

Makes 10 slices about ⅞-inch thick each. Serving size is 1 slice.

Per Serving: 195 calories, 27 mg. cholesterol, 3 g. dietary fiber, 8 g. fat, 189 mg. sodium.

Chocolate-Chip Cookies

PREPARATION TIME: 15 MINUTES.   BAKING TIME: 8 TO 10 MINUTES.

It would be hard to imagine a dessert chapter that didn't include an example of a recipe for one of America's favorites, chocolate-chip cookies. We think our version of this traditional recipe came out just fine; we cut the fat by one-quarter and the sugar by half.

¾ cup margarine, softened
½ cup brown sugar, firmly packed
½ cup granulated white sugar
1 teaspoon vanilla
1 teaspoon water
2 eggs

1 cup whole-wheat flour
1 cup all-purpose flour
1 teaspoon baking soda
1 teaspoon salt
8 ounces chocolate chips
⅔ cup chopped nuts

1. Preheat the oven to 375 degrees.
2. In a large bowl, combine the margarine, sugars, vanilla, and water. Beat in the eggs.
3. In another bowl, combine the flours, baking soda, and salt. Gradually add this to the wet ingredients, blending well. Stir in the chocolate chips and the nuts.
4. Drop by rounded teaspoonsful onto Teflon or ungreased baking sheets. Bake until golden brown, about 8 to 10 minutes.

VARIATION: Add a couple of teaspoons of grated orange rind to the batter before baking, for Orange Chocolate-Chip Cookies.

Makes 3 dozen cookies, about 2 inches in diameter.

Per Cookie: 131 calories, 15 mg. cholesterol, 1 g. dietary fiber, 8 g. fat, 133 mg. sodium.

Chocolate-Drop Peanut Butter Cookies

PREPARATION TIME: 30 MINUTES.   BAKING TIME: 10 MINUTES.

What a combination: chocolate chips AND peanut butter! Kids of all ages like the way these Chocolate-Drop Peanut Butter Cookies look, with the four chocolate chips in the middle.

⅓ cup margarine
⅓ cup brown sugar, firmly
   packed
⅓ cup granulated white sugar
1 egg, beaten
⅓ cup peanut butter
1 tablespoon skim milk
1 tablespoon water

1 teaspoon vanilla extract
1 cup all-purpose flour
¾ cup whole-wheat flour
1 teaspoon baking soda
½ teaspoon salt
3 ounces chocolate chips (about
   ½ cup)

1. Preheat the oven to 375 degrees.
2. Cream the margarine and sugars in a large bowl. Beat in the egg, peanut butter, milk, water, and vanilla.
3. In another bowl, combine the flours, baking soda, and salt. Add gradually to the wet ingredients, mixing well.
4. Form the dough into small balls, about 1-inch in diameter. Place the balls on an ungreased baking sheet, and make a depression in each ball by pressing your thumb in the center. Drop 4 chocolate chips into each ball.
5. Bake for about 10 minutes, until the cookies begin to brown on the bottom.

Makes about 3 dozen cookies, about 1½ inches in diameter.

Per Cookie: 79 calories, 8 mg. cholesterol, 1 g. dietary fiber, 4 g. fat, 76 mg. sodium.

German Apple Cake

PREPARATION TIME: 45 MINUTES.   BAKING TIME: 50 MINUTES.

Many recipes call for a little salt to bring out the flavors of the other ingredients. However, this recipe is delicious with no added salt.

4 medium apples, unpeeled
Juice of 2½ lemons (about 6 tablespoons)
3 tablespoons butter
  OR margarine, softened
¾ cup granulated white sugar
2 eggs, separated
Grated peel of ½ lemon
½ cup whole-wheat flour

1 cup all-purpose flour
1 teaspoon baking powder
¾ cup skim milk
1 tablespoon rum
Nonstick vegetable cooking spray
1 teaspoon vegetable oil
2 teaspoons powdered sugar

1. Slice the apples in thin wedges, remove the cores, and place in a bowl. Sprinkle with two-thirds of the lemon juice, and set aside.
2. Cream the butter and sugar together. Then gradually beat in the egg yolks, the remaining lemon juice, and the lemon peel.
3. Sift together the flours and the baking powder in one bowl, and combine the milk and rum in another. Gradually add the dry ingredients to the butter-sugar-egg mixture, alternating with the milk-and-rum mixture.
4. Beat the egg whites until they form stiff peaks. Fold into the batter.
5. Spray a springform pan with cooking spray, or lightly oil it with vegetable oil. Pour in the batter and decorate the top with the sliced apples. Lightly brush the apples with the teaspoon of vegetable oil. Bake at 350 degrees in the center of your oven for about 40 minutes, then move to a higher rack in the oven and bake 10 minutes more to finish cooking the apples.
6. Let cool for a few minutes, then remove from the pan, and sprinkle with powdered sugar. (You can use a sifter to evenly distribute the sugar over the top.)

12 servings.

Per Serving: 184 calories, 54 mg. cholesterol, 2 g. dietary fiber, 5 g. fat, 80 mg. sodium.

Peach Cobbler

PREPARATION TIME: 15 MINUTES.   BAKING TIME: 30 MINUTES.

4 cups sliced peaches, fresh or
   canned, unsweetened,
   drained
2 tablespoons lemon juice
½ cup whole-wheat flour
⅓ cup brown sugar

1 teaspoon cinnamon
2 tablespoons butter
   OR margarine
6 tablespoons plain low-fat
   yogurt (optional)
Dash cinnamon (optional)

1. Preheat oven to 375 degrees.
2. Place the peaches in a 9-inch pie pan or shallow casserole
   dish and sprinkle with lemon juice.
3. In a bowl, blend the dry ingredients. Cut in the butter
   with two knives or a pastry blender, to make a coarse,
   crumbly texture. Spread over the peaches.
4. Bake about 30 minutes.
5. If desired, top each serving with a tablespoon of yogurt
   and a dash of cinnamon.

6 servings. Serving size is about ¾ cup.

Per Serving: 161 calories, 10 mg. cholesterol, 4 g. dietary fiber,
4 g. fat, 40 mg. sodium.

Kahlua Chocolate Cheesecake

PREPARATION TIME: 30 MINUTES.   BAKING TIME: 1¼ HOURS.

This cheesecake tastes as good as it sounds . . . maybe even
better!

¾ cup graham cracker crumbs
   (about 9 squares)
1 teaspoon brown sugar
1½ tablespoons melted butter
   OR margarine
½ cup semisweet chocolate
   chips

1 container (15 ounces)
   part-skim ricotta cheese
¾ cup plain low-fat yogurt
2 eggs OR substitute 4 egg
   whites
⅓ cup Kahlua
   OR other coffee liqueur

¼ cup firmly packed brown
  sugar
¼ cup granulated white sugar

1 tablespoon cornstarch
Fresh strawberries (optional)

1. Preheat the oven to 350 degrees. Combine the crumbs, the 1 teaspoon of brown sugar, and the melted butter or margarine in a small bowl. Press firmly into the bottom of a 10-inch springform pan. Bake for 10 minutes, then set aside and let cool. Leave oven on.
2. Melt the chocolate chips in a double boiler.
3. Whir the ricotta cheese and yogurt in a blender or food processor, adding small amounts at a time. Blend until smooth. Add the eggs and blend briefly.
4. Combine the cheese mixture and melted chocolate in a large bowl. Stir in the Kahlua, sugars, and cornstarch, and pour over the baked crust.
5. Bake for 1 hour and 15 minutes, or until cake sets in the middle. Turn off oven, leave cake inside with oven door open, and let cool for 2 hours.
6. Chill for at least 4 hours. Release sides of pan, and garnish the cake with fresh sliced strawberries if desired.

12 servings.

Per Serving: 204 calories, 63 mg. cholesterol, 1 g. dietary fiber, 9 g. fat, 150 mg. sodium.

Crêpes with Fresh Strawberries (Julian's)

PREPARATION TIME: 30 MINUTES.   COOKING TIME: 15 MINUTES.

This recipe uses barley-malt sweetener in place of sugar. You may be able to find it in a well-stocked supermarket; if not, use sugar instead. Try serving this dessert with the Grilled Duck Breast (p. 183).

The crêpes:

1 egg
2 egg whites
1¼ cups skim milk
¼ cup unbleached white flour
1½ teaspoons vanilla extract

The filling:

about 1 to 1¼ cup strawberries to yield ¾ cup fresh-strawberry purée (see step 3)
1½ cups low-fat cottage cheese
24 fresh strawberries, sliced in halves

The sauce:

1 cup plain low-fat yogurt
2 tablespoons fresh orange juice
1 teaspoon orange rind
1 teaspoon lemon rind
4 teaspoons honey
A pinch or two of barley-malt sweetener
Fresh mint, if available, for garnish

1. Combine all the crêpe ingredients in a blender and blend for 2 minutes. Set aside, and let the mixture rest for 2 hours.
2. Cook the crêpes in a 5-inch nonstick crêpe pan for 30 seconds each. (The batter yields about 12 crêpes.) Set aside and let cool.
3. Meanwhile, whir enough fresh strawberries in a blender to make ¾ cup of purée. Set aside. Prepare the sauce by combining all ingredients in a small bowl, mixing well.
4. Spread 2 tablespoons of cottage cheese over half of each cooled crêpe. Add 1 tablespoon of strawberry purée, and 4 strawberry halves. Fold the crêpe in half. Spread about 2 tablespoons of the sauce over and around each crêpe.

(When we asked how much sauce they used, the answer was, "About 2 tablespoons—whatever looks good!") Garnish with a sprig of fresh mint.

12 servings. Serving size is 1 crêpe.

Per Serving: 77 calories, 26 mg. cholesterol, 1 g. dietary fiber, 1 g. fat, 156 mg. sodium.

Honey-Orange Bran Bread

PREPARATION TIME: 15 MINUTES.   BAKING TIME: 50 MINUTES.

2 cups all-purpose flour	1 cup All-Bran cereal
1 teaspoon baking powder	½ cup honey
½ teaspoon baking soda	¾ cup orange juice
¾ teaspoon salt	1 egg
¾ teaspoon ground cinnamon	2 tablespoons vegetable oil
¼ teaspoon ground cloves	1 teaspoon grated orange peel

1. In a small mixing bowl, combine the flour, baking powder, soda, salt, cinnamon, and cloves. Set aside.
2. In a large mixing bowl, combine the cereal, honey, and orange juice. Let stand for 2 minutes. Beat in the egg, vegetable oil, and orange peel. Add the flour mixture. Stir only until moistened. Spread the batter evenly into a lightly greased 9 × 5 × 3-inch loaf pan.
3. Bake at 350 degrees for 50 minutes, or until knife inserted in center comes out clean.

Makes 1 loaf of 16 slices. Serving size is 1 slice.

Per Serving: 120 calories, 20 mg. cholesterol, 2 g. dietary fiber, 2 g. fat, 290 mg. sodium.

Almond Drops

PREPARATION TIME: 25 MINUTES.   BAKING TIME: 15 MINUTES.

Here is an example of a cookie in which we revise the original recipe by blending flours, reducing salt by half, and sugar and fat by 25 percent. Try this approach in your own cookie recipes. These cookies are great with a cup of fresh coffee.

1 cup whole-wheat flour
1½ cups all-purpose flour
½ teaspoon baking soda
½ teaspoon salt
¾ cup granulated white sugar
¾ cup margarine

1 egg
¼ cup skim milk
1 teaspoon almond extract
⅓ cup almonds, chopped or
    slivered

1. Preheat oven to 325 degrees.
2. In a large bowl, sift flours, baking soda, salt, and sugar together. Cut in the margarine with a pastry blender or two knives until the mixture looks like fine cornmeal.
3. Lightly beat together the egg and the milk, and add to the above mixture, along with the almond extract and almonds. Mix well, and shape into small balls, about ¾-inch in diameter. Place them on an ungreased baking sheet, and press them down with your hand to flatten them slightly.
4. Bake for about 15 minutes, or until golden brown on the bottom. Cool on a wire rack.

Makes about 4 dozen cookies, about 1 to 1½ inches in diameter.

Per Cookie: 68 calories, 6 mg. cholesterol, 1 g. dietary fiber, 4 g. fat, 67 mg. sodium.

Carrot-Nut Tea Bread

PREPARATION TIME: 15 MINUTES.   BAKING TIME: 45 TO 55 MINUTES.

This is a mildly sweet quick bread.

2 eggs
¾ cup granulated white sugar
⅓ cup vegetable oil
⅓ cup water
1 cup whole-wheat flour
½ cup all-purpose flour
1 teaspoon baking soda
1 teaspoon baking powder

1 teaspoon salt
1 teaspoon cinnamon
1 cup grated carrots (about 3
  medium)
⅓ cup chopped nuts
Nonstick vegetable cooking
  spray

1. Preheat the oven to 375 degrees. Spray a 9 × 5-inch loaf
   pan with cooking spray and set aside.
2. Beat together the eggs, sugar, oil, and water.
3. In another bowl, combine the flours, soda, baking powder,
   salt, and cinnamon. Add the dry ingredients to the liquid
   ingredients.
4. Stir in the grated carrots and the chopped nuts. Pour the
   batter into the pan.
5. Bake for 45 to 55 minutes, testing for doneness by insert-
   ing a knife or toothpick into the center of the loaf to see
   if it comes out clean. The top should be evenly browned
   when done.

12 servings. Serving size is 1 slice about ¾-inch thick.

Per Serving: 193 calories, 44 mg. cholesterol, 2 g. dietary fiber,
10 g. fat, 287 mg. sodium.

Oatmeal Pecan Cookies

PREPARATION TIME: 10 MINUTES.   BAKING TIME: 12 TO 15 MINUTES.

We mixed this dough in a matter of minutes one night. A slightly crumbly and crisp cookie.

½ cup vegetable oil
½ cup brown sugar, firmly
  packed
¾ cup granulated white sugar
1 egg
¼ cup water
1 teaspoon vanilla extract

1 teaspoon rum (optional)
3 cups rolled oats
¾ cup whole-wheat flour
½ teaspoon baking soda
¼ cup chopped pecans
  OR other nuts

1. Combine oil, sugars, egg, water, vanilla, and rum in a large bowl, blending well. (A fork works fine for this.)
2. Stir in the remaining ingredients.
3. Drop by rounded teaspoonfuls onto an ungreased baking sheet, and bake at 350 degrees for about 12 to 15 minutes.

Makes approximately 3 dozen cookies, about 2 inches in diameter.

Per Cookie: 96 calories, 8 mg. cholesterol, 1 g. dietary fiber, 4 g. fat, 15 mg. sodium.

Lemon-Lime Coconut Pie

PREPARATION TIME: 40 MINUTES.   REFRIGERATION TIME: 1 HOUR.

1 tablespoon butter
  OR margarine
1¼ cups flaked coconut
1 tablespoon fresh lemon juice
5 tablespoons fresh lime juice
Water
1 envelope unflavored gelatin

⅓ cup granulated white sugar
½ teaspoon vanilla
1 tablespoon grated lime rind
  (about 2 limes)
2 cups plain low-fat yogurt
1 teaspoon grated lemon rind

1. Preheat the oven to 325 degrees. Put the butter or marga-

rine in a 9-inch pie plate, place the plate in the oven, and melt the butter.

2. Remove the plate from the oven, add the coconut, and mix with the butter to coat. Press the coconut onto the bottom of the plate (it will not stick to the sides), return to the oven, and bake for 15 minutes, or until slightly brown. Let cool.

3. Meanwhile, combine the lemon and lime juices in a measuring cup. Add enough water to make ¾ cup, then pour the liquid into a saucepan. Pour in the gelatin, and let stand for a few minutes to soften. Add the sugar, and cook the mixture over low heat until the gelatin and sugar are dissolved, stirring constantly.

4. Remove the pan from the heat, stir in the vanilla and the lime rind, and let cool for about 10 minutes. Then place in the refrigerator or freezer until partially set, about 10 more minutes. It will reach the consistency of raw, unbeaten egg whites.

5. Beat the gelatin mixture with an eggbeater or electric mixer, until fluffy. Fold in the yogurt, and beat the mixture again until smooth. Pour into the cooled crust, sprinkle with the lemon rind, and chill the pie in the refrigerator at least 1 hour, until firm.

8 servings.

Per Serving: 132 calories, 7 mg. cholesterol, 2 g. dietary fiber, 7 g. fat, 58 mg. sodium.

Pineapple Ice

PREPARATION TIME: 10 MINUTES.   FREEZING TIME: 3 HOURS.

This recipe is "easier than pie"—and has a lot fewer calories. It's also refreshing when frozen into ice cubes and served in beverages.

1 large, ripe pineapple, cut up   2 to 4 tablespoons honey
2 teaspoons lemon juice   (optional)

1. Place the pineapple chunks and the lemon juice (and the honey, if the pineapple doesn't seem very sweet) in a blender or food processor. Purée until smooth.
2. Pour into a plastic container or ice-cube trays, and freeze for about 1 hour.
3. When mixture is slushy-frozen, purée again in the blender until creamy. Pour it back into your freezer containers, and freeze at least 2 hours more.

6 to 8 servings, depending on the size of the pineapple. Serving size is about ½ cup.

Per Serving (8) 54 calories, no cholesterol, 1 g. dietary fiber, no fat, 1 mg. sodium.

Mandel Bread

PREPARATION TIME: 25 MINUTES.   BAKING TIME: 35 TO 45 MINUTES.

Actually, this is not a bread, but cookies that are first baked in
a loaf form, and then cut into slices or bars, and baked again.
A traditional Jewish recipe, modified for lower fat and sugar
content, this is another winner with a good cup of fresh-ground
coffee.

¾ cup margarine, softened to
  room temperature
¾ cup granulated white sugar
4 eggs
1 teaspoon vanilla
1½ teaspoons ground
  cinnamon

2 cups whole-wheat flour
2 cups all-purpose flour
1 teaspoon baking powder
½ cup chopped almonds

1. In a large bowl, cream together the margarine and the
   sugar. Beat in the eggs, vanilla, and cinnamon.
2. In another bowl, combine the flours and baking powder.
   Add to the wet ingredients, mixing well. Stir in the almonds.
3. Form the dough into a long loaf about 1-inch high and 4
   inches wide.
4. Place on an ungreased baking sheet, and bake at 375 degrees until browned on the bottom, about 25 minutes.
5. Remove the bread from the oven, place it on a cutting
   board, and cut it into 26 ½-inch thick slices. Arrange the
   slices on the baking sheet, and bake until toasted on one
   side. Turn them over, and toast the other side. Cool on a
   wire rack.

Makes about 26 cookies, about 3 × 1½ inches.

Per Cookie: 163 calories, 42 mg. cholesterol, 2 g. dietary fiber,
8 g. fat, 87 mg. sodium.

Old-Fashioned Blueberry Betty

PREPARATION TIME: 12 TO 15 MINUTES.   BAKING TIME: 30 MINUTES.

One of our taste-testers' favorites! Use a metal pan for this recipe, as the blueberries may stain white porcelain or stoneware casserole dishes.)

2 cups blueberries, fresh or frozen (thawed)
¼ cup granulated white sugar
Juice of one lemon
4 cups whole-wheat bread cubes, about ½-inch square

⅓ cup firmly packed brown sugar
1 teaspoon ground cinnamon

1. In a large bowl, combine the blueberries, white sugar, and lemon juice. In another bowl, combine the bread cubes, brown sugar, and cinnamon.
2. Fill an 8- or 9-inch-square metal baking pan by alternating the two mixtures, starting with half the blueberries, then half the bread cubes, and so on.
3. Bake at 350 degrees for about 30 minutes.

8 servings. Serving size is about ¾ cup.

Per Serving: 159 calories, no cholesterol, 3 g. dietary fiber, 1 g. fat, 165 mg. sodium.

Cookie-Crust Fruit "Pizza"

PREPARATION TIME: 35 MINUTES.   BAKING TIME: 10 MINUTES.

A thick cookie crust is made attractive with a creamy topping and a stunning arrangement of colorful fresh fruit. You can prepare the crust ahead of time, since it needs to be refrigerated for several hours. Once the fruit is cut up, it tends to begin turning brown, so the "pizza" is at its best served the same day, although the cut-up fruit will keep in a bowl of water mixed with about a tablespoon of lemon juice. Then put the fruit on the crust just before serving.

This is a great recipe for kids because it looks so good and it's fun to eat.

The crust:

¾ cup confectioners' sugar
½ cup soft margarine (light variety)
3 tablespoons skim milk
1 teaspoon vanilla extract

½ teaspoon almond extract
1 cup whole-wheat flour
¾ cup all-purpose flour
½ teaspoon cream of tartar
½ teaspoon baking soda

The topping:

6 ounces Neufchatel cheese, softened
½ teaspoon vanilla extract.
2 tablespoons sugar
OR honey

Mixed fresh fruit of choice (e.g., 1 cup pineapple chunks, 2 kiwi fruit, 1 sliced banana, ½ cup fresh strawberries, 4 ounces Mandarin oranges)

1. For the crust, cream the sugar and margarine together until fluffy. Add the milk and extracts.
2. In another bowl, sift the dry ingredients and add to the creamed mixture until well blended. Cover and refrigerate for 4 to 6 hours.
3. Press the dough into a 12- or 13-inch pizza pan, or use a similar-sized square pan if necessary. Press the edges of the dough slightly upward to resemble a pizza crust.
4. Bake at 375 degrees for about 10 minutes, or until golden.
5. Meanwhile, prepare the topping by creaming together the Neufchatel, vanilla, and sugar or honey.
6. Let the crust cool, and spread the topping over it.
7. Slice your favorite fruits into bite-sized pieces, and decorate the pizza with fruit in any pattern you like. Use your imagination! One of our favorite combinations is a mix of fresh pineapple, kiwi fruit, bananas, strawberries, and mandarin oranges. We've also used grapes, peaches, or other berries in season.

8 servings. Serving size is ⅛ pizza.

Per Serving (using the selection of fruits suggested above): 350 calories, 17 mg. cholesterol, 4 g. dietary fiber, 17 g. fat, 276 mg. sodium.

Sweet Pineapple Squares

PREPARATION TIME: 20 MINUTES.   BAKING TIME: 40 MINUTES.

¾ cup whole-wheat flour
¼ cup soy flour
¾ cup all-purpose flour
2 teaspoons baking powder
½ teaspoon salt
2 tablespoons brown sugar
1 egg

⅓ cup honey
⅓ cup vegetable oil
1 can (16 ounces) crushed
   unsweetened pineapple, plus
   juice
Nonstick vegetable cooking
   spray

1. In a large bowl, sift together the dry ingredients.
2. In another bowl, beat the egg, then beat in the honey and the oil.
3. Drain the pineapple carefully to get ⅔ cup juice. Add the juice to the egg, honey, and oil mixture. Blend mixture into the dry ingredients.
3. Spray an 8-inch-square baking pan with nonstick vegetable cooking spray. Spread the batter in the pan, and top with the pineapple. Bake at 350 degrees for about 40 minutes.

12 servings of about 2 × 2⅔ inches.

Per Serving: 180 calories, 22 mg. cholesterol, 2 g. dietary fiber,
7 g. fat, 140 mg. sodium.

Curried Fruit Compote

PREPARATION TIME: 10 MINUTES.   COOKING TIME: 1 HOUR AND 20
                                                                    MINUTES.

This is a "day before" recipe. It's best after it has been baked, chilled overnight in the refrigerator, and reheated, as directed. It's also good cold, so you may find it mysteriously disappearing from your refrigerator before you have a chance to reheat it.

You may use 2 teaspoons of a commercially prepared curry

powder, of course, but we highly recommend making the investment in the various spices and mixing your own. Try the special blend we've selected, and see how you like it. Once you discover the difference between this and the commercial blends, you may end up always preparing your own, as we do.

1 can (16 ounces) unsweetened peach slices

1 can (16 ounces) unsweetened pear halves

1 can (17 ounces) unsweetened apricot halves

1 can (16 ounces) unsweetened pitted dark cherries

1 can (15½ ounces) unsweetened pineapple chunks

½ cup chopped or slivered almonds

½ cup firmly packed brown sugar

½ teaspoon ground cinnamon

½ teaspoon ground coriander

¼ teaspoon ground cardamom

¼ teaspoon ground ginger

¼ teaspoon cumin

⅛ teaspoon turmeric

⅛ teaspoon cayenne pepper

¼ cup melted butter
OR margarine

1. Drain all liquid from each can of fruit. Pour the fruit into a 9 × 13-inch baking dish, and stir. Top with almonds.
2. In a small bowl, combine the brown sugar, spices, and melted butter. Sprinkle this mixture over the fruit.
3. Bake at 350 degrees for 1 hour. Let cool at room temperature, then refrigerate overnight. Twenty minutes before serving, reheat at 350 degrees, until bubbly.

16 servings. Serving size is about ½ cup.

Per Serving: 144 calories, 8 mg. cholesterol, 3 g. dietary fiber, 5 g. fat, 39 mg. sodium.

Lemon Pudding

PREPARATION TIME: 20 MINUTES.   COOKING TIME: 25 TO 30 MINUTES.

1 cup granulated white sugar
2 tablespoons butter
  OR margarine, softened
Grated rind of 2 lemons
4 tablespoons lemon juice

4 tablespoons whole-wheat
  flour
4 eggs, separated
Nonstick vegetable cooking
  spray

1. Cream together the sugar and butter. Add the lemon rind, juice, flour, and egg yolks, blending well.
2. Beat the egg whites until stiff, and fold into the batter.
3. Spray an 8 × 8-inch baking dish or 8 pudding dishes with nonstick cooking spray, and pour the batter in. Place in a larger oven-proof baking dish that has about 1 inch of hot water in it.
4. Bake at 350 degrees for 25 to 30 minutes (15 to 20 minutes if the individual serving dishes are used), or until set and slightly browned on top.

VARIATION: Substitute grated rind of one orange for the lemon rind, and 4 tablespoons orange juice for the lemon juice.

8 servings. Serving size is about ½ cup.

Per Serving: 176 calories, 145 mg. cholesterol, no dietary fiber, 6 g. fat, 65 mg. sodium.

Bread Pudding

PREPARATION TIME: 20 MINUTES.   BAKING TIME: 40 MINUTES.

Bread pudding has always been a favorite in the Katahn family, along with noodle pudding. As a child, when I was really yearning for a sweet topping, I added a bit of New York State or Vermont maple syrup. I occasionally still do this. And, to be honest, nothing quite compares with maple syrup on bread or noodle pudding, perhaps because of the childhood memories it conjures.

You can top this version in a satisfying and healthful way with fresh fruit, unsweetened applesauce, or a dollop of low-fat plain yogurt mixed with a dash of cinnamon. This is a truly lean bread pudding (Grandma's had PLENTY of butter in it), so if it tastes a bit austere with skim milk, don't abandon the basic recipe, but use low-fat milk on the second go-round. Also, notice that this is, in reality, a combination bread-and-fruit pudding. As usual, we use whole-wheat bread, which adds both a nutty flavor and a form of dietary fiber with a different nutritional effect from the fiber in the fruit.

3 cups skim milk	½ teaspoon salt
3 eggs	Dash of ground ginger
3 tablespoons honey	Dash of mace
2 tablespoons brown sugar	4 cups coarsely crumbled stale
Juice of ½ lemon	whole-grain bread
2 teaspoons vanilla extract	1½ cups chopped apple
1 teaspoon cinnamon	¼ cup raisins

1. Beat together the milk, eggs, honey, sugar, lemon juice, vanilla, cinnamon, salt, ginger, and mace.
2. In a 9 × 13-inch baking pan, combine the bread crumbs, apple, and raisins. Pour the milk mixture over the crumb mixture, stirring well.
3. Bake at 350 degrees for 40 minutes. Serve hot or cold.

12 servings. Serving size is about ¾ cup.

Per Serving (without topping): 142 calories, 70 mg. cholesterol, 3 g. dietary fiber, 3 g. fat, 287 mg. sodium.

Cocoa Zucchini Cake

PREPARATION TIME: 20 TO 25 MINUTES.   BAKING TIME: ¾ TO 1 HOUR.

This cake is moist, lightly sweet, with a satisfying, rich texture.

1¼ cup granulated white sugar
½ cup vegetable oil
1 teaspoon vanilla extract
1 egg
2 egg whites
½ cup low-fat milk
1 teaspoon baking soda
1 cup all-purpose flour
1½ cups whole-wheat flour

¼ cup cocoa powder
½ teaspoon cinnamon
½ teaspoon salt
2 cups grated zucchini, unpeeled (about 1½ squashes)
Nonstick vegetable cooking spray or oil

1. Combine first 6 ingredients in a large bowl.
2. In another bowl, sift together the dry ingredients, and add alternately with the zucchini to the first mixture.
3. Bake at 350 degrees for 1 hour in a lightly oiled bundt pan, or bake 45 minutes in a 9 × 13-pan. Remove from oven when a toothpick inserted in the center of the cake comes out clean. Let stand 5 to 10 minutes before removing from pan.

24 servings.

Per Serving: 136 calories, 11 mg. cholesterol, 1 g. dietary fiber, 5 g. fat, 90 mg. sodium.

Orange-Coconut Dip

PREPARATION TIME: 25 TO 30 MINUTES.

4 tablespoons crushed almonds, toasted
2 fresh navel oranges

¼ cup honey
7 tablespoons shredded coconut

1. To toast the almonds: spread them on a baking sheet and place in a 350-degree oven for 5 to 6 minutes.

2. Peel and section the oranges.
3. Place the honey in a small bowl. In another small bowl, combine the coconut and toasted almonds.
4. Brush each orange section with honey, using a pastry brush, then lightly roll each section in the nut mixture. Arrange on a serving dish or individual plates.

4 servings. Serving size is ½ orange.

Per Serving: 169 calories, no cholesterol, 4 g. dietary fiber, 7 g. fat, 3 mg. sodium.

Date Bran Bars

PREPARATION TIME: 15 MINUTES.   COOKING TIME: 30 MINUTES.

1 cup all-purpose flour
1½ teaspoons baking powder
¾ cup chopped dates
½ cup boiling water
¼ cup margarine, softened

1 teaspoon vanilla extract
1 egg, slightly beaten
⅓ cup orange juice
1½ cups All-Bran cereal
¼ cup chopped nuts

1. In a small mixing bowl, stir together the flour and baking powder. Set aside.
2. Stir together the dates and the boiling water. Set aside.
3. In a large mixing bowl, combine the margarine, vanilla, and egg. Beat well. Alternately add the flour mixture and the orange juice. Mix well. Fold in the dates, cereal, and nuts. Spread the mixture evenly in a lightly greased 8 × 8 × 2-inch baking pan.
4. Bake at 350 degrees for about 30 minutes or until a wooden toothpick inserted in the center comes out clean. Cool in the pan; cut into 24 bars.

24 servings of about 1⅓ × 2 inches.

Per Serving: 80 calories, 10 mg. cholesterol, 2 g. dietary fiber, 3 g. fat, 170 mg. sodium.

Chewy Bran-Raisin Bars

PREPARATION TIME: 15 MINUTES   STANDING TIME: ABOUT 1 HOUR.

2 cups All-Bran cereal
⅔ cup raisins
½ cup chopped nuts
1 tablespoon margarine

½ cup honey
¼ cup peanut butter
1 teaspoon vanilla flavoring
½ teaspoon ground cinnamon

1. Stir together the cereal, raisins, and nuts. Set aside.
2. In a large saucepan, combine the margarine, honey, and peanut butter. Stir over medium heat until the mixture is well blended. Remove from heat. Stir in the remaining ingredients.
3. Press the mixture into a lightly greased 9 × 9 × 2-inch pan. Let cool. Cut into 20 bars when cooled. Store covered in the refrigerator.

MICROWAVE DIRECTIONS: In a large glass mixing bowl, combine the margarine, honey, and peanut butter. Cover loosely with wax paper or microwave-safe plastic wrap. Microwave on full power for about 2 minutes until the mixture is well blended. Stir in the remaining ingredients. Press the mixture into a lightly greased 9 × 9 × 2-inch pan. Cut into bars when cooled. Store in the refrigerator.

20 servings of about 2¼ × 2 inches.

Per Serving: 110 calories, no cholesterol, 3 g. dietary fiber, 4 g. fat, 90 mg. sodium.

Orange-Chocolate Pudding

PREPARATION TIME: 25 MINUTES. REFRIGERATION TIME: 2 HOURS.

4 ounces semisweet chocolate (squares or chips)

3 tablespoons brown sugar, packed

1¾ cups low-fat milk

3 tablespoons cornstarch

¼ cup orange juice

1. Combine the chocolate, sugar, and milk in a large saucepan. Heat slowly over medium heat, stirring constantly (preferably with a wire whisk, if you have one; otherwise use a spoon) until chocolate is melted and milk is just beginning to scald, not boil.
2. Measure the cornstarch into a bowl, and pour in about ⅓ of the hot chocolate mixture. Whisk vigorously until the cornstarch is dissolved, then whisk back into remaining hot chocolate mixture in the saucepan.
3. Cook over very low heat for about 8 more minutes, stirring constantly. As the pudding thickens, you may need to switch to stirring with a spoon (if you've been using a whisk).
4. When the pudding is thick, remove from heat and stir in the orange juice. Pour into a serving bowl or individual pudding cups. Chill for at least 2 hours, and serve.

VARIATIONS: Use 2 cups of low-fat milk, and add ½ teaspoon of almond extract in place of the orange juice for Chocolate-Almond Pudding. Garnish each serving with a teaspoon of toasted almonds if desired. For Mocha Pudding, use vanilla extract instead of almond, and add a couple teaspoons of strongly brewed coffee.

4 servings. Serving size is about ½ cup.

Per Serving: 263 calories, 10 mg. cholesterol, 1 g. dietary fiber, 12 g. fat, 62 mg. sodium.

Poppy-Seed Cake

PREPARATION TIME: 20 MINUTES.   BAKING TIME: 45 MINUTES.

Believe it or not, we often come up with a recipe that works perfectly the first time we try it! This confection had all our taste-testers smiling (mouths full) right away.

Nonstick vegetable cooking
  spray
Whole-wheat flour
⅓ cup vegetable oil
¾ cup granulated white sugar
2 eggs, separated

1 teaspoon vanilla
1 cup whole-wheat flour
½ teaspoon salt
½ teaspoon baking soda
⅔ cup plain low-fat yogurt
⅓ cup poppy seeds

1. Spray an 8-inch tube pan with nonstick vegetable cooking spray, and dust lightly with whole-wheat flour.
2. Blend the oil and sugar in a large bowl. Add the egg yolks one at a time, beating well. Add the vanilla.
3. In another bowl, sift together the flour, salt, and baking soda. Alternately fold the flour mixture and the yogurt into the oil and sugar mixture. Set aside.
4. Beat the egg whites until stiff. Fold into the batter. Fold in the poppy seeds. Pour the batter into the pan.
5. Bake at 350 degrees for about 45 minutes, until top is nicely brown, and a toothpick inserted in the center comes out clean.

20 servings. Serving size is 1 slice about ⅜ inch thick.

Per Serving: 106 calories, 28 mg. cholesterol, 1 g. dietary fiber, 5 g. fat, 87 mg. sodium.

Gingersnaps

PREPARATION TIME: 20 MINUTES.   BAKING TIME: 10 TO 12 MINUTES.

Compared with chocolate-chip cookies, gingersnaps generally run a poor second in popularity. Not these! They disappeared first in our tasting session.

½ cup vegetable oil
½ cup granulated white sugar
¼ cup brown sugar, firmly
  packed
¼ cup light molasses
1 egg, well-beaten
1½ cups all-purpose flour

½ cup whole-wheat flour
¼ teaspoon salt
2 teaspoons baking soda
1 teaspoon cinnamon
1 teaspoon ground cloves
1 teaspoon ground ginger

1. Preheat the oven to 350 degrees.
2. In a large mixing bowl, combine the oil, sugars, and molasses. Beat in the egg.
3. In another bowl, combine the flours, salt, baking soda, and spices. Stir into the wet ingredients, mixing well.
4. Form the dough into balls about 1-inch in diameter, and place them about 2 inches apart on ungreased baking sheets. Bake for about 10 to 12 minutes.

Makes 3 dozen cookies, about 2 inches in diameter.

Per Cookie: 75 calories, 8 mg. cholesterol, no dietary fiber, 3 g. fat, 64 mg. sodium.

Whole-Grain Goody

PREPARATION TIME: 20 MINUTES.   BAKING TIME: 25 TO 30 MINUTES.

This has a nutty flavor and a chewy texture because of the rolled oats. It goes almost too well with a glass of milk.

3 eggs
¼ cup firmly packed brown
  sugar
¼ cup molasses
1 cup rolled oats
1 cup whole-wheat flour
½ teaspoon baking powder
Grated rind of 1 orange
Juice of ½ orange

1 teaspoon vanilla extract
1 teaspoon rum
½ cup buttermilk
2 tablespoons melted butter
  OR margarine
½ cup raisins
Nonstick vegetable cooking
  spray

1. Beat the eggs with the sugar and molasses until smooth.
2. In another bowl, combine the oats, flour, and baking powder.
3. Add the orange rind and juice, the vanilla and the rum, and mix well. Stir in the buttermilk, butter, and raisins. Add to the egg-sugar mixture, blending well.
3. Pour into a pie tin that has been sprayed with nonstick vegetable cooking spray, or greased very lightly with oil.
4. Bake at 375 degrees for 25 to 30 minutes, until set.

8 servings.

Per Serving: 232 calories, 111 mg. cholesterol, 3 g. dietary fiber, 6 g. fat, 101 mg. sodium.

The Rotation Diet Activity Program or How to Have Your Cake and Eat It, Too

I simply could not imagine writing a book that had anything to do with health and weight management and failing to discuss the importance of physical activity. So, this may be the first cookbook that has recipes for physical activity as well as for the dinner table![1]

At the beginning of this book, on page 10, I made a very important point: if you are, or have been, a *sedentary* overweight person, I don't believe there's a cookbook in existence that can show you how to sustain a significant weight loss and maintain desirable weight unless you are willing to change your ways and become active. Without additional physical activity, no matter what style of cooking you choose, you will have to deprive yourself forever and ever of most of the really good tasting things you can put on your table.

The human body was *not* designed for sedentary living! From the beginning of our existence on this planet up until the invention of the automobile and the availability of electricity in our homes, the average person had to move the energy equivalent of seven to eight miles of walking every day, *just to get the job of living done.* Today we can get by with a mile or two, and, compared with life just 100 years ago, that's an energy expenditure difference of several hundred calories each day!

[1]After writing this chapter I discovered that Jane Brody, in her excellent and most comprehensive *Good Food Book: Living the High-Carbohydrate Way,* published by W. W. Norton and Co., Inc., also includes a chapter on the importance of physical activity.

Our appetites for fat and sugar, however, have not diminished to compensate for our decrease in physical activity! Quite the contrary: for many of us, when there is little physical work to do, appetites seem to increase. If anything, high-calorie foods are more available to more people in the United States now than have ever been available to large numbers of persons in the history of humankind.

Thus, we have an epidemic of *overnutrition*—OBESITY—as *the* major nutrition problem in this country. Fortunately, the problem has a solution.

In order to match appetite and energy expenditure, to put them in sync, the average sedentary person needs to add about 45 minutes of some sort of brisk physical activity to his or her daily routine. In about 45 minutes of brisk walking, a person who weighs about 150 pounds will burn about 200 calories over and above the calories required to just sit still; if you weigh more than 150 pounds, you burn more in physical activity; if you weigh less, you burn less.

THAT 200 CALORIES IS VERY IMPORTANT FOR WEIGHT MAINTENANCE. That's because it takes about 200 calories a day to keep around 40 to 50 pounds of fat alive in the human body. Fat is relatively inactive tissue and only about 200 calories of your total daily food intake will be used to keep 40 to 50 pounds alive, on the average. I cannot be more exact in this average estimation because there is a great deal of metabolic variability. At the extremes, some people may need only 100 calories a day to maintain 40 to 50 pounds of excess fat, while others may need 300; metabolic needs really do vary by that amount.

Let's assume you have lost extra pounds. The key to weight maintenance, without deprivation at the dinner table, is to exercise enough EACH DAY to burn up the same number of calories it used to take to keep you fat! It's simple arithmetic: if you were 40 to 50 pounds overweight and are now at desirable weight and want to stay that way, exercise 200 calories-worth every day. IF YOU DON'T, THE FAT WILL CREEP RIGHT BACK ON AGAIN, ON THE AVERAGE OF 200 CALORIES-WORTH EVERY DAY. That's an average of about

2 pounds a month. It means that sometime within the next year or two, all the weight you struggled to lose will be right back on again, unless you restrict yourself to an extremely low food intake for the rest of your life—and who can do that? And who would *want* to?

Physically active people can eat like normal human beings.[2] Yes, there is room for dessert every day, especially if you make it one of the healthier, less fatty desserts included in the previous chapter. I know I am being repetitious, but if it helps just one person who has lost a significant amount of weight to stay motivated, it's worth warning you once again: if you do not become active and stay active, YOU ARE GOING TO GET FAT ALL OVER AGAIN.

End of lecture. Time now for a few words of encouragement and a little practical advice.

The best activities for weight management, as well as for cardiovascular health, are those in which you continuously move your whole body through space, or those which move the large muscle groups in your thighs and buttocks. Walking, bicycling, swimming, rowing (in a boat, or with a machine using your legs as well as your arms), are at the top of the list. I don't recommend jogging for overweight persons because of the risk of injury. Bouncing on a minitrampoline is fine, but be careful not to become too vigorous until your legs become accustomed to this type of exercise.

You get the best effects, while assuring cardiovascular and pulmonary conditioning as well as safety, when you exercise within what is called your **target** or **training range**. This range is determined to be between 60 and 85 percent of your maximum heart rate. For most persons, maximum heart rate will be about 220 minus their age. For example: the average maximum speed that the heart is capable of beating is about 180 beats per minute at maximum exertion for persons 40 years old.

To determine your own target heart rate for physical activ-

[2]Women of about 128 pounds who follow the Rotation Diet Activity Program will require an average of about 1800–2000 calories per day to maintain their weight. Men at about 154 pounds will require an average of around 2400. Heavier people will need more, lighter people less.

ity, subtract your age from 220. Then multiply that figure first by .60 to get the bottom of the range, and then by .85 to get the top. Thus, for a person of 40 years, the range will be .60 × 180, or 108 beats per minute, to .85 × 180, or 153 beats per minute at the maximum. When that person goes for a *brisk* walk, swim, or other aerobic activity, he or she should strive to keep the heartbeat between 108 and 153 beats per minute.

To find your pulse and determine your heart rate (pulse and heart rate are almost invariably the same) place the first two fingers of one hand on the inside of the other wrist, along a vein leading back from the thumb. Only light pressure is required to detect the pulse. Count the beats for 10 seconds, and then multiply by six to get the rate in beats per minute.

Most experts feel that you can improve cardiovascular endurance by exercising within your target range a minimum of three times a week, for 20 minutes at a time. You should warm up for at least 5 minutes before working up into that range, and cool down afterwards for about 5 minutes before stopping, by walking or doing some other exercises less vigorously. A few minutes of gentle stretching exercises in addition may help to prevent injury, especially if you tend to be tight in the joints.[3]

However, weight management requires more than cardiovascular conditioning in terms of time and frequency, as I have said. While it is important for cardiovascular health that you exercise within the target range at least three times a week, it is quite acceptable for weight control that you exercise on other days as well, at the bottom of that range or even below, for comfort.

THE FIRST RULE OF PHYSICAL ACTIVITY IS TO GO AS VIGOROUSLY AS YOU CAN *WITHOUT HURTING YOUR-SELF.*

We advise people who are sedentary to start slowly and increase gradually. Aim for 15 minutes a day during your first week, increase gradually toward a goal of 30 minutes a day the second week, and end up at 45 minutes a day in the third

[3]For a good book on stretching, I recommend Jean Couch and Nell Weaver's *Runner's World Yoga Book,* reprinted by Anderson World Publishers in Mountain View, Calif.

week. Taking a day off is, of course, in order, if you don't feel well or have overexerted on a previous day!

It may seem strange to you that we suggest you check with your doctor before doing something so simple as going out for a walk, BUT WE DO! We do because we want you to get as vigorous as you can *without hurting yourself.* Sedentary, overweight persons should check with their doctors before going on any diet or starting any activity program. Obesity is related to a number of physical illnesses, some of which may be undetected unless you have had a recent physical. These include heart disease and hypertension, as well as diabetes. Although physical activity can be helpful in dealing with these illnesses, their presence, as well as the presence of a number of other physical problems (arthritis, kidney disease, other circulatory problems) will require a physician's supervision as you become more active.

It seems best from both a physical and psychological standpoint to exercise for at least 30 minutes at a time. That amount of activity may stimulate your metabolism to burn a few more calories round the clock, and it seems to be the amount of time required in order to feel truly relaxed and refreshed.

However, don't be concerned: you can break up your activity to fit your schedule and still get at least 98 percent of all its benefits. Just get up out of your chair 5 minutes on the hour each hour during the workday, climb a flight of stairs or two and walk the hallways as vigorously as you can without causing chaos! You will end up burning close to the extra 200 calories a day that helps guarantee weight maintenance. Plus, the break will refresh you and you will probably be more productive during the rest of the hour.

Time of day for physical activity has little practical meaning, although some research suggests you may burn a few more calories exercising between four and eight o'clock when the metabolic rate tends to be a bit higher for most people. If you exercise in the morning, you will be more alert and ready for productive work; if you exercise late in the afternoon, you will be relaxed and refreshed at night, and you'll probably sleep better, *unless* you have overexerted. Indeed, just about everyone who completes the workday feeling tired, and perhaps irritable, reports feeling incredibly better after some exercise. (And their spouses and friends report that they are much easier to live with, too!)

Physical activity may not feel good at first if you are overweight or out of shape. Terri and I have both been overweight and inactive. So we both know from experience that once you've gotten used to daily physical activity, it will become one of the high points of your day.

Here are a few facts to help you stay motivated for physical activity until the pleasure of doing it takes over.

When you go for a walk at just 3 miles per hour, you burn about three times the calories that you burn sitting still. If you walk briskly at 4 miles per hour, you burn almost five times the calories burned when you sit still.

The average person can count on burning a total of around 100 calories for every fifteen minutes of brisk activity, that is, while doing things that are equivalent to walking at 4 miles per hour. A good game of singles tennis, played at a strong intermediate level, is about equivalent. Racquetball and squash are even more vigorous. Doubles tennis, on the other hand, may be good for your social life, but, unless played very vigorously, doesn't burn nearly as many calories as continuous walking.

Perhaps the reason that jogging is so effective in weight management (and remember, we DO NOT recommend jogging for overweight persons; get down to desirable weight first) is that even at a 6-mile-per-hour pace, which is quite gentle once you get into it, you burn from nine to ten times the calories of sitting still. Jogging at that pace will burn 100 calories, or more, every ten minutes. It adds up to a total of 600 to 800 calories an hour. And, for many people, this level of activity, at this intensity, does leave a residual metabolic elevation that burns up 50 to 100 more calories than normal, as the body recovers from activity over the next several hours.[4]

---

[4]In the examples we have just given, we are referring to total calories burned in activity. This *includes* the amount it would have taken if you had just sat still. Earlier,

A time for activity always goes down first on my daily calendar, and on Terri's. It means more to us than just improving our physical condition and increasing our flexibility. As the years go by and I have grown busier and busier, the time I take for a jog or a walk has become more and more important. It's the most creative and refreshing part of my day. Although we encourage people to get active together when they first start and to form "buddy systems" to support and motivate each other, physical activity may well become a time for you to be alone, to relax, and to completely separate yourself from the rest of the day's activities.

So, we hope you will use and enjoy our recipes for good healthy cooking AND for physical activity. It's the only way you can have your cake and eat it, too!

when we spoke of the need to exercise for around 45 minutes a day, we spoke of 200 calories being burned in that period of time *in addition* to the sitting requirements. For simplicity's sake, and in view of the great metabolic variability, we are rounding figures to the nearest 100 in these last examples.

Sample Menus for Weight Loss and Weight Maintenance

OVERVIEW OF THE QUICK-WEIGHT-LOSS ROTATION DIET

Included in this chapter (pp. 403–9) are sample menus for 600-, 900-, 1200-, 1500-, and 1800-calorie rotations on the Rotation Diet. These menus are different from, but interchangeable with, the original Rotation Diet menus, as well as those appearing in the supermarket version of the Rotation Diet and the Rotation Plus program.

In order to be sure that the instructions for implementing the Rotation Diet for quick-weight-loss are all in one place and easily available for reference, we must of necessity repeat certain nutritional guidelines and cooking suggestions that appeared separately in various parts of this book. We hope the integration will be useful to you and that you forgive the occasional redundancy.

The Rotation Diet is a twenty-one-day, quick-weight-loss diet that is safe for overweight people who are otherwise in good health. The average weight loss is approximately 12.5 pounds during this three-week period. Heavier people lose faster than lighter people, and men tend to lose faster than women of equal weight.

For women: During the first three days of the diet, the core menu contains approximately 600 calories. During the next four days it contains approximately 900 calories. In Week 2 you go up to 1200 calories, and then, in Week 3, you repeat Week 1.

In addition to the core menu (see pages 402–5), you may eat unlimited *free vegetables* with any meal or as snacks, and you choose a *safe fruit,* also to be used as a snack, whenever you feel hungry or need a lift. (Additional information on *free vegetables* and the *safe fruit* is on pages 394–95.) In Week 4 you make a transition to maintenance, eating approximately 1200 calories for three days, followed by 1500 for about four days. Then you increase until your weight stabilizes.

It is very important that you take a "vacation" from dieting and allow your weight to stabilize for one to two weeks before repeating the Rotation Diet. This prevents the metabolic slow-down that can occur with prolonged dieting, and "vacation-ing" will help you maintain your motivation. You will learn how to maintain your losses and avoid feelings of deprivation.

On the average, women who implement the complete Rota-tion Diet recommendations for the correct balance of foods and 45 minutes a day of physical activity will find that their weight stabilizes when they eat around 1800 to 2000 calories per day.

For men: Men add 600 calories a day to the basic menus for women. Thus, the calorie levels for men are 1200 calories for three days, 1500 calories for four days, followed by 1800 calo-ries for a week. In Week 3, you return to Week 1 levels. Then, in the fourth week, men also take a "vacation" from dieting by going up to 1800 calories for three days, 2100 for about four days, and then stabilizing somewhere around 2400 calories. Additional instructions appear on page 397.

SUBSTITUTIONS are allowed on the Rotation Diet if you don't like a particular food or if a particular food does not agree with you. However, you must substitute within the same food group. That is, if you don't care for the vegetable that appears on any menu, substitute another vegetable; if you don't care for one protein food (fish, poultry, or meat), substitute another, and so on. **Substitution lists appear in this chapter, on pages 411–23.**

Serving sizes are given with the food items on the daily menus. It is a good idea to weigh and measure your food for the first few days of the diet if you are unsure of the "look" of these portion sizes. However, if you don't wish to weigh and measure, choose a moderate, "restaurant-size" portion, such as you would find at a cafeteria, and you will be fairly accurate. A dish followed by an asterisk (*) in the sample menus means the recipe—with other nutritional information—appears in the recipe section of this book.

THE ROTATION-DIET INSURANCE POLICY

So everyone can follow the Rotation Diet and never feel hungry, we have designed an "insurance policy" that will help you overcome temptations and achieve good results. This insurance policy has two clauses.

Clause #1 is *free vegetables*. If you are ever tempted to eat anything that isn't on the diet during the next three weeks, you may eat all you want of the *free vegetables* with any meal and at any time of the day as snacks (see the list that follows). They contain vitamins, minerals, and beneficial amounts of fiber, with fewer than 25 calories per half-cup serving. Eat them plain or use only no-cal salad dressings on the 600-calorie days, and no- or lo-cal dressing on any other days.

Unlimited Free Vegetables

Asparagus	Bean Sprouts	Beets
Beet greens	Broccoli	Brussels sprouts
Cabbage	Carrots	Cauliflower
Celery	Chard	Chicory
Collards	Cucumbers	Dandelion greens
Eggplant	Endive	Escarole
Green pepper	Kale	Lettuce
Mushrooms	Mustard greens	Okra
Onions	Parsley	Radishes
Rhubarb	Rutabaga	Spinach
String beans	Summer squash	Tomatoes

Turnips	Turnip greens	Watercress
Wax beans	Zucchini	

Clause #2 in our insurance policy is the *safe fruit*. Start by choosing *one* fruit from this list, *or any other fresh fruit that is easily available to you,* as your *safe fruit*. Carry one with you at all times as a snack. Eat up to *three* servings a day, in addition to whatever different fruits are called for in the menus of the Rotation Diet, when you need a lift, feel unbearably hungry, or are tempted to stray from your diet for any reason. (A serving size is one piece of fruit, or standard "restaurant" portions for such fruits as berries, melons, etc.)

Safe Fruits

Apple	Banana	Blackberries
Blueberries	Canteloupe	Cherries
Grapefruit	Grapes	Honeydew melon
Kiwi	Mango	Orange
Papaya	Peach	Persimmon
Pineapple	Plum	Raspberries
Strawberries	Tangerine	Watermelon (and other melons)

Weight loss tends to be quicker if you limit yourself to one fruit as your safe fruit, because you will probably get bored with it and hence, will not overeat. But, to be sure you can stick with the diet and not go back to high-calorie snacks, *feel free to substitute any fresh fruit at any time as your safe fruit if it means you will be able to avoid junk-food snacks for the full three weeks of the diet.* Indeed, most persons can eat almost unlimited quantities of fresh fruit during the Rotation Diet and, although they may not lose an average of two-thirds of a pound a day, they will still lose a considerable amount of weight.

HOW TO COOK FOR THE ROTATION DIET

To insure the quickest and safest possible weight loss, prepare everything on these daily menus simply, without additional fat or sugar. Some recipes do call for fat and/or sugar, but these menus have been analyzed to fall within the calorie guidelines. This advice is especially for menu items for which there is no recipe. It is the added fat and sugar in your diet that provides concentrated calories and no bulk.

Use low-fat products and remove the skin from chicken, preferably before cooking as the skin contains much of the fat. Use the portion sizes in the menus and recipes as a guide when eating out. Weights in the menus are all cooked weights for cooked foods such as meat, fish, and poultry, which shrink when cooked.

The portion sizes in the menus are for women. You may add unlimited free vegetables and as many as three extra servings of fruit each day and still stay within the guidelines of the diet. Fruits and vegetables provide a great deal of bulk but minimal calories; make up your mind to use fruit and vegetables, not junk food, for snacks, and it will help you be successful on the Rotation Diet. Fresh is best, but frozen fruit and canned fruit, unsweetened, in its own juice still have high bulk and low calories.

When a dinner salad is called for, start with about 1 cup of any fresh salad vegetables of your choice. (Remember, vegetables don't make you fat; you really can eat unlimited quantities of them.) "No-cal" salad dressings have fewer than 10 calories per tablespoon, while "lo-cal" dressings have about 35. No-cal salad dressings can be added at any time, so they are not always indicated.

As a general rule, whether dieting or not, we suggest that you add little or no salt to your foods. Our recipes call for a "touch" of salt, just to help enhance the flavor of the herbs and spices.

INSTRUCTIONS FOR MEN AND FOR COUPLES USING THE DIET TOGETHER

The diet for men contains 1200 calories for the first three days and 1500 calories for the next four days. Men can use the basic Rotation Diet menus for women by adding approximately 600 calories each day according to the following instructions. This also permits couples to use the diet together by simply preparing larger quantities of the basic foods. (Men can also use the 1200-, 1500-, and 1800-calorie menus that we've supplied as examples and guides for the construction of additional menus.)

To the 600- and 900-calorie-diet menus for women, men should add, each day:

—two more servings of grain (bread, cereal, or crackers)
—50 percent larger portions of meat, fish, or poultry
—1 tablespoon of butter, oil, or regular salad dressing
—three *safe fruits* (these are optional for women, but should be included to be sure men add the extra 600 calories to their diets).

SPECIALLY RECOMMENDED FOODS FOR THE ROTATION DIET

The menus are designed to maximize nutritional value while maintaining variety and good taste. Certain substitutions can, however, make the diet even more healthful.

For example, fortified breakfast cereals (of course, NOT the sugared variety) can always be substituted for a grain product at breakfast, or whenever bread or crackers are called for. Check the labels of your favorite cereals. Look for fortification at around 25% of the recommended dietary allowances for most vitamins and minerals. For instance, the Special K Breakfast, which was especially designed with weight management in mind, would be a good choice with fruit. Remember that you can increase the fiber content of your own favorite cereal by adding fruit or by adding 2 to 3 tablespoons of a high-fiber cereal. Our favorites for this latter purpose are All-Bran and Bran Buds. For variety in higher fiber cereals, sample the Kellogg's Fiber Pack Assortment. (You can, of course, use your own favorite fiber cereals for additional fiber.)

Fish and poultry can always be substituted whenever beef is called for. This will greatly lower the saturated fat and cholesterol in your diet—two of the goals for reducing the risk of cancer and heart disease. You may also substitute tofu, or complementary-protein foods such as beans and rice, or any grain served with beans, seeds, or nuts in place of meat. (Complementary-protein cooking is discussed on page 234.)

We do not feel, however, that you have to eliminate beef in order to design a healthy diet. We choose lean cuts such as top or bottom round, top sirloin, eye of round, London broil, and flank steaks in our own cooking. We use hamburger that is truly lean (10% fat or less, by weight). We do not recommend sweetbreads because they tend to be higher in either fat or cholesterol.

If the store where you usually buy your meat does not customarily provide well-trimmed beef (they will advertise something like "¼-inch trim," "lean trim," or "light beef" if they do), then you must request a lean trim or trim your beef yourself. In some of the fatty cuts, as much as 80% of the calories come from fat, not protein!

The identification "light beef" on meat may mean even less fat than "¼-inch trim," or "lean trim." Although trimming well will remove a large percentage of the fat from meat, there is still a considerable amount intertwined with the muscle in prime and high-grade choice steaks and roasts. You can tell this from the white streaks or "marbling." Light beef in some stores may mean beef that has been specially bred for reduced marbling. However, to our knowledge, there is as yet no standard practice in the industry. You will have to ask your meat department personnel for help and information as to the meaning of the various labels in your store.

THE VEGETARIAN ROTATION DIET

Many vegetarians easily use the Rotation Diet by substituting their usual protein foods whenever meat, poultry, or fish is called for. Use standard "restaurant"-size portions of complementary protein foods, dairy products, or tofu or other soy products. For example, ½ cup beans with ½ cup rice would be about the equivalent of a serving of meat, fish, or poultry.

BEVERAGES

Drink eight 8-ounce glasses of water a day. *Drinking plenty of water is one of the most important things you can do in your efforts to lose weight and keep it off, as well as in your pursuit of overall good health.* Use only no-cal beverages (black coffee, black tea, herbal teas, seltzer, water with a twist of lemon or lime, low-sodium bouillons), except when milk is called for. Limit your use of caffeinated coffee or tea to two cups each day, because more may cause stomach upset on low-calorie days. Also, too much caffeine can add to nervousness, irritability, and other health problems. If decaffeinated coffee and tea do not upset your stomach, you can use these beverages, but only in moderation, since the health implications of using decaffeinated beverages are still in question. Finally, if black coffee upsets your stomach, one or two teaspoons of milk will not hurt.

Artificially sweetened diet drinks, and artificial sweeteners and sugar, should also be used in moderation. Our experience indicates that people who have been accustomed to drinking large quantities of sweet-flavored drinks are better able to manage their weight when they reduce, or eliminate, their consumption and start drinking plain water or unsweetened herbal teas.

If you find the taste of your tap water objectionable and have difficulty drinking it, ice or refrigerate it, add a twist of lemon, or drink seltzer. Clean, fresh-tasting water is a pleasure to drink, so you also might look into bottled water or a much more reasonably priced alternative: a portable or kitchen-sink filtration unit that removes chlorine and other objectionable organic matter from your tap water.

HOW TO BE COMFORTABLE ON THE ROTATION DIET

The Rotation Diet is a fun diet and a "feeling-good" diet! You do not have to be uncomfortable in order to succeed. If you feel tired, grouchy, or headachy, INCREASE YOUR CALO-RIES. Dip into the *free vegetables* and your *safe fruit.* Have a bowl of cereal and milk. If necessary, go up to 1200 calories a day if you are a woman or 1800 if you are a man. *You will still lose weight* in a way that will amaze you if you just substitute healthy low-calorie, high-fiber foods, such as safe fruits and free vegetables, for desserts, candy, junk-food snacks, and alcohol.

VITAMIN AND MINERAL SUPPLEMENTATION

We strongly recommend the use of a multiple vitamin and mineral supplement, especially for persons who will use the Rotation Diet several times in a row. Choose a supplement that provides approximately 100 percent of the Recommended Dietary Allowances (RDAs) of the essential vitamins and minerals. Calcium and iron may require additional supplementation in the form of a separate calcium tablet and an iron tablet. Do not use megadoses of vitamins without the advice of a physician, and if you need help, discuss the choice of a supplement with your physician, pharmacist, or nutritionist.

READ THIS BEFORE USING THE ROTATION DIET

The Rotation Diet is safe for overweight persons who are otherwise in good health; however, no one should undertake this or any other weight loss program without consulting his or her physician.

The Rotation Diet should not be used by:

Pregnant or nursing women
Children or teenagers
Diabetics
Underweight or normal-weight adults
Persons recovering from surgery or trauma

Persons presently under a physician's care and taking prescription medication should check with their doctor before changing their diet in any way. Dietary changes can cause changes in the effects of medication.

The Rotation Diet is not appropriate for highly active persons; for example, those who run five miles or more a day. In order to lose weight, such persons should not cut their normal intake by more than 500 calories per day.

People who are not overweight should not use the Rotation Diet. Normal-weight persons who wish to reduce body fat, and tone up their bodies, should consult a fitness expert and enter a well-rounded physical conditioning program.

THE ROTATION DIET ACTIVITY PROGRAM

Physical activity is absolutely essential for weight management and overall good health.

Be sure to read about physical activity on pages 388–89 for more tips on getting started safely and comfortably. IF YOU ARE A SEDENTARY PERSON WITH A WEIGHT PROBLEM, YOU MUST MAKE A LIFETIME COMMITMENT TO AN INCREASE IN PHYSICAL ACTIVITY.

Briefly, the Rotation Diet activity program requires you to increase total *daily* physical activity by 15 minutes each week, until you reach a daily average of about 45 minutes in Week 3. Week 1 calls for 15 minutes per day; in Week 2 you build to 30 minutes per day; and in Week 3 you reach your goal of 45 minutes per day.

If you feel that your physical condition prevents you from engaging in the Rotation Diet Activity Program, we recommend that you first consult a physical therapist to determine what, if anything, in the way of exercise might be suitable and enjoyable for you. If you are an overweight person who cannot be active and must control your weight through diet alone, you may never be able to increase your intake to the maintenance levels attainable by more active persons. Thus you will be restricted to a low-calorie, potentially inadequate diet. Under these conditions, you will do well to seek the advice and supervision of a registered dietitian, who can help you design the most satisfying diet possible.

SAMPLE ROTATION DIET QUICK-WEIGHT-LOSS MENUS

Here are some sample menus for quick weight loss. In order to maximize nutritional value on 600- and 900-calorie days, we suggest a fortified breakfast cereal with milk in these menu examples. **You may, however, substitute according to the substitution guidelines given on pages 393 and 397–98. Use the following sample daily menus to help you construct additional menus, using the substitution lists for variety.** Be sure to eat a wide variety of foods: many different fruits and vegetables, along with whole-grain products, skim or low-fat dairy products, and lean meats. The complete Rotation Diet can be found in *The Rotation Diet,* by Martin Katahn, Ph.D., published in hardcover by W. W. Norton and Co., Inc. and in paperback by Bantam Books.

Menu selections followed by an asterisk (*) are recipes included in this cookbook.

The serving sizes in the *recipes,* however may not always correspond exactly to the suggested serving size on these *menus.* This will be true most frequently on the menus containing fewer than 1500 calories per day. The serving sizes in the recipes are the typical sizes used in nutrient analyses and are geared more toward weight-maintenance diets than calorie-restricted diets. You're on your honor to adjust portion size when you use these Rotation Diet menus for losing weight!

SAMPLE 600-CALORIE DAY FOR WOMEN

Breakfast
1 ounce fortified cereal
8 ounces skim or low-fat milk
½ cup berries or other fresh fruit
no-cal beverage

Lunch
¾ cup plain low-fat yogurt
½ banana, sliced
1 tablespoon high-fiber cereal or wheat germ
no-cal beverage

Dinner
Broiled or poached fish (3 ounces cooked):
Broiled Cod with Shallots,* Lime-Steamed Fish Fillets*
or other fish fillet of choice
½ cup rice (wild or brown)
1 cup broccoli, steamed
1 cup tossed salad plus unlimited free vegetables
no-cal salad dressing
no-cal beverage

SAMPLE 900-CALORIE DAY FOR WOMEN

Breakfast
1 ounce fortified cereal
8 ounces skim or low-fat milk

½ cup sliced peaches or other fruit
no-cal beverage

Lunch
2 ounces salmon (canned)
unlimited free vegetables
1 teaspoon mayonnaise or 1 tablespoon Paprika Dressing*
1 slice whole-grain bread
1 orange
no-cal beverage

Dinner
Baked chicken (3 ounces cooked):
Happy Heart Chicken,* Lime-Light Chicken,* or Patti's
Roast Chicken*
½ cup pasta, brown rice, or other cooked grain
Cheese-Baked Cauliflower*
1 cup greens (spinach, mustard, kale, turnip, or other)
1 apple
no-cal beverage

SAMPLE 1200-CALORIE DAY

This is an example of a basic Week-2 day on the Rotation Diet
for a woman, or a Day 1, 2, or 3 of Week 1 for a man.

You may use 1 tablespoon of butter, margarine, or other fat,
and include 3 servings of a safe fruit. Or, in place of 2 servings
of fruit, you can have an ounce of breakfast cereal and ½ cup
of low-fat milk. With these additions, we aim for a total of
between 1200 and 1300 calories per day.

Breakfast
½ whole-grain English muffin
1 tablespoon peanut butter
8 ounces skim or low-fat milk
½ cup fresh fruit:
Creative Fruit Salad* or other fruit cup
no-cal beverage

Lunch
Barley Chicken Soup,* Spinach-Egg Drop Soup,* or Quick
Clam Soup*
Toasted Open-Face Sandwich:
1 ounce cheese, 1 slice whole-grain bread, 1 tomato slice
1 orange
no-cal beverage

Dinner
Baked Flank Steak* or other lean meat (4½ ounces cooked)
Sweet Spiced Beets*
Shades of Green*
½ cup sliced peaches
no-cal beverage

SAMPLE 1500-CALORIE DAY

This is an example of a menu appropriate for women on the
first three days of Week 4 as they make a transition to maintenance. It is also appropriate for men on Days 4 through 7 of
Week 1 during the fast-weight-loss period. As usual for all
menus of 1200 calories and above, you add 1 tablespoon of fat
and your safe-fruit snacks to the stated menu.

Breakfast
8 ounces skim or low-fat milk
1 cup hot cereal
cinnamon
2 tablespoons raisins
½ grapefruit
no-cal beverage

Lunch
4 sardines
sliced tomato
unlimited free vegetables
1 slice whole-grain bread
1 apple
no-cal beverage

Dinner
Baked Bass with Lemon-Wine Bouillon* or
other fish fillet (4½ ounces cooked)
Broccoli with Water Chestnuts*
1 cup yellow squash
½ cup brown rice
2 Gingersnaps*
8 ounces skim or low-fat milk

SAMPLE 1800-CALORIE MENUS

Here are some examples of 1800-calorie menus that are appropriate for most women who implement the complete Rotation Diet and Activity Program for weight maintenance. You add to these menus additional fat or oil, up to a total of a tablespoon per day, and your fruit or cereal snacks. You may also be able to add an occasional higher calorie dessert or a glass of wine. HOWEVER, YOU MUST EXPERIMENT TO FIND YOUR CORRECT MAINTENANCE LEVEL. As you begin to increase your food intake, get on the scale every day. If you go up 2 or 3 pounds and stay up for two or three days, YOU HAVE EXCEEDED YOUR MAINTENANCE LEVEL. Sorry, you will have to cut back. Catch it quickly! Additional instructions follow the menus.

For men: These menus can be used during Week 2 while you are on the quick weight loss Rotation Diet. When you reach Week 4, add calories slowly until you reach maintenance. Additional instructions follow the menus.

1800-CALORIE MENU #1

Breakfast
Great Shake* or
8 ounces plain low-fat yogurt with 1 cup berries
1 whole-grain bagel
no-cal beverage

Lunch

Japanese-Style Crab Salad* or
2 ounces water-packed tuna or salmon
2 slices whole-grain bread
unlimited free vegetables
low-cal salad dressing
choice of fruit
no-cal beverage

Dinner

Baked Horseradish Chicken* (4½ ounces baked chicken)
Spinach Bake*
Honey-Nut Glazed Carrots*
2 Chocolate-Chip Cookies*
8 ounces skim or low-fat milk

1800-CALORIE MENU #2

Breakfast

8 ounces skim or low-fat milk
1¼ cups fortified cereal
½ cup fresh fruit
Honey Bran Muffin* or
1 slice whole-grain toast with 1 teaspoon margarine or
butter
no-cal beverage

Lunch

Chunky Tomato Soup* (1½ cups soup)
Spinach Salad:
1½ cups fresh spinach, ¼ cup sliced mushrooms, ½ cup
mandarin orange sections, 1 tablespoon slivered almonds
with Poppy-Seed Dressing* or other dressing
5 whole-wheat crackers
no-cal beverage

Dinner
White-Bean Casserole,* Tofu Manicotti,* or
Swiss-Mozzarella Bake* (or ½ cup beans, ½ cup rice, 2
ounces cheese)
1 cup Yellow Squash with Dill*
1 cup Dinner Salad*
no- or low-cal dressing
1 slice Poppy-Seed Cake* or choice of fruit
8 ounces skim or low-fat milk

1800-Calorie Menu #3

Breakfast
8 ounces skim or low-fat milk
½ banana
1 tablespoon peanut butter
2 slices whole-grain bread
no-cal beverage

Lunch
Oriental Tofu Soup* or Winter Bean Soup* or other soup
(1½ cups soup)
Combination Sandwich*
unlimited free vegetables
1 orange
no-cal beverage

Dinner
Mexican Red Snapper* (6 ounces cooked fish)
1 medium baked potato
Cherry Tomato Bake*
Artichoke-Spinach Salad*
no- or low-cal dressing
Serving of Old-Fashioned Blueberry Betty*
8 ounces skim or low-fat milk

1800-CALORIE MENU #4

Breakfast
"English Danish":
½ cup low-fat cottage cheese
½ teaspoon ground cinnamon
½ cup fresh or water-packed sliced peaches or other fruit
on
2 halves whole-grain English muffin
8 ounces skim or low-fat milk
no-cal beverage

Lunch
Tuna Salad with Fruit-Vinaigrette Dressing* (2 ounces fish)
1 whole-grain 6-inch pita bread
unlimited free vegetables
½ canteloupe
no-cal beverage

Dinner
Veal Scaloppine Dijon* (4½ ounces cooked meat)
1 cup fettucini
1 cup zucchini
1 cup Dinner Salad*
no- or low-cal dressing
1 slice Kahlua Chocolate Cheesecake*
8 ounces skim or low-fat milk

GENERAL MAINTENANCE GUIDELINES FOR WOMEN

The preceding 1800-calorie menus are meant to serve as illustrations of a healthy weight maintenance diet. Design your own by building your daily diet around the following selection of foods. Use the Food Substitution Lists (pp. 411–23) for information on serving sizes and nutritional equivalence.

- Four servings per day of whole grains or their equivalents.
- Two to three servings of skim or low-fat milk products.
- Five to seven ounces of lean meat, fish, or poultry (cooked weight) per day. Or use complementary protein substitutes of grains and legumes.
- Two servings of vegetables, including a dark green vegetable for vitamin A and extra calcium.
- Two servings of fruit, including a citrus fruit for vitamin C.
- To this basic diet you may add 1 tablespoon of butter, margarine, oil, regular salad dressing, or other fat of your choice per day.
- These selections will total between 1200 and 1400 calories. To arrive at about 1800, add unlimited free vegetables and safe fruit snacks, or another serving or two of a grain product, up to a total of about 300 calories more (see the following substitution lists for approximate calorie contents). This leaves you room for between 100 and 200 calories in desserts (pp. 354–84) or one to two glasses of dry wine at dinner (about 90 calories per 4-ounce serving).

MAINTENANCE GUIDELINES FOR MEN

- Six servings per day of whole grains or their equivalents.
- Two to three servings of skim or low-fat milk products.
- Eight to ten ounces of lean meat, fish, or poultry (cooked weight) per day. Or use complementary protein substitutes of grains and legumes.
- Two servings of vegetables, including a dark green vegetable for vitamin A and extra calcium.
- Two servings of fruit, including a citrus fruit for vitamin C.
- To this basic diet you may add 1 tablespoon of butter, margarine, oil, regular salad dressing, or other fat of your choice per day.
- Depending upon whether you select the smallest suggested quantity of leanest meats and skim milk products, or the upper limit, calories in the above recommendations can vary from a low of around 1325 to a high of 1750. The average

male will need between 2100 and 2400 calories per day to maintain his weight. To arrive at your maintenance level, add unlimited free vegetables and safe fruit snacks, or another serving or two of a grain product, up to a total of about 300 calories more (see the following substitution lists for approximate calorie contents). This should leave you room for between 200 and 300 calories in desserts (pp. 354–84), or one to two glasses of dry wine at dinner (about 90 calories per 4-ounce serving).

FOR EVERYONE

- *Desserts, high-calorie snacks, and alcoholic beverages should never replace the foods in this basic dietary plan.* They can be added as treats to this diet at a level that doesn't lead to weight-gain.

FOOD SUBSTITUTION LISTS

Milk and Dairy Products

Whether you are using the Rotation Diet for quick weight-loss, or following our suggestions for weight maintenance, our menus include skim or low-fat dairy products daily. The maintenance menus recommend two to three servings a day.

Milk is the leading source of calcium in the diet. However, since not everyone wishes to have two or three glasses of milk each day, the following list indicates possible substitutions for milk, from the daily group of foods, that are approximate equivalents in terms of calories. The dairy products in this list contain from about 80 to about 115 calories per serving, with an average of about 105 calories. Skim-milk products have the fewest calories, and those with 5% butterfat will have the most.

Substituting another dairy product for milk may, however, compromise calcium content to a certain extent. For this reason, we list the calcium content of the items in parenthesis for comparison.

Women need over 1000 milligrams of calcium a day for strong, healthy bones and men need around 800 milligrams each day. If your calcium consumption consistently falls short of recommended levels, you may require a calcium supplement. You do not need to obtain all of your calcium from milk products. Deep green vegetables such as collards, kale, spinach, and other greens are also good sources of calcium, as are fish with bones, such as sardines and canned salmon.

Type of Dairy	Calcium Content	Amount for Calorie Equivalent*
Skim or non-fat milk	(302 mg.)	1 cup
Low-fat (1%) milk	(300 mg.)	1 cup
Powdered, non-fat dry	(316 mg.)	
(before adding 1 cup water)		1/3 cup, dry
Canned, evaporated skim milk	(368 mg.)	1/2 cup
Buttermilk	(285 mg.)	1 cup
Plain, low-fat yogurt	(415 mg.)	6 oz.
Cheeses		
Greater than 5% butterfat, such as:		
Swiss	(272 mg.)	1 oz.
Parmesan	(207 mg.)	3 T.
Cheddar	(204 mg.)	1 oz.
American	(174 mg.)	1 oz.
Less than 5% butterfat, such as:		
Mozzarella (part-skim)	(183 mg.)	1 1/4 oz.
Ricotta (part-skim)	(169 mg.)	1/4 cup
Farmer	(160 mg.)	1 1/4 oz.
Sapsago	(160 mg.)	1 1/4 oz.
Cottage (low-fat)	(155 mg.)	1/2 cup

*Note: T. = level tablespoon; t. = level teaspoon.

Neufchatel	(63 mg.)	3 T.
Specialty reduced-fat cheeses such as:		
"Weight Watchers"	(30 mg.)	2 oz.
"Lite Line"	(320 mg.)	2 oz.

FAT FACTS: The fat content of dairy products varies with the amount of butterfat present. Skim and low-fat products have had some or all of the butterfat removed. Limit your consumption of dairy foods made from whole milk or cream; although these provide approximately the same vitamin and mineral content as their low-fat counterparts, an equivalent serving size gives you substantially more calories, fat, and cholesterol.

Protein Foods

This list encompasses substitutes for various protein foods such as beef, pork, poultry, and fish. Also included are plant-protein sources with comparable calories for the given serving sizes. Substitutions for approximate protein equivalence are listed in quantities for one ounce cooked. Since the serving size at meals varies from 3 to 4.5 ounces, sometimes even 6 ounces, depending on whether you're a man or a woman, or which calorie rotation you're on, you can figure protein equivalency ounce by ounce.

Always choose lean, well-trimmed cuts of meats, which will contain about 55 calories per ounce. (The fatty cuts, untrimmed, have over 100 calories per ounce.) Most types of fish tend to contain fewer calories than meats. Remove skin from poultry before cooking. Bake, broil, boil, or poach rather than fry. Avoid adding fat when cooking; avoid high-fat sauces and gravies. Follow the Rotation Diet menus and recipes for specific serving sizes; in general, women may include 5 to 7 ounces of protein foods per day (except on 600- and 900-calorie days while on the weight-loss diet) and men may include 8 to 10 ounces a day.

Type of Protein Food	Amount for Protein Equivalent
Beef, lean (less than 10% fat), well-trimmed cuts such as: flank steak, tenderloin, top or bottom round, rump	1 oz.
Lamb, lean cuts such as: leg, rib, sirloin, loin, shank, shoulder	1 oz.
Pork: rump, center shank, lean ham, lean rib or loin chops	1 oz.
Veal: leg, loin, rib, shank, shoulder, cutlets	1 oz.
Poultry, without skin chicken, turkey, cornish hen, guinea hen, pheasant	1 oz.
Fish, fresh or frozen, any kind	1 oz.
canned tuna, salmon, crab, lobster	¼ cup
Clams, oysters, scallops, shrimp	5 shellfish (or 1 oz.)
Sardines, drained	3 sardines (or 1 oz.)
Egg (high in cholesterol)	1
Peanut butter (high in fat)	1 T.
Cheeses, less than 5% butterfat	1 oz.
Legumes, dried beans or peas	¼ cup
Tofu	3 oz.

FAT FACTS: Americans get as much as 40% of the total fat they eat from meats, primarily red meats. Limit red meat to three or four times a week, replacing it with lower fat, lower cholesterol animal alternatives such as fish and poultry, and plant proteins such as tofu. Experiment with our recipes that use meat as a garnish rather than as the center of the meal.

Vegetables

Here again is your complete unlimited *free-vegetable* list! It contains all the vegetables that have 25 or fewer calories per ½ cup serving. Trade any vegetable in this list for any other that appears in the list.

You will note that there are some vegetables that contain fewer than 25 calories for a full 1-cup serving! They are marked with an asterisk. Some vegetables not listed here contain more calories and are included in the Grain List, since they are considered "starchy" vegetables. Use the other "starchy" vegetables in the Grain List as a substitute for breads.

Asparagus	Bean sprouts	Beets
Beet greens	Broccoli	Brussels sprouts
Cabbage	Carrots	Cauliflower
Celery	Chard	Chicory*
Collards	Cucumbers*	Dandelion greens
Eggplant	Endive*	Escarole*
Green pepper	Kale	Lettuce*
Mushrooms	Mustard greens	Okra
Onions	Parsley*	Radishes*
Rhubarb	Rutabaga	Spinach
String beans	Summer squash	Tomatoes
Turnips	Turnip greens	Watercress*
Wax beans	Zucchini	

FIBER FACTS: On average, most of the above vegetables contain about 2 grams of fiber per serving. We need 20 to 35 grams of fiber a day for good health; most Americans get less than 10!

FAT FACTS: Vegetables are essentially fat free. Don't mess up nature's blessing by covering them with added fats or high-fat sauces. Season with your favorite herbs and spices, and use the recipes appearing in this cookbook. If you do season with but-

*Serving size = 1 cup

ter or margarine, go easy; one tablespoon will flavor four to six servings of vegetables.

Fruits

The portion sizes for fruits in the following list all contain about 40 calories. You can see that there is considerable difference in portion sizes for 40 calories, since fruits vary in the amount of sugar they contain per unit of size or weight.

Choose fresh fruits rather than canned fruit or fruit juices whenever possible. Fresh fruit is a good source of fiber and "fills you up." The fiber content has been included for most of the listed fruits. When using canned fruits, choose those canned in their own juice or in water. Fruits canned in syrup may have as much as twice the calories of their fresh equivalents.

Although the quantities listed are equal to about 40 calories, most people choose larger pieces of fruit. A large apple is about twice the size of a small apple and, therefore, would have around 80 calories (in fact, it is almost impossible to find a 40-calorie apple). Our daily calorie calculations in the Rotation menus reflect these larger servings, since they are customary. The list below is meant to serve as a basic guideline to illustrate the portion size for equivalent calories in various fruits.

Fruit	Amount (average 40 calories)	Fiber (grams)
Apple	1 small	1.5
Applesauce (unsweetened)	½ cup	1.7
Apricots, fresh	2 medium	1.6
Apricots, dried	4 halves	3.4
Banana	½ small	1.5
Blackberries	½ cup	3.8
Blueberries	½ cup	1.0
Canteloupe (6-inch diameter)	¼ melon	1.0
Cherries	10 large	1.2

Cranberries, no sugar	½ cup	4.0
Dates, dried	2	2.4
Fruit cocktail or		
fresh mixed fruit	½ cup	2.1
Figs, fresh	1	2.0
Grapefruit	½	2.6
Grapes (large)	12	.6
Grapes (small, seedless)	40	.9
Honeydew melon	⅛ medium	1.5
Mandarin orange sections		
(canned)	½ cup	.1
Mango	½ small	1.0
Nectarine	1 medium	.5
Orange	1 small	1.2
Papaya	¾ cup	1.8
Peach	1 medium or ½ cup	1.3
Pear	1 small or ½ cup fresh, sliced thin	2.8
Persimmons	½ cup	.4
Pineapple	½ cup or 2 slices	1.5
Plums	2 medium	2.0
Prunes	2 medium	1.3
Raisins	2 tbsp.	2.0
Raspberries	½ cup	4.6
Strawberries	¾ cup	3.9
Tangerine	1 medium	.3
Watermelon	1 cup	.5

Juices (unsweetened; fiber content is negligible in juice):

Apple cider or juice	⅓ cup
Cranberry juice	¼ cup
Fruit nectars	⅓ cup
Grape juice	¼ cup
Grapefruit juice	½ cup
Lemon juice	¾ cup
Lime juice	½ cup
Orange juice	½ cup

Pineapple juice	⅓ cup
Prune juice	¼ cup
Tomato juice	1 cup
Vegetable-juice cocktail	1 cup

FIBER FACTS: Fresh fruits, especially those that have peels and seeds you can eat, are excellent sources of fiber. Try to obtain at least 5 grams of fiber a day from this naturally sweet group food.

FAT FACTS: Fruits contain no fat, with the exception of avocados, coconuts, and olives (found in the Fat Substitution List). A rich source of many vitamins and minerals, and convenient to carry everywhere with you (they come in their own natural wrappers!), fruits are the perfect alternative to higher fat, higher calorie desserts or snacks.

Grains

Over three-fourths of the world's population center their diets around starches or grains (and they tend to be thinner than those who don't). Grains are sources of carbohydrate, protein, vitamins, minerals, and fiber. Nutritionists are encouraging the American public to eat more carbohydrate-rich foods in place of fatty foods because grains contain little fat. And, except for complete protein and vitamin B_{12}, grains have the same nutrient spectrum as the more fatty foods in the meat group.

The following foods are interchangeable in the portion sizes indicated, and, other than the exceptions noted, contain about 70 calories in the indicated serving sizes. Choose whole-grain, unprocessed products whenever possible.

Note that some items, indicated by an asterisk, count as a serving of a teaspoon of fat as well as a bread choice. These contain about 115 calories per serving instead of 70 calories, as for a bread serving alone.

Type of Grain	Amount (average 70 calories)	Fiber (grams)
Breads		
Bagel	½ average	1.0
Bread, white (including Italian and French bread)	1 slice	1.0
Bread, wheat and rye	1 slice	3.0
Bread, pumpernickel	1 slice	2.0
Bread crumbs	¼ cup	1.0
Croutons	¼ cup	.5
Buns		
Hot dog	½	1.0
Hamburger	½	1.0
Rolls		
Dinner*	2-inch diameter	1.0
Hard	2-inch diameter	1.0
Kaiser	½, 4-inch diameter	1.0
Muffins		
English	½	1.0
Plain*	1 small or ½, 3-inch diameter	1.0
Bran*	1 small or ½, 3-inch diameter	2.0+
Corn*	1 small or ½, 3-inch diameter	2.0
Biscuit*	1, 2-inch diameter	1.0
Cornbread*	2 × 2 × 1-inch square	2.0
Tortilla	1, 6-inch diameter	2.0
Pancake*	1, 5-inch diameter (½-inch thick)	1.0
Waffle*	1, 5-inch diameter (½-inch thick)	1.0

Crackers

Arrowroot	3	NA
Graham Crackers	2, 2½-inch square	1.4
Matzoh	½, 4 × 6-inch	NA
Oyster	20	.1
Pretzels, very thin		
sticks	25	.1
Round, thin	5	.2
Ry-Krisp	3	.2
Saltines	5	trace
Soda	4, 2½-inch square	trace

Cereals

All-Bran	⅓ cup	3.0
Bran Flakes, Raisin Bran	½ cup	3.0
Cooked cereals	½ cup	2.0
grits, rice, oatmeal, barley		
Cereals, dry	¾ cup	1.0
unsweetened, ready-to-eat		
Cornmeal, dry	2 T.	2.0
Cornstarch	2 T.	0
Flour, all-purpose	2½ T.	.2
Flour, whole-wheat	2½ T.	1.8
Pasta, cooked	½ cup	.2
(lasagna, macaroni,		
noodles, spaghetti)		
Pasta, cooked,		
whole-wheat	½ cup	2.8
Popcorn, popped, no fat		
added	2 cups	2.0
Rice, white	½ cup	.2
Rice, brown	½ cup	2.0
Wheat germ	¼ cup	.7

Starchy Vegetables

Beans, peas, lentils		
dried and cooked**	½ cup	4.0

Corn

hominy	½ cup	.4
on the cob	1 small ear	2.1
whole kernel	½ cup	2.1
Lima beans	½ cup	3.7
Mixed vegetables	½ cup	2.5
Parsnips	⅔ cup	3.0
Peas, green	½ cup	3.8
Potato, white	1 small	3.1
Potato, mashed	½ cup	3.7
Potatoes, french fries*	8 pieces	.4
Pumpkin	¾ cup	5.3
Succotash	⅓ cup	2.1
Winter squash, acorn, butternut	½ cup	3.5
Yam or sweet potato	¼ cup	2.0

FIBER FACTS: Whole, unprocessed grains provide an excellent source of dietary fiber. Including a serving or two at each meal can help to achieve a healthy fiber content in your diet each day.

FAT FACTS: Prepared or commercial bread or grain products can contain substantial amounts of added fats. And, since humans like fat, food processors tend to "sneak" it into their recipes in order to increase their products' attractiveness to the consumer. If you truly want to reduce the fat in your diet, forego the butter-topped, sweetened, or cake-like breads, except on special occasions. The bread and muffin recipes in this book illustrate how delicious breads and muffins can be with minimal amounts of fat.

*These items, prepared according to standard recipes, contain about 35 calories of fat in addition to the basic calories contained in the grains from which the product is produced.

**Legumes (beans, peas, any variety of plants that have seeds growing in pods) are a significant source of protein as well as carbohydrate. Although the protein is incomplete, that is, not completely available to the body as is the protein in milk, eggs, or meat, combining legumes with grains, nuts, or seeds, or a small amount of meat or dairy products makes them as nourishing as meat, with far less fat and cholesterol, and far fewer calories.

Fats

Fats provide more than twice as many calories per equal weight as carbohydrates or proteins. The American diet typically contains more than 40% of its calories as fat. Many overweight people get over half their daily calories from fat. For weight maintenance as well as for the prevention of cardiovascular disease and certain forms of cancer, health authorities recommend that fewer than 30% of calories should come from fat.

In general, avoid using more than 135 calories of added fat each day (3 teaspoons). Cutting back on fats in the diet is essential to long-term weight management as well as to good health. Cut fat whenever possible in your own recipes. The recipes in this book are all lowered in fat, compared with standard recipes of a similar nature.

There are about forty-five calories in the serving sizes for fats in the following list. Note that the list is divided into two categories. The first listing contains fats and fatty foods that contain little or no saturated fat and cholesterol. If and when you use added fats in cooking, vegetable oils such as corn, safflower, sunflower, soybean, olive, or peanut, are the preferred choices. The second listing includes foods that contain significant amounts of saturated fat and cholesterol. Unfortunately, butter is in this list. Because butter has such an attractive flavor, we frequently blend a bit with a vegetable or fruit fat from the first list, such as olive oil, when we want a touch of butter flavor in our recipes.

High-Fat Foods	*Amount (45 calories)*
Avocado, 4-inch diameter	⅛
Vegetable oil	1 t.
Margarine, reduced-calorie	2 t.
Margarine, regular	1 t.
Mayonnaise	1 t.
Nuts, pecans, walnuts	4 whole or 1 T.
Olives	5 small
Peanuts, shelled	1 T.

Salad dressings	2 t.
Italian, French, oil & vinegar, blue cheese, thousand island	
Sunflower seeds	1 T.
Tartar sauce	2 t.

The following fat choices contain significant amounts of cholesterol and/or saturated fat. Use them sparingly.

Very High-Fat Foods	*Amount (45 calories)*
Bacon, crisp	1 slice
Butter	1 t.
Chocolate, unsweetened	1 t.
Cococut, shredded	2 T.
Cream cheese	1 T.
Cream	
Heavy, unwhipped	1 T.
Heavy, whipped	2 T.
Light, unwhipped	2 T.
Fat back	1 slice 2 × 1 × ½ inches
Gravy	2 T.
Half-and-half	¼ cup
Lard	1 t.
Sour cream	2 T.
Whipped topping, commercial	3 T.

Index

Indian spice blend, 334
storing, 38
traditional Italian herb blend, 335
sedentary life-style, 385–86
seeds, 235, 237–38, 398
in complementary protein combinations, 234
sprouts from, 236
toasting, 237–38
see also specific seeds
serving platters, 32
serving sizes:
for fruits, 416
for protein foods, 413
in Rotation Diet, 393–94, 403
sesame seed(s), 36
in complementary protein combinations, 234
ginger lamb chops, 160
poppy-seed loaf, 315
shades of green, 268
shakes, 350–51
fruit 'n' juice, 350–51
orange-banana, 350
shark steaks, Oriental, 206
shellfish, 193
linguine with, 224–25
oyster stew, 214–15
see also clam(s); crab(meat); shrimp
shepherd's pie, Australian, 188–89
shortenings, solid, 355
shrimp:
curried, 204
and mushroom dinner, easy, 203
skimpy, 211
spread, 341
tofu and, 257
silverware, storing, 39
600-calorie day menu, 403
skillets, stir-frying in, 31
slaw, vegetable, 93
smoked foods, 331–32
snacks:
free vegetables as, 22–23, 393, 394–95, 400, 415

fruits as, 418
safe fruits as, 22, 393, 395, 418
sodium intake, 25, 26, 330–31
see also salt intake
soufflés, zucchini, 247
soups, 63–83
as aid to prevent overeating, 64
asparagus, 67
barley chicken, 74
chunky tomato, 68–69
clear vs. cream, 64
cold tomato (Julian's), 74–75
David's chili, 70
English cucumber, 75
French onion, 71
gazpacho, 76
Manhattan clam chowder, 83
meatless chili, 81
minestrone, 76–77
New England clam chowder, 82
Oriental tofu, 260
Patti's vegetable, 73
potato and cheese, 72
quick clam, 69
spinach egg-drop, 80–81
split-pea, with vegetables, 78
thickeners for, 64
vichyssoise, 79
winter bean, 80
see also stocks
South American turkey stew, 189
soybean oil, 355
soy flour, 234
soy sauce, 25–26, 331
spaghetti squash Parmesan, 267
Spanish rice, 287
Special K breakfast, 397
spiced:
coffee, Irish, 352–53
tea, 351
spices, 15, 34–36, 330–32
garam masala, 332–33
Indian blend, 334
storing, 38, 332
spinach:
artichoke salad, 85
bake, 275